Manuscript Genetics, Joyce's Know-How, Beckett's Nohow

The Florida James Joyce Series

UNIVERSITY PRESS OF FLORIDA

Florida A&M University, Tallahassee
Florida Atlantic University, Boca Raton
Florida Gulf Coast University, Ft. Myers
Florida International University, Miami
Florida State University, Tallahassee
New College of Florida, Sarasota
University of Central Florida, Orlando
University of Florida, Gainesville
University of North Florida, Jacksonville
University of South Florida, Tampa
University of West Florida, Pensacola

Manuscript Genetics, Joyce's Know-How, Beckett's Nohow

Dirk Van Hulle

Foreword by Sebastian D. G. Knowles, Series Editor

University Press of Florida
Gainesville/Tallahassee/Tampa/Boca Raton
Pensacola/Orlando/Miami/Jacksonville/Ft. Myers/Sarasota

Copyright 2008 by Dirk Van Hulle
Printed in the United States of America on acid-free paper

All rights reserved

First cloth printing, 2008
First paperback printing, 2009

Library of Congress Cataloging-in-Publication Data
Hulle, Dirk van.
Manuscript genetics: Joyce's know-how, Beckett's nohow /
Dirk Van Hulle; foreword by Sebastian D. G. Knowles.
p. cm.—(Florida James Joyce series)
Includes bibliographical references and index.
ISBN 978-0-8130-3200-9 (cloth, alk. paper)
ISBN 978-0-8130-3414-0 (pbk.)
1. Joyce, James, 1882–1941—Criticism, Textual.
2. Joyce, James, 1882–1941—Technique. 3. Joyce, James, 1882–1941—Manuscripts. 4. Beckett, Samuel, 1906–1989—Criticism, Textual. 5. Beckett, Samuel, 1906–1989—Technique. 6. Beckett, Samuel, 1906–1989—Manuscripts.
7. Criticism, Textual—Methodology. I. Title.
PR6019.O9Z589 2008
823'9129–dc22   2007043552

The University Press of Florida is the scholarly publishing agency for the State University System of Florida, comprising Florida A&M University, Florida Atlantic University, Florida Gulf Coast University, Florida International University, Florida State University, New College of Florida, University of Central Florida, University of Florida, University of North Florida, University of South Florida, and University of West Florida.

University Press of Florida
15 Northwest 15th Street
Gainesville, FL 32611-2079
http://www.upf.com

It is doubtful whether in the course of the centuries, though we have learnt much about making machines, we have learnt anything about making literature. We do not come to write better; all that we can be said to do is to keep moving, now a little in this direction, now in that.

Virginia Woolf, *Modern Fiction*

Contents

List of Tables ix
Foreword by Sebastian D. G. Knowles xi
Acknowledgments xiii
Abbreviations xv
Transcription Conventions xvii
Introduction 1

I. Genetic Criticism 7

1. Genetics and Poetics 9
2. Methodology 24
3. Strategies and Typologies 47

II. Joyce's Know-How 53

4. Introduction: "Work in Progress" 55
5. Decomposition 77
6. Recombination: S, M, L 83

III. Beckett's Nohow 115

7. Introduction: "Work in Regress" 117
8. Recollection 128
9. Decomposition: L, M, S 162

Notes 195
Works Cited 207
Index 227

Tables

4.1. Interaction between the Private and Public Aspects of "Work in Progress"   73

6.1. "Decomposition" of Reviews in Notebook VI.B.06 (Landuyt 1999)   85

6.2. Genetic Classification of the Four Stacks of "Notesheets (First set)"   94

6.3. Decomposition and Subsequent Recombination: Indirect Usage   95

6.4. Distribution of Deleted Notes on Page VI.C.01:11, Originally Derived from Gallois' *La poste*   97

Foreword

Genetic criticism is an explosive field in modernist studies. Technology has caught up with writers like Joyce and Beckett in its ability to record, research, sift through, and present data on notebooks, archival material, and variant editions: what was previously known to a handful of people who had the time to go to Buffalo, Texas, and Dublin can now be revealed to all. Dirk Van Hulle is one of the best of today's genetic critics: by taking advantage of this newly disseminated knowledge, he is able to tell us something about how these authors tick. What is more, Van Hulle is a writer of extraordinary lyrical gifts, with a stylistic agility that is often, and especially at the end of a chapter, quite breathtaking. The tensile strength of his literary line is astonishing: with the critical equivalent of a quick flick of the wrist, he turns from an airy lightness to a stark confrontation with the profoundest implications of his argument, stunning the reader into wonder.

The links between Joyce and Beckett have been forged many times before, but this is a book that is only tangentially interested in biography, that takes as read the parallel thematics in the two writers' works. Van Hulle is interested in the text: how it is generated, how it is composed, how it progresses, and what that tells us about the way that Joyce and Beckett worked. When is a text finished? How does a writer begin? To provide compelling answers to these questions, you need a scholar who knows the field, who can communicate ideas on the nanolevel to those used to reading on the macrolevel, and who can clearly and inventively state what is at stake. The heart of Van Hulle's book is a chronological survey of *Finnegans Wake* arranged by writing process, wherein each section is summarized in terms of its main action. This is as good a synopsis of the *Wake* as I have seen, and all supported by genetic evidence: a crowning demonstration of the benefits of the genetic approach.

The contrast between Joyce and Beckett is as exquisite as that between the viceroy and Lady Dudley in the viceregal cavalcade, Beckett's pearl gray nicely setting off Joyce's eau de Nil. Or to use Murphy's metaphor, the two writers play figure and ground, Joyce's white to Beckett's black, throughout this book. Where one writes by addition, the other writes by deletion: Joyce's whole is Beckett's hole; one man's plenum is another man's vacuum.

Where there is a divide between two genetic camps, Joyce straddles the divide: he is both a syncretist and a step-by-step writer, both a minimalist and a maximalist. Any time there are two ways of doing things, Joyce does both: *Finnegans Wake* is a published work in the public domain before it is finally declared *bon à tirer*. And on Beckett's side, whenever there is a divide, Beckett widens it into an abyss: any time there are two ways to do something, Beckett does neither. So Joyce and Beckett are perfect foils for one another, working in counterpoint together, and the reader learns through them how an author writes a book and how important the process of composition is to our final sense of a completed work. Van Hulle establishes that Joyce's notebooks are provisional in an entirely unexpected sense of the word: not as preliminary sketches, but as sustenance, providing the necessary provisions for Joyce's journey through the *Wake*. In Dirk Van Hulle, we could not have a better guide.

Sebastian D. G. Knowles

Acknowledgments

The study of modern manuscripts almost inevitably implies the question of whether it is not inappropriate to enter an author's workshop and study his drafts. In a conversation with James Knowlson during my first research visit to the Samuel Beckett Archives at the University of Reading, I asked him this question. He replied that, on the contrary, Beckett even encouraged this kind of research and therefore gave his manuscripts to the university library. I would like to thank James Knowlson, not only for his initial reassurance but for his unremitting support and his encouragement of manuscript genetics as well. I especially want to thank Mark Nixon and John Pilling for all their help. I also wish to express my gratitude to the University of Reading and the Beckett International Foundation, Ronan McDonald, Julian Garforth, Cedric Brown, Michael Bott, Verity Andrews, Brian Ryder, and the whole staff of the RUL Archives; to the Estate of Samuel Beckett, notably to Edward Beckett, for his openness to new developments in the genetic study of Samuel Beckett's manuscripts; to Tom Staley, Richard Oram, Richard Workman, Debbie Armstrong, and the friendly staff of the Harry Ransom Humanities Research Center; to the National Library of Ireland and Trinity College, Dublin; to the Poetry/Rare Books Collection in Buffalo; to Isabelle, Oscar, and Lina for all their patience; to Chris Ackerley, Louis Armand, Helen Astbury, Carle Bonafous-Murat, Barbara Bordalejo, Julia Briggs, Marius Buning, Bill Cadbury, Martine de Clercq, Tom Cousineau, Luca Crispi, Matteo D'Alfonso, Burghard Dedner, Jed Deppman, João Dionisio, Paolo D'Iorio, Chris Eagle, Bart Eeckhout, Paul Eggert, Matthijs Engelberts, Matthew Feldman, Daniel Ferrer, Anne Fogarty, Ruth Frehner, Robert Fulton, Mikio Fuse, Hans Walter Gabler, Stan Gontarski, Karine Germoni, Almuth Grésillon, Warwick Gould, Molly Hardy, David Hayman, Stacey Herbert, Luc Herman, Ruud Hisgen, Sjef Houppermans, Daniel Katz, Onno Kosters, Charles Krance, Ingeborg Landuyt, Sean Lawlor, Françoise Leriche, Pat McCarthy, John McCourt, Cécile Meynard, Wim Van Mierlo, Vincent Neyt, Rüdiger Nutt-Kofoth, Nathalie Mauriac Dyer, Alois Pichler, Bodo Plachta, Lois Overbeck, Magessa O'Reilly, Ondrej Pilný, Jean-Michel Rabaté, Friedhelm Rathjen, Peter Robinson, Cioran Ross, Danièle de Ruijter, Pascale Sardin, Fritz Senn, Peter Shillingsburg, Sam Slote, Erik

Tonning, Tom Toremans, Anthony Uhlmann, Edward Vanhoutte, Walter Verschueren, Adriaan van der Weel, Shane Weller, and Ursula Zeller for all the stimulating conversations and expert advice. Above all, I wish to thank Sebastian Knowles for his encouragement to write this book, which could only be about genetic Joyce and Beckett studies thanks to the unremitting support of Geert Lernout.

Abbreviations

James Joyce

FW   *Finnegans Wake*. Quotations are taken from the first Faber and Faber paperback edition in which Joyce's errata are incorporated (London: Faber and Faber, 1975). Whenever comparisons are made to the first (1939) or another edition, the bibliographical reference is indicated.

FWNB   *Finnegans Wake Notebooks at Buffalo*. Edited by Vincent Deane, Daniel Ferrer, and Geert Lernout. Turnhout: Brepols, 2001.

FDV   The first drafts of each section of *Finnegans Wake* were transcribed by David Hayman in his indispensable edition of *A First Draft Version of "Finnegans Wake."* London: Faber and Faber, 1963. Quotations from this edition observe Hayman's transcription system.

JJA   This abbreviation, followed by volume and page number, refers to the facsimile edition of Joyce's manuscripts, *The James Joyce Archive*, edited by Michael Groden, Hans Walter Gabler, David Hayman, A. Walton Litz, and Danis Rose. New York: Garland, 1977–79. The *Archive*'s draft catalogue system is used to refer to a specific draft stage:
e.g. I.5§2.*0 = book I, chapter 5, section 2, first draft; the asterisk indicates an autograph document.

BL   The number following the abbreviation *BL* indicates the number of the manuscript, preserved at the British Library.

BL Add.   British Library, Additional Manuscript, followed by the folio number.

L I   *Letters of James Joyce*. Vol. 1. Edited by Stuart Gilbert. London: Faber and Faber, 1957.

L III   *Letters of James Joyce*. Vol. 3. Edited by Richard Ellmann. London: Faber and Faber, 1966.

NLI   National Library of Ireland

TD   *The Textual Diaries of James Joyce*. Edited by Danis Rose. Dublin: Lilliput Press, 1995.

U   *Ulysses*. Critical and Synoptic Edition. Edited by Hans Walter Gabler et al. New York: Garland, 1984.

Samuel Beckett

CDW   *Collected Dramatic Works*. London: Faber and Faber, 1986.
CSP   *The Complete Short Prose 1929–1989*. New York: Grove Press, 1995.
HRHRC   *Harry Ransom Humanities Research Center*. References to the manuscripts kept at the HRHRC are followed by the name of the collection, the box, folder, and folio number.
RUL   *Reading University Library*. References to the manuscripts kept at the RUL are followed by the MS number from the catalogue *Beckett at Reading: Catalogue of the Beckett Manuscript Collection at the University of Reading*, edited by Mary Bryden, Julian Garforth, and Peter Mills. Reading: University of Reading, Whiteknights Press, and the Beckett International Foundation, 1998.
TCD   *Trinity College Dublin*. References to the manuscripts kept at TCD are followed by the archive number.
TN   *The Theatrical Notebooks of Samuel Beckett*. Edited by James Knowlson. Vol. 1, *Waiting for Godot*, edited by Dougald McMillan and James Knowlson. New York: Grove Press, 1993. Vol. 2, *Endgame*, edited by S. E. Gontarski. London: Faber and Faber, 1992. Vol. 3, *Krapp's Last Tape*, edited by James Knowlson. London: Faber and Faber. Vol. 4, *The Shorter Plays*, edited by S. E. Gontarski. London and New York: Faber and Faber, and Grove Press, 1999.

Transcription Conventions

The aim of the linear transcription as applied in this book is to represent holograph drafts with a minimum of diacritical signs, crossing out ~~deletions~~; indicating ~~deletions within deletions~~ with double strikethrough; using bold type for **overwritings** (immediately following the word or letter over which the substitution was written); and carets for ^additions^. Square brackets indicate an [uncertain reading] of a word. An illegible word is represented by square brackets enclosing two xxs: [xx].

Introduction

Imagine this were a manuscript of "Imagine." Imagine how much it would be worth. In July 2005, John Lennon's handwritten lyrics for "All You Need Is Love" were auctioned. All you needed was $1 million to become its owner. Similar amounts of money are being paid for manuscripts by authors such as James Joyce or Samuel Beckett. Whenever a manuscript is sold, critics are duly worried about the potential fragmentation of an author's estate and the dispersal of valuable pieces of information into unknown safe-deposit boxes. But in the meantime, thousands of literary manuscripts are resting untouched in fireproof archive vaults.

The most direct appeal of a holograph manuscript is undoubtedly its aura, as Walter Benjamin called it. The "here and now" of the unique original constitutes its authenticity. And as Mark Z. Danielewski notes in the opening section of *House of Leaves*: "While enthusiasts and detractors will continue to empty entire dictionaries attempting to describe or deride it, 'authenticity' still remains the word most likely to stir a debate" (2000: 3). But there is a difference between holding manuscripts in reverence and treating them as fetishes. Manuscripts are not relics, even though their auction at exorbitant prices may sometimes resemble the flourishing and lucrative medieval relic business.

In the Middle Ages, most manuscripts were produced by scribes to circulate a work. They had a public function. In French *critique génétique* (genetic criticism, or the study of writing processes), a clear distinction is made between this kind of medieval manuscript and the so-called modern manuscript. From the eighteenth century onward, authors started keeping their drafts more systematically. This international phenomenon reflects an enhanced self-consciousness. As a result, literary modernism is the golden age of the modern manuscript. This type of document has a more private function than the medieval manuscript and belongs to the intimate atmosphere of the writing process.

Because of this private nature, manuscript research is sometimes compared to prying into an author's wastepaper basket. But it is precisely because some authors did *not* throw away their manuscripts that they constitute such a considerable research corpus. As the invaluable Garland facsimile edition of Joyce's manuscripts shows, the *James Joyce Archive* is a wealth of information. So is the Beckett archive at the University of Reading, Trinity College Dublin, the Harry Ransom Humanities Research Center, and several other institutions. Samuel Beckett's decision to entrust his manuscripts to university archives was a well-considered choice. It seems important not to ignore this decision, which is part and parcel of his authorship and a crucial aspect of his poetics.

His example is not an isolated case. Louis Aragon, Michel Butor, Ernst Jünger, Hans Joachim Schädlich, and many others offered their manuscripts to special archives such as the French IMEC (Institut Mémoires de l'Edition Contemporaine) and the German Literaturarchiv in Marbach, usually of their own accord. That this kind of donation is less likely to give rise to inheritance disputes is probably not the only reason why these authors entrust their manuscripts to an archive. Implicitly their gesture expresses the wish that their writings will be studied as more than just marketable products. For, more often than not, these finished products are the result of long, laborious composition processes.

The process of writing is the focal point of genetic criticism. Manuscript research is instrumental in this critical approach. Traditionally, it was taken for granted that manuscript research was only part of scholarly editing and textual criticism. But it does not need to be exclusively at the service of editing. The interpretation of a published text can often benefit from textual information that can only be obtained by an examination of its early versions. Moreover, investigating the genesis of literary works may shed a new light on an author's poetics, defined in its most basic, original sense as "the art of making" (from Greek *poiein*, "to make, to create").

An excellent introduction to genetic criticism is the book of that title, edited by Jed Deppman, Daniel Ferrer, and Michael Groden (2004). This great collection of essays focuses mainly on French authors. In *Manuscript Genetics, Joyce's Know-How, Beckett's Nohow*, I discuss the methodology of genetic criticism and apply it to two European authors whose works can hardly be linked to one particular language or literature.

By comparing the writing methods of James Joyce and Samuel Beckett, I aim to demonstrate that the composition process is an integral part of what these authors' works convey. Joyce's attempt to write a history of the world focuses on rumors and different versions of the facts. His view of history is reflected in his own working method. He was well aware that the mechanics of time and history also applied to the time he invested in his own writing, notably the seventeen-year composition process of *Finnegans Wake*, also known as "Work in Progress."

In many respects, Beckett's works are quite the opposite of Joyce's, yet he too elaborated on the idea of a "work in progress." Although he thoroughly questioned the idea of teleology implied in the word "progress," preferring the expression "work in regress" instead, Beckett did retain and develop the idea of a work in motion, and even radicalized it: he applied it to his oeuvre in its entirety. In his early essay *Proust*, Beckett pointed out that the individual consists of a succession of versions. The transition periods from one version to another represent the "perilous zones in the life of the individual, dangerous, precarious, painful, mysterious and fertile" (Beckett 1999 [1931]: 19). This idea finds its textual equivalent in successive versions and composition variants, especially when the writing process is thematized in the published text. In *Manuscript Genetics*, I examine the role of the composition history and its equal importance in the works of two authors with quite divergent poetics. The aim of the book is to show how Joyce used the textual history to write a history of the world, and how Beckett made a direct link between the development of the text and that of the individual.

In order to do so from a twenty-first-century vantage point, it is important not to ignore the inevitable (dis)advantages of hindsight. Genetic criticism owes a great deal to experimental literary developments in the 1960s and 1970s, such as the French poet Francis Ponge's idea of presenting all the failures to describe a bar of soap as a literary work in its own right (*Le savon*, 1967), or of publishing all the preparatory versions of his poem "Le pré" as a process rather than as a product (*La fabrique du pré*, 1971). One of the issues that should be addressed here is the extent to which genetic Joyce and Beckett studies are a form of back-shadowing. In *Foregone Conclusions*, Michael André Bernstein defines back-shadowing as the retrospective tendency to project the shadow of recent developments backward onto the preceding period. Such a tendency may be at play when *Finnegans Wake* is studied as a "Work in Progress" or when Beckett is said to have constantly avoided formal completion in his work. The purpose of this analysis is to investigate to what degree this approach is a retrospective projection or to what extent it is inspired by these authors' own oeuvre.

Since any attempt to look inside a writer's mind is doomed to fail, genetic criticism does not try to reveal what an author wanted to write, but focuses instead on what he has written. And what he has written can be studied only on the basis of what is still extant. As a consequence, the material evidence of the writing process will play a central role in this book. These documents include the dozens of notebooks, containing the most diverse excerpts and jottings; the drafts in copybooks and on loose sheets of paper; the numerous typescripts, corrected galleys, and revised page proofs; the installments in magazines, different editions, omitted passages, errata, and self-translations. Sometimes letters will also be helpful in determining the chronology of particular textual versions. Epistolary material, however, is employed only insofar as it relates to the writing process. Manuscript genetics is not a new form of biographism, although it does acknowledge the important fact that a text needs an author in order to be written. By reconstructing the writing process, this genetic approach may add a new perspective to what H. Porter Abbott has termed "autography," or self-writing.

In *Beckett Writing Beckett*, H. Porter Abbott suggests that Beckett's art is to a large extent focused on "undoing the illusion of sequential time" (19). In this respect, he also had a direct example: James Joyce's *Finnegans Wake*. Abbott rightly suggests a revaluation of the impact of "Work in Progress" on Beckett's works. He argues that the "continuing incompletion" of "Work in Progress" may be a much more fundamental element in this artistic relationship than the somewhat too neat dichotomy—partly construed by Beckett himself—between the supreme artist in control of his material and the rebellious disciple. Abbott suggests replacing this "tale" with "a long tableau of shared company in the shadow of a project outside the closure of time and fictional form" (20). Indeed, the circular structure of *Finnegans Wake* was a cunning trick to put an end to what essentially remains a process. The notion of progress usually implies amelioration, which the book seems to question by means of its circular structure. An even more critical attitude toward progress characterizes Samuel Beckett's work. Still, Beckett's writing also expresses an acute awareness of the tension between his criticism of "onwardness" and his own creative urge to write on. The writing process thus becomes an inherent part of these authors' works.

As a consequence, the published text is not necessarily considered better than its preceding drafts, but merely a version among other versions—which is reflected in titles such as *Residua*, *Disjecta*, *Fizzles*. According to Abbott, "Beckett continually avoided formal completion. And although, like Joyce, he saw his works bound and published, these 'finished' works contain everywhere notes and questions for the author" (20). Several other characteristics illustrate the pro- and regressive character of Beckett's works, such as the numerous intratextual references to previous works and the self-translations—which may be regarded as continuations of the composition process even after publication of the original. Moreover, Beckett apparently attached enough importance to his manuscripts and typescript versions to donate many of them to university libraries, fully aware that these institutions are likely to regard documents of this kind as research objects and may consider them as part and parcel of an author's literary legacy.

Within the fairly unexplored field of comparative genetic criticism, the composition processes of writings by Joyce and Beckett are a particularly interesting case, especially given the authors' close cooperation at a moment when Beckett was still developing his own poetics. *Manuscript Genetics* offers an introduction to this relatively young field of research, applies it to these two authors, and focuses on a remarkable aspect of their works: the process as an integral part of the product.

To study their writings accordingly, genetic criticism offers an appropriate methodology, which is discussed in part 1. The metaphors employed by authors to describe their writing methods often shed some light on their poetics. A short history of these metaphors in chapter 1 charts the ways in which authors have looked at their own writing throughout the previous centuries. Chapter 2 locates genetic criticism within the field of literary studies. Its methodology is discussed in chapter 3, focusing on different typologies of manuscripts and writing strategies. This introduction to genetic criticism is not only meant to be a preamble to parts 2 and 3, but the latter are also an illustration of part 1.

Part 2 discusses Joyce's expansive writing method, notably the long composition history of *Finnegans Wake*, which Daniel Ferrer—in his paper at the "Genetic Joyce and Beckett Studies" colloquium (University of Antwerp, 16–17 March 2006)—has shown to be paradigmatic for genetic criticism. To illustrate how the theories of genetic criticism relate to the practice of writing, one of the typologies discussed in chapter 3 will be confronted with this "Work in Progress" par excellence. Joyce's veiled description of the book's writing process serves as a guideline for examining its composition. In the last part of *Finnegans Wake*, Joyce writes: "Our wholemole millwheeling vicociclometer (. . .) receives through a portal vein the dialytically separated elements of precedent decomposition for the verypetpurpose of subsequent recombination" (*FW* 614). The decomposition of source texts in notebooks and notesheets is the subject of chapter 5, whereas chapter 6 examines the recombination of this decomposed lexical material, concentrating on three sizes of textual units from small to large, corresponding with Joyce's expansive writing method.

Part 3 focuses on Beckett's textual "nohow," a pun suggested by Beckett in *Worstward Ho*. Chapter 7 starts from the periods of cooperation with Joyce, during which Beckett developed his own writing method by gradually taking his distance from Joyce's. Here, the guideline is a passage from *Molloy*: "It is in the tranquillity of decomposition that I remember the long confused emotion which was my life" (1955–58: 25). The overt allusion to the Preface of the *Lyrical Ballads* inverts Wordsworth's view on "successful composition," which "takes its origin from emotion recollected in tranquillity." One and a half centuries later, Beckett seemed less interested in successful composition than in a reverse creation. This "decreation" is analyzed in two phases: recollection and decomposition. Chapter 8 focuses on the recollection of both personal reminiscences and intertextual memories. The subsequent decomposition is analyzed in chapter 9, following the work's regress from large to small, closing with Beckett's last text, *Comment dire/what is the word*, a deliberately unfinished attempt to write a single sentence.

The nature of this study necessitates a few expeditions into the chaos of Joyce and Beckett's manuscripts. The point of these explorations is one of convergence. In spite of the opposite tendencies of their respective works in pro- and regress, both Joyce *and* Beckett can be regarded as paradigmatic authors for genetic criticism. No matter how their poetics may diverge, the role of the writing process in their works is equally important.

PART I
Genetic Criticism

Il s'agit de comprendre une oeuvre par son devenir et non par son seul aboutissement.
Louis Hay, *La littérature des écrivains*

1
Genetics and Poetics

Genetic criticism (*critique génétique*) is a confusing term, often associated with biogenetics instead of literary studies. The relationship between both disciplines may be a vaguely similar fascination with creation or procreation, but the thoroughly different nature of their respective research objects suggests a merely metaphorical connection. Nevertheless, metaphors may be a useful instrument to study the way in which we conceive of our own activities. They reflect the ways in which we look at things, and as such they can also have a profound impact on the way we understand those things. As a consequence, new fields of research in the early stages of their conceptualization are typically marked by a frequent change in the use of metaphors. This also applies to genetic criticism, a relatively young discipline that was developed in France by scholars such as Louis Hay, Almuth Grésillon, Daniel Ferrer, Pierre-Marc de Biasi, and Jean-Louis Lebrave, working together as a team in the Institut des Textes et Manuscrits Modernes (ITEM) in Paris. As Almuth Grésillon points out, the metaphors that were employed to give shape to this new discipline can be divided into two categories: an organic and a constructivist type (1992: 11). But these two types have a much longer history that marks the development of poetics in general.

The history of representations of the creative process shows a constant tension between imitation and originality. The Greeks and Romans "outsourced" the notions of inspiration and creative impulse to what they called "the Muses." This view was dominant from Homer's "Tell me, Muse" until the first half of the eighteenth century. In Swift's *Battle of the Books*, the bee gets the full support of the Ancients, against the Modern spider who pretends to be able to create ex nihilo. In his *Imitations of Horace* (1733–38), Alexander Pope suggested studying Homer to find the Muses among the Ancients: "Be Homer's Works your Study, and Delight, / Read them by Day, and meditate by Night, / Thence form your Judgment, thence your Maxims bring, / And trace the Muses upward to their Spring."

Around the middle of the eighteenth century, the scales were drastically tipped and the stress on imitation was replaced by a radical emphasis on originality, as in Edward Young's *Conjectures on Original Composition* (1759). The metaphors he uses are almost exclusively organic. According to Young, "the mind of a man of Genius is a fertile and pleasant field (. . .); it enjoys a perpetual Spring" (§34). Moreover, "an Original may be said to be of a vegetable nature; it rises spontaneously from the vital root of Genius; it grows, it is not made" (§43). This development is contrasted with what Young calls "Imitations," which are "a sort of Manufacture, wrought up by those Mechanics, Art, and Labour, out of pre-existent materials not their own" (§43).

A century after Young's *Conjectures*, his suggestion that an original "is not made" but "grows" was exemplified in the works of Walt Whitman. The organic metaphors employed by Whitman also apply to the "growth" of the successive editions of *Leaves of Grass*, and even to Whitman studies, which are marked by a long tradition of organic metaphors. This tradition is examined in *The Growth of "Leaves of Grass"* by M. Jimmie Killingsworth, who points out that Whitman critics have often unquestioningly absorbed the author's organic metaphors.

In Killingsworth's typology, three variations on the theme of growth are clearly discernible: the genetic, the progressive, and the cyclic. The genetic type "implies that the work of the poet grows from an essential center of being" (1993: 1). According to this view, each poem, each stanza, each line by the same poet is imbued with an identity that links it to "an informing center." The entire oeuvre radiates from this center, which is compared to a gene. Because of this analogy, Killingsworth calls this conception of poetry "genetic"—which further confuses the term "genetic criticism." The second category in his typology stresses the sequential aspect of growth, as in concepts such as progress and evolution, which contrast sharply with the image of radial growth. This second concept of growth implies amelioration and a form of teleology. According to this view, the steady progress culminates in completion. The third category in its turn dismisses this "ascending narrative" and prefers a cyclic view on organic growth. This "modern" approach includes both maturation and decline, "admitting loss as well as gain as a consequence of organic growth" (1).

In Whitman studies, the transition from the progressive to the cyclic view is marked by a gradual rejection of the so-called "death-bed edition" (1891–92) of *Leaves of Grass* as the culmination of the work's growth. The alternative conception of this work's development starts with its first appearance in 1855, reaching maturity in the third (1860) or the fourth (1867) edition, which was followed by a long period of decline: "The poems added in the 1870s and 1880s added weight without muscle. The revisions obscured rather than enhanced the accomplishment and radical energy of the earlier poems" (6).

Jerome McGann has pointed out that the phenomenon of critics absorbing the metaphors of the authors they study is particularly striking in the study of English Romantic poetry. In *The Romantic Ideology*, he argues that the second category (the progressive view) has been predominant in criticism of Romanticism, which tends to "show (say) Keats's or Byron's progress from certain interesting but undeveloped ideas, through various intermediate stages, to conclude in some final wisdom or 'achievement'" (1983: 135).

The progressive view, however, is not necessarily linked to organic metaphors. If Romantic poets' self-representations have had an influence on critics, the constructivist metaphors cannot be neglected either. Other nineteenth-century views on writing emphasize architectonic design and mathematical calculation, and in spite of Young's *Conjectures*, imitation was certainly not generally regarded as an inferior practice. Authors such as Mary Shelley did acknowledge that "everything must have a beginning," and "Invention, it must be humbly admitted, does not consist in creating out of void, but out of chaos." In the "Author's Introduction"[1] to her most famous book, *Frankenstein, or the Modern Prometheus*, Mary Shelley refers to the nature of the so-called "principle of life" and explicitly employs the term "manufacture" that Edward Young so fiercely rejected: "perhaps the component parts of a creature might be manufactured, brought together, and endued with vital warmth" (8).

Mary Shelley compared her own book to her protagonist's monster by calling it her "hideous progeny." This is quite an important aesthetic statement, for it expresses a changing view in modern poetics, referring to organic material, but applying constructive metaphors to it. Frankenstein's monster is not bred; it is composed by means of limbs of inanimate material, of different dead human beings. This also applies to Mary Shelley's book. For instance, a description of Lake Geneva toward the end of the book is taken almost literally from Percy Shelley's notebook. On 23 June 1816, he writes about his boat trip with Lord Byron around Lake Geneva:

> I/We could observe its [the river Drance] path thro the chasm of the mountains & the glens of the lower hills, until The mountains here came closer to the lake, & we could see the eastern boundary enclose

its waters so that & we approached the amphitheatre which of mountains which forms its eastern boundary. The spire of Evian shone in/under the woods that surrounded & the range of mountain above mountain which overhung it. (Percy Shelley in M. Shelley 1996: lxxix; transcription by C. E. Robinson)

In Mary Shelley's *Frankenstein* this became:

we passed the river Drance, and observed its path through the chasms of the higher, and the glens of the lower hills. The Alps here come closer to the lake, and we approached the amphitheatre of mountains which forms its eastern boundary. The spire of Evian shone under the woods that surrounded it, and the range of mountain above mountain by which it was overhung. (1992: 187)

Evidently the most difficult part to write was the textual creation of the creature or monster.

A new creation would bless me as its ~~maker~~ ^creator^ and source; many happy and excellent creatures would owe their existence ~~in~~ to me (M. Shelley 1996: 85)

During a first stage of revision, Mary Shelley replaced the word "maker" with "creator" in the left margin, thus emphasizing the desire to be a god of one's own creation. But because of this change, the succession of "creation," "creator" and "creatures" was a bit repetitious. Mary's partner, Percy, then made several changes to this draft, replacing "creation" and "creatures" with synonyms, so that the word "creator" stands out more clearly: "creation" is replaced by "existence"; the "creatures" are outlived by "beings." Because of the first replacement, "existence" also had to be changed, so it was replaced by "being." But since the previous line already had "beings," these had to be changed into "natures."

A new ~~creation~~ ^*existence*^ would bless me as its maker ^creator^² and source; many happy and excellent ~~creatures~~ ^*beings*^ ^*natures*^ would owe their ~~existence~~ ^*being*^ in to me. . . (M. Shelley 1996: 85; emphasis added).

Eventually yet another change was made so that in the first edition of 1818, "existence" is replaced by "species": "A new species would bless me as its creator." The method to create and animate that species was inspired by contemporary scientific discoveries with regard to electricity and galvanism. In the era of modernity, the metaphors that are used to describe artistic creation are increasingly modeled after contemporary evolutions in science. In the middle of the nineteenth century, Edgar Allan Poe presented the composition of his poem "The Raven" as a scientific endeavor. In "The Philosophy of Composition," he insists on mathematical precision from the outset: "It is my design to render it manifest that no one point in its composition is referrible either to accident or intuition—that the work proceeded, step by step, to its completion with the precision and rigid consequence of a mathematical problem" (1986: 482). One of the very first considerations before the actual writing, according to Poe's own account, was "the proper *length* for my intended poem—a length of about one hundred lines" (483). Poe presents his writing process as pure teleology, a straight progress toward accomplishment: "Here then the poem may be said to have its beginning—at the end, where all works of art should begin" (487).

But the eagerness with which he undertakes this enterprise makes his argument suspicious. The only deviation from the straight course toward accomplishment he admits, is the momentary consideration of using a parrot instead of a raven to repeat the refrain "Nevermore." Considering the smoothness of the writing process as presented in "The Philosophy of Composition," this small spot in the otherwise unruffled surface cannot avoid the impression that it hides an iceberg of other hesitations and deviations in the "Composition" that did not fit in with Poe's "Philosophy." Nonetheless, Poe's emphasis on craftsmanship is an important statement in that it represents a break with the early-nineteenth-century tendency to consider the creation of poetry as the result of "an ecstatic intuition" (481).

Because Poe's "Philosophy" draws attention to his composition's underlying chalk marks, it can be seen as a precursor of a particular aspect of modernism, which Rosalind Krauss refers to as "the grid." According to Krauss, the structure of the grid is "emblematic of the modernist ambition" (1985: 9). The grid used to serve as a tool to create a successful reality effect by means of perspective. Once the work of art was finished, the grid was erased. As opposed to this mimetic practice, modern artists tend to focus on the discontinuity between reality and its representation. According to Krauss, modernist art is not just antimimetic but also "antinarrative" and "antidevelopmental" (22).[3] Because the grid states the autonomy of the realm of art, Krauss argues that it is even "antinatural": "It is what art looks like when it turns its back on nature" (9).

In the visual arts, the grid may have been the most prominent structure, with Piet Mondrian's work being the most obvious example. Many poets, however, seem to have taken recourse to music. Louis Zukofsky's "A"—especially "A"-12—is a good example of both a pronounced interest in mathematical precision[4] and an unhidden grid. In the middle of his poem, Zukofsky makes the metapoetical statement that he has a plan (to write twenty-four books, twelve of which he has now finished), implying that he clearly intends to complete his project. But this statement is immediately followed by the undermining comment, suggesting that this division into twenty-four books is just "a kind of childlike play," an arbitrary structure imposed on the "gathering of 12 summers." It is interesting that Zukofsky's self-deconstruction of his own constructivist, mathematical division of "A" is analyzed by Burton Hatlen in organic terms: "a 'gathering,' a gestation, of twelve years has at last brought forth this new birth" (1997: 217).

The comparison of literary creation with the birth of a child is probably the most frequently employed organicist metaphor throughout literary history. In one of his notebooks, Marcel Proust remarks: "Le travail nous rend un peu mères" (The work more or less turns us into mothers). And the Belgian modernist author Willem Elsschot noted: "In the arts, one doesn't try. (. . .) One can try and bake a bread, but one doesn't try a creation. Nor does one try and give birth. If there is pregnancy, childbirth follows automatically, in due time" (2003: 7). This may be the way a particular author sees his particular creation, but from an editor's perspective it is certainly not the average scenario. The metaphor of childbirth applies only to short texts, and even then the extant material gives a distorted image of the "labor" that preceded the work's birth, for Elsschot often destroyed his earliest drafts—just like, for instance, Thomas Mann. The work is not always a steadily growing entity. Each new version contains new elements or variants vis-à-vis the previous version, but it also copies the elements that remain unchanged.

Around the beginning of the twentieth century, other scientific developments suggested new metaphors—the discovery of X-rays, for instance. When Hans Castorp in *The Magic Mountain* sees the X-ray of his cousin Joachim, he feels "stirrings of uneasy doubt, as to whether it was really permissible and innocent to stand here in the quaking, crackling darkness and gaze like this" into the inside of a human being (Mann 1960: 218). Dr Behrens, who takes the X-rays, appears to be an amateur painter; he has the scientific knowledge of what is hidden underneath the skin, and he manages to apply this knowledge to his art. As a result, his portraits seem to show a shimmer of all the underlying arteries and veins, a suggestion of all that is lurking behind or underneath the surface. The scientific discovery of the X-ray turned out to be an adequate metaphor for Mann's own writing method, notably his so-called technique of layers (*Schichtentechnik*) to create the illusion of temporal depth.

A similar layering technique characterizes the writing process of *Finnegans Wake*. Joyce saw himself as an engineer, and "one of the greatest engineers, if not the greatest, in the world" (16 April 1927; *L I* 251). He also called himself a "scissors-and-paste man." But, at the same time, he also emphasized the self-generative power of his work. About his first sketches for *Finnegans Wake*, he famously wrote: "I work as much as I can because these are not fragments but active elements and when they are more and a little older they will begin to fuse of themselves" (to Harriet Shaw Weaver, 9 October 1923; *L I* 204).

This somewhat organic notion of "fusion" that is such a crucial part of Joyce's writing strategy corresponds to what is sometimes called "osmosis" with reference to the writing method of Marcel Proust. In *Proust dans le texte et l'avant-texte*, Jean Milly emphasizes the "tendency toward osmosis" (1985: 17) in Proust's writing and its effect on punctuation (184). Proust uses the verbs *mêler* (to mix) and *fondre* (to melt; to merge) to denote the blending or fusion of textual units.[5] But Proust regards this fusion as an active intervention by the author. To what extent Joyce counted on the self-generative power of his "active elements" to "fuse of themselves" will be one of the focal points of the genetic examination in part 2.

Joyce's explicit poetical statements are rather rare. As a young man, the artist referred to Aristotle's famous dictum "e tekne mimeitai ten fusin," which he said is usually wrongly translated as "art is an imitation of nature"; instead, he suggested a more dynamic translation: "Aristotle does not here define art: he says only 'Art imitates Nature' and means that the artistic process is like the natural process" (*NLI* MS 36,639).[6] If the "antinatural" grid is emblematic of the modernist ambition, as Krauss argues, and if some aspects of Joyce's early aesthetic statement can still be said to resonate in his later modernist poetics, the question is how both statements can be reconciled. In terms of poetics, the question is also why one would need art at all, if it just imitates what can be found anywhere? Another modernist had a clear answer to this question. According to Marcel Proust, we need art because it shows us how this process works. The problem is that our perception, our senses standardize the world around us; Proust uses the verb *uniformiser*. If we encounter something new, we try to recognize it by making it uniform with a class of things we already know. Proust strongly believed in the power of art to defamiliarize this habitual perception. So in art he tries to find what he had vainly sought in life: diversity and variety: "La variété que j'avais en vain cherchée dans la vie" (Proust, First Pléiade edition 3: 159). As indicated in *Textual Awareness*, the manuscripts of the preceding draft stages show that this piece of art indeed imitates nature in the sense that it evolves through variation. In one of his notebooks, he jotted down: "La variété, la différence, que nous cherchons en vain dans l'amour, dans le voyage, la musique nous l'offre" (Carnet 4, f. 4r; Proust 2002: 344). In his drafts, Proust first wrote "Diversité," crossed it out, added "différentiation," crossed it out as well, replaced it by "Cette variété," crossed it out again, and replaced the specific variety by the more universal "La variété."[7] "Variété" is the version that was eventually published. But when Gilles Deleuze quoted this line in his book *Proust et les signes* in order to illustrate the importance of this crucial notion in Proust's aesthetics, he misquoted it, replacing "variété" by the word "diversité" (1973: 41; 1976: 54). And in the transcriptions of the relevant manuscript in the Pléiade edition, the "variété" is transcribed as "vérité."[8] If there is any "truth" in this "vérité," it is its textual memory of the "variété," "différence," "différentiation," and "diversité," as well as the copying mistakes that preceded it.

In both literary criticism and editorial theory, this textual evolution is simply to be avoided, but from a point of view of aesthetics it is quite interesting. If—as Joyce and Aristotle suggest—the artistic process is like the natural process, then this erroneous textual evolution indeed shows the "truth"—if truth is understood in Karl Popper's sense as correspondence to the facts. In this case, the fact is that while DNA molecules are awfully good at copying, even they sometimes make a mistake, and these mistakes make evolution possible.

In *The Selfish Gene*, Richard Dawkins paraphrases the notion of "the survival of the fittest" as a special case of the more general law of "the survival of the stable." Every new version can be considered as a modified copy of the previous one. Just how unstable or "unfit" a version can still be at the very last stages of the composition process is analyzed with microscopic precision in *The Dublin Helix*. Focusing on the textual inflation of the "Aeolus" episode in *Ulysses*, Sebastian Knowles draws attention to what in meteorological terms would probably be called a stiff breeze. Between the second and third versions of the placards "HARP EOLIAN" (*JJA* 18: 20) became "O, HARPEO LIAN A!" (*JJA* 18: 32). The intended modification was "O, HARP EOLIAN!" The extra *A* in "LIAN A!" is the printer's misinterpretation of what Knowles compares to messenger RNA: "the messenger RNA, in this case the letter A, has been read as actual text rather than as a carrier of information; its function as transmitter has been confused with the mark which it transmits. The result is a defective gene and a defective line of genetic text" (2001: 35).

In *Finnegans Wake*, Joyce thematized this textual type of messenger RNA. Apart from the letter *A*, he frequently used the letter *F* as an insertion mark. In chapter I.5 it is referred to as "that fretful fidget eff, the hornful digamma," followed by the parenthesis "(used always [. . .] throughout the papyrus as the revise mark)" (*FW* 120.33–121.02). As Sam Slote notes, it is "a mark that sacrifices itself for the sake of further text" (1997: 299). Part of this messenger RNA's message is that it needs to be "exscribed" as soon as the information it carries has been inserted and its (trans)mission is accomplished. Transmissional variants show resemblances with biological evolution, which is the result of a sort of copying mistake. Many popularizing books on genetics compare genetic evolution to printing processes and their inevitable mistakes or transmissional variants. But a clear distinction should be made between transmissional variants on the one hand, and genetic or compositional variants on the other. In the majority of cases, printing mistakes and other transmissional variants, not unlike variation or mutations in biology, simply "happen." As Richard Dawkins points out, there is nothing that "wants" to evolve; evolution is something that takes place in spite of all the efforts of the genes to prevent it.

In this respect, genetic variants (that is, variants in the manuscripts) are quite different. Here, in the majority of cases, a modification is intentional. Many authors claim that their writing is self-generative and that the fragments "fuse of themselves." To a certain extent, this may be true, but that is evidently not enough to write a complete work. Rather than the development of an embryo, a complex literary genesis is like the development of a new species in fast-forward mode, that is, there is intentional modification. That is why I think the metaphor of genetic manipulation, with trial and error, is applicable to writing processes of modern texts.

Germline gene therapy—"changing genes in places where they would be passed on to future generations" (Ridley 2000: 250)—in the form of genetically modified soybeans or mice, is sometimes called "Frankenstein technology" by its detractors (251). This is again just a metaphor that serves as an ethical warning. It is based on the popular image of the overconfident scientist who thought he could be a god of his own creation. But it is not informed by manuscript research, which shows Mary and Percy Shelley's pretty refined writing technology. The metaphor works better in the other direction. The comparison of literary genesis with genetic engineering may be just a metaphor, but as such it may also provide a more nuanced view of the act of literary creation. In the history of representations of the creative process, the metaphor of the writer as a genetic engineer is quite unique in that it combines both organicist and constructivist elements. It acknowledges the fact that to a certain extent the writing generates itself, but it also draws attention to the artificial nature of the intentional modifications that speed up the textual evolution.

From an editorial perspective, the development of a work has traditionally been visualized as a family tree or a stemma. This idea runs parallel with the presentations of species evolution in the nineteenth century, such as the phylogenetic tree created by Ernst Haeckel in 1866, shortly after the publication of Darwin's *On the Origin of Species*. Philology has traditionally been interested in the stem of the tree, which corresponds in biology with the most recent common ancestor of the descendants, often depicted as a so-called "rooted" phylogenetic tree. Since this common ancestor is usually postulated, the stem, or "root," is sometimes omitted, resulting in an "uprooted" phylogenetic tree. Since in classical and medieval philology the common ancestor often has to be postulated as well because the original manuscript is lost, Peter Robinson applied the "uprooted" method to the stemma of the surviving manuscripts of Chaucer's *Canterbury Tales*.

The image of the family tree would imply that the writing process, with its more private and "underground" nature than the "public" aspect of the published version, should be compared to the *roots* of that tree. Thomas Mann indeed compared his composition process to the double movement of downward drilling and upward absorbing.[9] The root, or "radix," metaphor is implied in the term "radical philology," which Geert Lernout suggested to designate the contextualization of Joyce criticism: "A radical philology limits the inquiry to the original desire-to-say of any form of writing *and* to its participation in a saturable and constraining context. If it did not, it would forfeit all relevance" (1994: 25). Three decades earlier, David Hayman employed the root metaphor in the opening paragraphs of his article "Tristan and Isolde in *Finnegans Wake*":

> It is hard to separate the roots of literary experience from the soil which surrounds them. It is harder to establish the virtues of those elements in the soil which helped to nourish the plant while it was growing. Doubtless this is more true than usual of Joyce's last book, and any attempt to sort out and evaluate all the sources and influences manifested by the records available to the student of *Finnegans Wake* would be unthinkable. But, if we limit our inquiry to a single theme

(...) we achieve a new understanding of the mechanics of influence and the integration of sources as well as of Joyce's book and of his mind. (1964a: 93).

Apart from Hayman's faith in the possibility of understanding an author's mind by making use of manuscript material, the interesting botanical metaphor[10] has some theoretical implications, to which A. Walton Litz drew attention in his article "Uses of the *Finnegans Wake* Manuscripts":

> All our metaphors of growth—"root" ideas, "skeleton" structure—imply that the meaning of the *Wake* can be discovered if, somehow, we can successfully trace the stream of composition to its source. In other words, the *Finnegans Wake* manuscripts pander to our love of paraphrase, and offer the tempting security of "intentions": yet no work ever lost more through paraphrase than *Finnegans Wake*. Just as many of the leading ideas of the book seem flat and commonplace when stated, so do the early drafts seem flat in comparison with the texture of the finished work. How exciting to learn that a "plain" version of Anna Livia's letter resides in the early manuscripts, and how dull to read it. Although many of us may insist that Joyce carried his methods of verbal elaboration beyond effective limits, there can be no doubt that the life of the *Wake* lies in this elaboration. (1966: 103)

Litz's emphasis on the textual elaboration rightly suggests that the traditional metaphors are too reductive. The "root" metaphor may be applicable to the search for sources of information exterior to the writing. But it is perhaps not quite adequate to visualize the processing of pretextual material in the drafts. Once the author has decided that he may use a specific source text, the subsequent process is the most complex aspect: the incorporation of this foreign material in the drafts. This process should be visualized from the other direction—not top down, but bottom up—to show how a foreign element is integrated and where it ended up in the published text; or how it eventually did *not* make it into the final version after all by ending up in a textual cul-de-sac or an aborted section that fell out of the direct line of textual descent.

In the case of James Joyce, a good example is the line "Rolando's deepen darblun Ossian roll" (*FW* 385.36). By retracing the composition history of this sentence counterclockwise (or "top down"), one eventually arrives at the line: "Roll on, thou deep and dark blue ocean – roll!" which is a quote from Lord Byron's *Childe Harold's Pilgrimage* (Canto 4, stanza 179, line 1603):

Counterclockwise reconstruction (top down)
Rolando's deepen darblun Ossian roll (*FW* 385.36)
↓
Rollon thoudeep anddark blueo ceanroll! (first typescript)
↓
Rollon thoudeep anddark blueo ceanroll! (third fair copy)
↓
Roll on thou deep and darkblue ocean, roll! (second fair copy)
↓
Roll on thou deep and darkblue ocean, roll (Byron, *Childe Harold's Pilgrimage*)

But genetic criticism is not so much (certainly not exclusively) interested in literary detective work and source hunting; the object of research is the writing process. At a certain moment, Joyce either reread or remembered Byron's line and started distorting it. This is only one among hundreds of source texts Joyce used (that is, one of the hundreds of extremities of the roots, if one sticks to the image of the family tree). In this case, Byron's line ended up completely distorted in *Finnegans Wake*: Apart from the final "roll," not a single word corresponds to the original line. As it happened, one stage in this line of textual descent became a genetic dead end: in a typescript, Joyce added the word "andamp," thus changing the pentameter into a hexameter: "Rollon thoudeep ^andamp^ anddark blueo ceanroll." But this typescript went missing.[11]

Chronological reconstruction (bottom up)
Rolando's deepen darblun Ossian roll (*FW* 385.36)
↑
→ Rollon thoudeep ᵃⁿᵈᵃᵐᵖ anddark blueo ceanroll (missing Ts)
↓
Rollon thoudeep anddark blueo ceanroll! (first typescript)
↑
Rollon thoudeep anddark blueo ceanroll! (third fair copy)
↑
Roll on thou deep and darkblue ocean, roll! (second fair copy)
↑
Roll on thou deep and darkblue ocean, roll (Byron, *Childe Harold's Pilgrimage*)

Perhaps Joyce simply forgot he ever made this change or he eventually decided that the hexameter was not a viable option and the variant "andamp" was neglected, creating a kind of dead end in the writing process. It is important for genetic research to draw attention to this variant and indicate that Joyce disrupted the pentameter at some point in the composition history, but it is equally important to indicate that Joyce eventually kept the original pentametric form. In fact, every single cancellation in a writing process is a kind of dead end. For every road not taken, it is necessary to observe both that the author did take it at a certain moment, and that he eventually decided to retrace his steps and continue in another, hopefully more viable direction.

This applies not only to words or sentences but also to the level of whole sections. During the writing process of Samuel Beckett's penultimate text *Stirrings Still*, another hexameter was the subject of a complete section that was elaborated in three successive versions but eventually aborted. The section is about an old man lying in a bed, apparently aware that there are two people who once in a while come and read to him. Fragments of what he hears he seems to have heard before. For instance, the hexameter "Mr Hackett turned the corner and saw his seat" (*RUL* MS 2935/2/3). Whereas the protagonist only seems to have heard it before, the author has definitely written it before, since this is part of the first sentence of Beckett's novel *Watt*: "Mr. Hackett turned the corner and saw, in the failing light, at some little distance, his seat." In the *Stirrings Still* manuscripts, the specifications "in the failing light, at some little distance" are omitted, and the resulting ellipsis is then shifted around with the following results:

Mr Hackett[12] turned the corner ... and saw his seat,
   or
Mr [Hackett] turned the corner and ... saw his seat.
   or
Mr [Hackett] turned the corner and saw ... his seat.
(*RUL* MS 2935/2/3)

On a separate notesheet, the different examples of how the position of the ellipsis changes the "lame hexameter" are followed by the exclamation: "How ~~elusive~~ ^various^ thus this simple set of words!" (*RUL* MS 2935/1/1).[13] The word "elusive" is replaced by the adjective "various." Both adjectives may be an indication that this hexameter, and by extension the whole section in which this hexameter is being discussed, would eventually turn out to be too unstable to survive. But that makes them all the more interesting. If there is any link between the two disciplines of biogenetics and manuscript genetics—or even more generally, if it is at all possible to find a link between life and art—the notion of variety or variation seems crucial.

The difference between medieval and modern manuscripts, based on their respective public and private functions, suggests a simple reversal of the traditional tree metaphor. But writing processes cannot be reduced to "underground" activities, as the French poet Francis Ponge has demonstrated, for instance, notably by publishing his drafts as an integral part of his published work. From a genetic perspective, the so-called *bon à tirer* moment (the moment the author decides his work is ready to be printed and to be confronted with the public) is perhaps less important than the moment an author finds a way to incorporate external material into his own composition. The most interesting moment in a botanical growth process is the point where the roots grow down and the rest of the plant grows up. Literary composition involves not just the downward movement, but the upward movement as well. The downward drilling, as Thomas Mann called it, includes looking for information, reading books, taking notes and excerpts. The absorption of this extratextual material is still part of the "underground" aspect of the genesis, but the selective incorporation, processing, and further elaboration in ever new versions is a matter of inflorescence. When an author makes a second draft or a fair copy, part of it will vary from the previous version, but part of it will simply be copied and remains the same.

One of the implications of this view is that the publication is not regarded as a once-only event—the eventual, long-awaited flowering of the work—but as just one in a series of versions. Instead of selling cut flowers, Francis Ponge changed his view on his own writing method by patterning it on botany (in *L'opinion changée quant aux fleurs*). Not unlike the growth of flowers, the urge to write is characterized by what he calls a "thirst for absolute perfection" (1992: 131). At the same time, Ponge realizes that the continued attempt of any flower to reach this absolute state can only lead to some kind of "relative perfection" (130). According to Ponge, the logical conclusion is reproduction. The urge to reach perfection culminates in the flower, but since the flower thrusts its reproductive organs into the air, it simultaneously gives evidence of the awareness that its perfection is only relative, and that it is condemned to die. To acknowledge death is to renounce absolute perfection, and what remains is repetition. This perspective on writing corresponds with what Killingsworth called the cyclic view, which does not deny decline but sees it as an integral part of the writing process.

In this sense, both Joycean composition and Beckettian decomposition can be said to belong to the cyclic type of growth in Killingsworth's typology. This does not mean they do not show any progressive characteristics

(Killingsworth's second type). As the preliminary title "Work in Progress" indicates, a literary work inevitably implies some kind of project, however vague. As a consequence it constantly "oscillates between an anticipatory perspective (. . .) and a retrospective vision" (Ferrer 1996: 225). Joyce and Beckett did not always have the final "telos" in mind from the start, but once the goal began to take shape, they tried to finish their project as well as possible by means of numerous revisions. Although this process can be said to entail the suggestion of "amelioration," neither Joyce nor Beckett ignored the relativity of perfection. The type of growth characterizing their writings can only be described as "genetic" (Killingsworth's first type) if this adjective includes the notion of textual descent with—both intentional and unintentional—modification.

2

Methodology

In the following attempt to chart the position of genetic criticism within literary criticism, it will be necessary to discuss a few controversial theoretical issues and get past a number of -isms and so-called "fallacies" such as positivism and intentionality, the Scylla and Charybdis of literary theory. But the Joycean advice that the longest way round is the shortest way home urgently calls for a digression—here to Ian McEwan's novel *Atonement* (2001), which lays out the terrain in a helpful and arresting way.

The painful precision with which McEwan describes the characters and the environment in the first and longest part of this literary triptych has a similar effect as the pounding migraine of Emily Tallis. On a hot summer day in 1935, the mistress of the house is taking a rest in her darkened room. With her overimpressionable senses in this camera obscura, she registers everything that goes on around the house in the sweltering heat, shimmering of unexpressed assumptions and expectations. Her eldest daughter, Cecilia, has just graduated and seems to be waiting aimlessly for whatever the future has in store. The youngest daughter, Briony, is thirteen and cannot wait to be an adult. The entire house is waiting, notably for the elder brother, Leon, and his friend Paul Marshall. *En attendant*, Briony is rehearsing one of her own plays together with her cousin Lola and Lola's younger twin brothers.

From her room, Briony sees how her sister Cecilia wants to fill a precious Ming vase in the fountain. She is in the presence of the cleaning lady's son, Robbie. Cecilia and Robbie are the same age and grew up together. Robbie has studied English literature, thanks to the support of father Tallis, and he is on the verge of studying medicine as well. At the fountain, he tries to help Cecilia fill the vase, but inadvertently snaps off two triangular pieces of china. Irritated, Cecilia suddenly undresses, climbs into the fountain, picks up the pieces of china from the bottom, takes off and leaves Robbie dumbfounded, confused, and excited. He has been feeling ill at ease and acting strangely the last few days.

To try to find an explanation for what is going on in his mind, he writes a short letter to Cecilia. But he needs more than one version to put his confused thoughts down on paper. When he is on his way to Cecilia, he meets Briony and asks her if she wants to give the letter to her sister. Of course, Briony cannot resist the temptation to open the envelope and have a secret glance at its contents. What she reads has such an impact that she interprets and reinterprets all the events of that day in a totally distorted way. A few moments after her reading of the letter, she witnesses an erotic scene between Robbie and Cecilia in the library. Briony misjudges the situation and thinks her sister is being raped. After supper, when the whole family is outside looking for the twin cousins, Briony finds her cousin Lola in the bushes, apparently assaulted by a dark figure. From a distance, Briony sees the figure running away. She cannot possibly discern who it is, but she "knows" it is Robbie. This certainty is based on her interpretation of the envelope's content, which becomes a crucial item of evidence when the police are called in. All persons present eventually get to read the letter. That very same night, Robbie is charged with attempted assault and arrested. Given the enormous consequences of Robbie's letter to Cecilia, the crucial question is of course: what was its content? To reveal this, McEwan relates its genetics:

First drafts: Imagine Robbie sitting down at his desk in his room. He feeds a sheet of paper and a carbon into the typewriter, types the date and the salutation, and formulates a conventional apology for what he calls his "clumsy and inconsiderate behaviour," continuing:

> If it's any excuse, I've noticed just lately that I'm rather light-headed in your presence. I mean, I've never gone barefoot into someone's house before. It must be the heat! (McEwan 2001a: 85)

He is not satisfied with the "self-protective levity" of these sentences, flicks the return lever and writes a second version:

> It's hardly an excuse, I know, but lately I seem to be awfully light-headed around you. What was I doing, walking barefoot into your house? And have I ever snapped off the rim of an antique vase before? (85)

He waits a minute before adding:

> Cee, I don't think I can blame the heat! (85)

Immediately sensing the melodrama of the exclamation mark, which is "the first resort of those who shout to make themselves clearer," he turns the drum, types an *x* and annuls the exclamation: "Cecilia, I don't think I can blame the heat." Without the exclamation mark, the humor is replaced by "an element of self-pity," so he considers reinstating the exclamation mark. *Fair copy*: He tinkers with the draft for another fifteen minutes until he decides to feed another sheet of paper into the typewriter and to type up a fair copy:

> You'd be forgiven for thinking me mad—wandering into your house barefoot, or snapping your antique vase. The truth is, I feel rather light-headed and foolish in your presence, Cee, and I don't think I can blame the heat! Will you forgive me? Robbie. (85)

He tilts back on his chair, thinks of a particular page in Gray's *Anatomy*, then suddenly drops forward and types:

> In my dreams I kiss your cunt, your sweet wet cunt. In my thoughts I make love to you all day long. (86)

Final version: This of course ruins the fair copy, and Robbie pulls the sheet of paper clear of the typewriter. He takes another sheet and writes the letter out in longhand, because after all a more personal touch seems more appropriate. When the letter is finished, Robbie starts polishing his shoes and prepares himself for the dinner at the Tallises, to which he is invited (86).

The chronological reconstruction of the writing process is one of the major tasks of genetic criticism, but this is only a prerequisite to interpreting what happened during this process, up to and including the publication of its textual result. In this respect, the context of its publication has to be taken into account, as well as "the enveloping facts themselves," as they are called in *Finnegans Wake* (*FW* 109.14). As McEwan illustrates, it is worthwhile looking "sufficiently longly" (*FW* 109.08) at the envelope as well. After the description of the different versions of the letter, McEwan inserts a digression with a flashback, diverting the reader's attention from the letter. Only after four pages does he return to the scene. In a deliberately long sentence, he describes how Robbie prepares himself for the dinner at the Tallises. The "snatching" and "folding" of the letter are mentioned only in passing, hidden in a long enumeration of methodical actions.[1]

Immediately after Robbie has given the envelope to Briony, he realizes he has folded the wrong version into the envelope:

> The handwritten letter he had rested on the open copy of Gray's Anatomy, Splanchnology section, page 1546, the vagina. The typed page, left by him near the typewriter, was the one he had taken and folded into the envelope. No need for Freudian smart-aleckry—the expla-

nation was simple and mechanical—the innocuous letter was lying across figure 1236, with its bold spread and rakish crown of pubic hair, while his *obscene* draft was on the table, within easy reach." (94; emphasis added)

The gravity of the word "obscene" is much more immense than the surface of this scene may suggest. On 12 September 2001—the year *Atonement* was published—Ian McEwan wrote a short text, describing what he had seen the day before. Or rather, what he had not seen. In "Beyond Belief," he acutely observed that one of the most horrifying aspects of the World Trade Center tragedy was "our safe distance from it all." In spite of the overabundance of images on television, the fear of the people inside the Twin Towers remained out of the picture. This offstage element turned the catastrophe into an obscenity: "The Greeks, in their tragedies, wisely kept these worst of moments off stage, out of the scene. Hence the word: obscene" (McEwan 2001b).

In *Atonement*, McEwan uses the adjective "obscene" when Robbie has just entrusted the letter to Briony, the moment he is no longer in possession of it. He suddenly realizes his mistake and still sees Briony from a distance, but when he calls her name she cannot hear him anymore. She is already too far away. The letter is out of reach, out of the scene. And that is precisely the moment when the version becomes obscene.

Briony opens the envelope and reads the wrong version of the letter.[2] With her newly acquired knowledge, she needs to reconsider everything that has happened in the course of the day, notably the scene by the fountain.[3] How it has to be reinterpreted is determined by one word—"See you in tea," as it is spelled out in *Ulysses* (*U* 15.1895). McEwan does not repeat the word but devotes a whole paragraph to it, starting as follows: "The word: she [Briony] tried to prevent it sounding in her thoughts, and yet it danced through them *obscenely*" (114; emphasis added). Again, the word and the version in which it occurs are "out of the scene," not only because in the meantime Briony has given the letter to her sister Cecilia, but also because the word has systematically been avoided in her presence. Up until now, the word has never entered the scene in the life of this thirteen-year-old girl.[4]

She analyzes the word and realizes what Beckett observed with reference to Joyce's last work: "Here form *is* content, content *is* form" (1929: 248). Or focalized through Briony: "the word was at one with its meaning (. . .). The smooth-hollowed, partly enclosed forms of its first three letters were as clear as a set of anatomical drawings" (2001a: 114). What bothers her, of course, is that the word is written by a man "confessing to an image in his mind" and the "irreducibly human, or male" principle that threatens the order of the scene. Before she read the letter, her world was confined to a safe home. Now that she has read it, this scene is marked by the presence of an offstage surrounding it: "With the letter, something elemental, brutal, perhaps even criminal had been introduced, some principle of darkness"—according to Briony—"and even in her excitement over the possibilities, she did not doubt that her sister was in some way threatened and would need her help" (113–14).

This "obscene" interpretation is in sharp contrast with the "onstage" interpretation by Cecilia, who "absorbs" its force and color, "derived from the single repeated word" (111). To her it is not so much the "See you in tea" of the prison gate girls' song in *Ulysses*, but rather an indication of the "word known to all men." It is the vanishing point that makes her see the whole scene in the right perspective. While the letter is unfolded in her hands, Cecilia interprets it as a most direct, heartfelt declaration of love. Then she folds it away and suddenly realizes how this might be interpreted by anyone else: "The act of folding it away brought her to an obvious realisation: it could not have been sent unsealed" (111).

If this were a fable, the moral might be that we should not read early versions, since apparently they only complicate matters that can easily be interpreted intuitively. But rather than a fable, McEwan's story is an exercise in empathy, one of the most important principles of literature, according to the author.[5] Perhaps more than any other form of art, literature is an invitation to try to put oneself in someone else's place. This "someone else" is not necessarily the author. Both readers and authors try to put themselves in the characters' shoes, or more precisely, in their minds. Together with the author, together with Briony, any reader is invited to interpret the "scene by the fountain"—as it is called in the book. And even the two characters involved in the scene have to interpret it. They have to interpret not only their actions, but above all the interactions between their respective minds. And as if that were not enough, they have to interpret their own minds as well, which is probably the most difficult of all forms of empathy.

As a remnant of Robbie's effort to get the picture and explain what is going on in his mind, the early version of the letter, reduced by Briony to one obscene word, is a literary equivalent of the hole in the canvas of Vermeer's painting *Lady Writing a Letter* (ca. 1670). A little hole in the canvas is covered by the lady's left eye, but still recognizable because of a dent in the paint (Wheelock and Broos 1995: 186). In fact, the eye was painted around the hole, which is the material trace of the painter's method to determine the vanishing point, that is, the point at which receding parallel lines seem to meet. This trace of the tools used by the painter to create the illusion of three dimensions called central perspective becomes a palpable absence, a spatial mark of the underlying temporal dimension. This kind of material evidence of the writing process is located by Peter Shillingsburg in "the hole at the center of textual and literary theory" (1997: 56). Shillingsburg designed a map that shows four major forms of "textual concern" (59), focused respectively on "The Language (Speech act theory, Signs, Semantics), The Reader (Time, Place, Interpretation), The Book (Bibliography, ...), and The Author (Time, Place, Intention)," arranged respectively to the north, east, south, and west of the center, "The Physical Documents for the Work" (58). The underlying idea is that "texts—both as physical and mental constructs—lie at the center of any attempt to record or communicate any knowledge" (60). With this map, Shillingsburg tries to open up the interests of textual criticism, which for a long time has been oriented toward the southwest. Shillingsburg makes a clear distinction between the physical documents (the "Material Text") and the reading experience (the "Reception Text"). The latter is only an approximation, "the only 'thing' that a reader can refer to when making comments about a work" (60). But even the material text is only a representation. It is not equivalent with the work (75), merely one of its many manifestations. Yet, what distinguishes it from these other manifestations is that it is the starting point where the process of "decoding or dematerializing the material text into some mental construct" begins (75–76). Shillingsburg's view is based on the idea that, since even the author's manuscripts are only the results of his attempt to record a mental process, the subsequent page proofs and publications are all results of printers' and proofreaders' mental reconstructions of the author's mental conception. As a consequence, the only thing that is at our disposal is a representation of something else.

Against this background, it becomes clear what French genetic critics mean by *avant-texte*. This central notion in genetic criticism is defined by Pierre-Marc de Biasi as "the work's process of production, insofar as it can be pieced back together by the analysis of the author's working manuscripts, and then interpreted following a defined critical method" called *critique génétique* (1996: 38). Although the empirical basis is crucial to this kind of research, it is important to note that the *avant-texte* is more than the sum total of all available material documents; it is only after critical analysis that the geneticist can read them "as successive moments of a process" (38).

Almuth Grésillon has pointed out the problematic nature of the term *avant-texte* in that it may create the deceptive presupposition that any creative process can be subordinated to a textual model. Genetic criticism is equally applicable to architecture, for instance; here, the notion of *avant-texte* is not quite suitable. Even within the realm of literature, it is not always clear what the "avant" relates to, since it is often hard to define the "text," for instance with reference to dramatic works. Beckett has brought this problem to a head, not only by directing (and making postpublication changes to) some of his own plays, but also by translating them and thus creating yet another authorial version of the text. Even though the term *avant-texte* has been adopted in English publications as well, Almuth Grésillon suggests the term *genetic dossier* (1994a: 109) to avoid the dominance of the textual model.

Use versus Interpretation

McEwan's story may perhaps serve as a warning to genetic critics that reading early versions is no guarantee of a "right" interpretation. And pragmatists might regard it as a case in point to prove Richard Rorty's opinion that "all anybody ever does with anything is use it" (1992: 92). This is Rorty's reply to Umberto Eco's suggestion that "use" is the opposite of "interpretation." With this distinction, Eco drew attention to what he called "the limits of interpretation," alerting readers to the dangers of "overinterpretation." To "interpret" a literary work or opus, Eco suggests taking into account what he calls the *intentio operis*. According to Eco, "it is possible to speak of text intention only as the result of a conjecture on the part of the reader," and to prove such a conjecture, the best way is "to check it against the text as a coherent whole" (1990: 58).

In *Le démon de la théorie: Littérature et sens commun*, Antoine Compagnon considers Eco's coinage *intentio operis* as a form of *intentio auctoris*, or authorial intention, in disguise (1998: 87). Peter Shillingsburg, on the other hand, regards it as "warmed up New Criticism" (1997: 191). One of the problems is the anthropomorphization of the work implied in the term *intentio operis*. "Texts do not themselves have either intention or meaning," as Peter Shillingsburg argues (2006: 55). Texts are meant to mean or made to mean by different agents. If a text does not mean anything until it is acted upon, its meaning becomes a matter of politics. As Humpty Dumpty explained to Alice, "The question is, which is to be master—that's all" (Carroll 1988: 196). Roland Barthes had presented the Author as an authoritarian Father or Master, from whom the reader—who had apparently been neglected in traditional criticism—finally liberated himself: "the birth of the reader must be at the cost of the death of the Author" (1977: 148). This liberation is presented as "revolutionary" and "anti-theological," whereas in fact the reader has always been in the position of a master. In "The Politics of Theories of Interpretation," E. D. Hirsch refers to Humpty Dumpty's notion of "which is to be master" to make a distinction between an a priori approach (interpretation based on ad hoc reader preferences) and an a posteriori approach (interpretation based on a cipher key chosen by somebody other than the reader). The former is referred to as the self-governing, or "autocratic," norm, the latter the other-governing, or "allocratic," norm (1982: 240).[6] But in both cases it is completely up to the reader to choose her or his approach. With the autocratic approach, the reader chooses to be free to project his or her own present hobbyhorses into the text; with the allocratic approach, s/he chooses to work with someone else as a norm.

This latter approach is the opposite of Jean-Paul Sartre's dictum: "L'objet littéraire n'a d'autre substance que la subjectivité du lecteur" (The literary object has no other substance than the subjectivity of the reader). This line is quoted by Louis Hay (2002: 8) to point out that the text can become an effect without cause when the critic is regarded as a reader among readers and the existence of the author is simply denied. For a long time, Hay argues, critical theory has almost obliterated the text in favor of reading (*la lecture*), which was seen as "the only reality of literary facts" (7). The task of the critic, according to Hay, is to be "the ferryman between the universe of writers and the universe of readers" (30).

Falsifiability

What Hirsch called an "allocratic" approach is necessarily historical, since it is based on decisions made in the past. Hirsch adds that this historical norm is "always open to revision" (1982: 240). This kind of revision is what Antoine Compagnon alludes to in the title of his article "Ce qu'on ne peut plus dire de Proust" (What Cannot Be Said about Proust Any Longer). Compagnon refers to Karl Popper's theory of falsifiability as set forth in *The Logic of Scientific Discovery*.[7] To the question of whether anything should be allowed in literary criticism, his reply is negative, which he illustrates by means of an example. He refers to a psychoanalytic interpretation of a passage from Proust's *Sodome et Gomorrhe* by Alain Roger. This interpretation was based on a note in the first Pléiade edition of *A la recherche du temps perdu*, which mentioned the presence of the word *succinctement* (succinctly) in the manuscripts. Since this word does not occur in the final version, Roger assumed that Proust deleted this word. According to Roger, this cancellation was a psychologically symptomatic act, but as Compagnon shows, the omission of this word was not a cancellation by Proust but the result of a typist's copying mistake.[8]

However, this example may create the false impression that the main aim of manuscript genetics would be to revise earlier interpretations. The concept of falsifiability is rather a rule of thumb to check one's own theories or interpretations, and a reminder of the humbling realization that scientific statements are not conclusively verifiable, merely falsifiable (according to the black swan paradigm: to verify the statement "All swans are white," one has to observe *all* white swans, but one single observation of one single black swan is enough to falsify the statement). By starting from material evidence, manuscript analysis allows researchers to make interpretive statements that can be proven wrong. That is, according to Geert Lernout, the reason "why a small number of *Wake* critics are turning to the notebooks: we are doing a type of research that is *falsifiable* and therefore scientific in Karl Popper's sense of the word. And it also explains why a sophisticated postmodernist critic such as Daniel Ferrer may suddenly find himself being 'absolutely certain'" (1995: 48). The latter statement is a reference to Daniel Ferrer's essay on Joyce's Freud notes in notebook VI.B.19, "The Freudful Couchmare," in which Ferrer argues that this material evidence "gives us at last some irrefutable evidence of a direct (and close) contact with Freud's text" and that "[w]e can now be absolutely certain that Joyce read attentively 'Little Hans' and 'The Wolf Man'" (1985: 367).

The first time Geert Lernout refers to Ferrer's moment of certainty, the focus is on "the notebook text": "If we look for sources we definitely do not open up *the notebook text* to the larger intertextual network: on the contrary, we ground the text by limiting the infinity of its possible meanings, we find 'irrefutable evidence' and end up being 'absolutely certain'" (1995: 33; emphasis added). The second time Geert Lernout refers to this certainty (48), he uses it to emphasize the difference between a "radical philological approach" and that of a literary critic "who manages to apply a fashionable theory to *a text*. The results of such interpretations are more or less interesting. Findings that derive from a radical philological approach belong to a different category: they are true in a different sense for the simple reason that they can be proven wrong" (48; emphasis added).

The difficulty is the discrepancy between "the notebook text" (33) and "a text" (48). Daniel Ferrer did not claim we can be absolutely certain about any interpretation of the (published) text of *Finnegans Wake*, only about Joyce's reading of Freud. If one of the Freud excerpts made it into a passage, the falsifiability principle only applies to tracing it back to Joyce's reading of Freud's "Little Hans" and "The Wolf Man." At the level of "the notebook text," we can indeed be quite certain of other readings as well. For instance, it seems safe to say that Joyce read at least large portions of Fritz Mauthner's *Beiträge zu einer Kritik der Sprache*. But this falsifiable statement does not lead to a "definitive" reading of the passages in which Joyce has incorporated his Mauthner notes. It is also possible to follow the processing of some of his Mauthner notes in the drafts and eventually the published versions of book IV. But to what extent this incorporation is an homage to Mauthner's linguistic skepticism or an ironic comment remains a matter of interpretation.

Limits of Interpretation?

According to Umberto Eco, "it is not true that everything goes" (1992: 144). In *The Limits of Interpretation*, he had already illustrated this by means of an example taken from Joyce criticism, more specifically a discussion regarding the word "berial" in *Finnegans Wake*. All the critics involved in this exemplary and stimulating debate used contextual and genetic evidence to corroborate their arguments, which led Eco to the following conclusion: "All the participants proved to be smart enough to invent acrobatic interpretations, but both, in the end, were prudent enough to recognize that their brilliant innuendos were not supported by the context. They won the game because they let *Finnegans Wake* win" (1990: 150).

The matter of limits was intensified in genetic Joyce studies when R. J. Schork made an explicit distinction between a "circumscribed" ("minimalist") and an "expansive" ("maximalist") approach. According to Schork, minimalists "tend to emphasize the detection of documentary sources" while maximalists "exercise considerable psychological ingenuity in explicating the connections between strings of entries" in Joyce's notebooks (1994: 108). Schork did not conceal his preference for the circumscribed method as an adequate means to avoid interpretations that "manipulate a text to signify anything one wishes" (106). Geert Lernout applied the circumscribed approach to notebook research and the discovery of source texts, which he contrasted with the approach of "the literary critic who finds a thought or a formula to describe a poem or a novel" (1994: 48). The expansive method is represented by researchers such as David Hayman, who argued:

Those who limit themselves to the philological tasks may perhaps see themselves as doing necessary spadework for which we others may be grateful, but we should not confuse this sort of activity with criticism. Unless the implications of such findings are used to disclose something about the text and its procedures, theirs is an endstopped activity. (1995: 8)

In a review of *Probes: Genetic Studies in Joyce*, Michael Groden gave an account of this "heated and healthy debate," concluding that from a maximalist perspective, "genetic research and scholarship inevitably become genetic criticism because it is focused ultimately not on the documents but on the creative process, on the interaction of that process with a theoretical framework, or on the relationship between the writing process and reading. On the other hand, Lernout is far less willing than Hayman to subordinate scholarship to criticism" (1996: 14).

This healthy debate also proves to be relevant to a wider circle of literary critics. Ortwin De Graef has reacted against Eco's "limits of interpretation" by arguing that interpreters or critics do not need to self-impose limits to the act of interpreting. De Graef criticizes the prescriptive nature of Eco's limits, which "*can* be transgressed by interpretation but *ought not* to be transgressed" (2001). On the other hand, "Deconstruction's limits are the limits interpretation runs into and *cannot* transgress." De Graef argues that the limits of interpretation are indicated or imposed by aporias in the text itself.

The question then is: What is the text itself? What if there are various editions? What if the author did not destroy his manuscripts? If a writer chooses not to destroy the early versions of his writing, they may be a valuable interpretive tool. If a researcher chooses not to consult these documents, is this choice another form of self-imposed limits? Since limits are a contested issue, how does literary criticism in general appreciate "preliminary" issues that are the subject of genetic criticism? To what extent can the early version of a text be regarded as part of the work? Is a work to be treated as a synchronic structure, or is its diachrony part and parcel of this structure? Not everyone agrees on the relevance of this temporal aspect. New Criticism focused on "the text itself" and logically did not study manuscript material as a matter of principle. For many decades, researchers agreed with the dominant New Critical point of view formulated by René Wellek and Austin Warren: "A study of variants seems to permit glimpses into an author's workshop. Yet if we examine drafts, rejections, exclusions, and cuts more soberly, we conclude them not, finally, necessary to an understanding of the finished work or to a judgement upon it" (1973: 91).

T. S. Eliot argued that "a knowledge of the springs which released a poem is not necessarily a help toward understanding the poem: too much information about the origins of the poem may even break my contact with it" (1969: 112). Consistent with this view, he wrote toward the end of his life: "As a general rule, to which I cannot perceive my own work to provide any exception, it seems to me that posterity should be left with the product, and not be encumbered with a record of the process" (quoted in Gardner 1978: v). But it is remarkable that he wrote this in a letter to the librarian of Magdalene College in Cambridge, asking him whether the university would be interested in the drafts of his *Four Quartets*. For a man who consistently advised against manuscript research, it is all the more remarkable that he kept his manuscripts and even presented several of them to a university library, knowing full well that this kind of institution might interpret such an offer as an invitation to study these documents. The reasons for this kind of gesture will vary from case to case. Financial motivations are certainly a factor that should not be underestimated. Apart from this financial aspect, an author may see it as a way of safeguarding, or at least presenting, some traces of his intentions. Since a text has no meaning unless it is acted upon by agents, it seems only natural—from a writer's perspective—that he may want to assert his role as an agent, especially when he is nearing his death. This may be even more pressing in the case of playwrights, such as Samuel Beckett, who have seen numerous performances that did not tally with their view of their own plays. When an author realizes that after his death his work will be acted upon unilaterally by the *intentio lectoris*, he may see a donation of his manuscripts as a way of presenting some traces of what the text was meant to mean, as a counterweight to what it will be made to mean.

With regard to Beckett's works, S. E. Gontarski refers to this kind of enlarged corpus of texts as a ghost canon, or "grey canon" (2005: 143): "Such expansion of the canon is precisely what Beckett at first sought to resist, since it re-inscribes the traditional presumption of authorial authority," yet "he finally extended such authority, insisting on the primacy of the playwright in the process of performance" (142–43). Steven Connor discussed this paradoxical attitude with reference to the entire bilingual oeuvre:

> The paradox here is that Beckett visibly exercised a high degree of proprietary concern and power over a body of texts which consistently

claim the condition of being uncontrolled, unmastered, or without origin in a responsible or authoritative "I." What focuses these problems for Beckett in particular are, first, his turn to French, with the resulting requirement to become his own translator, and, second, his turn to drama. In both cases, Beckett found himself no longer able simply to separate himself from his works after their completion but continued to work with them (and against them) in various ways. (1992: 155)

But apart from extending authorial authority, Beckett simultaneously extended its problematization. The paradox signaled by Connor and Gontarski relates not only to authority, but also to the concept of the "work." The important fact that Beckett continued to work with and against his texts also problematizes the notion of their completion and makes them a particularly suitable corpus for genetic criticism.

Authorial Intention

One of the main arguments against authorial intention is that the significance of a literary work is neither exhausted by, nor equal to, the author's intention. As W. K. Wimsatt and Monroe C. Beardsley argued in their essay "The Intentional Fallacy," an author's intention "is neither available nor desirable as a standard for judging the success of a work of literary art" (1954: 3). One of the examples to illustrate their theory is a line in T. S. Eliot's "Love Song of J. Alfred Prufrock" ("I have heard the mermaids singing, each to each"), which may be interpreted as a reference to a line in a poem by John Donne ("Teach me to heare Mermaides singing"). Wimsatt and Beardsley conclude that an attempt to find out whether or not this line is an allusion to Donne by asking T. S. Eliot "would have nothing to do with the poem 'Prufrock': it would not be a critical inquiry. Critical inquiries, unlike bets, are not settled in this way. Critical inquiries are not settled by consulting the oracle" (18).

Here, Wimsatt and Beardsley do not make a distinction between biographism and genetic research. With reference to the "Prufrock" example, the authors suggest two approaches: "There is (1) the way of poetic analysis and exegesis, which inquires whether it makes any sense if Eliot-Prufrock *is* thinking about Donne. (. . .) [W]e submit that this is the true and objective way of criticism, as contrasted to what the very uncertainty of exegesis might tempt a second kind of critic to undertake; (2) the way of biographical or genetic inquiry" (18). Since in this particular case, the "oracle" was still alive, Wimsatt and Beardsley lumped together "biographical or genetic inquiry." As opposed to this view, Geert Lernout emphasizes the difference between genetic criticism and biographism: "The power of the genetic approach lies precisely in the fact that it deals with what Joyce thought *in so far as it can be shown in the documents.* Geneticists are not interested in Joyce's psyche but in what he was doing when he was working on *Finnegans Wake*" (1998: 302).

A famous opponent of biographism was Marcel Proust. According to Antoine Compagnon, however, Proust's antibiographism had nothing to do with a rejection of the notion of authorial intention. Instead, Proust replaced a superficial intention by a profound one, of which the work was a better witness than the CV (1998: 95). In any case, intention remains a central concept, according to Compagnon. It is not limited to what an author resolved to write (for instance, in a kind of declaration of intent or in an interview), nor to the motivation that may have incited him to write, nor even to the textual coherence of the work (95). Authorial intention, according to Compagnon's definition, is what the author wanted to say with the words he actually employed. Since everyone has different pasts, words will arouse different "involuntary" memories, or significances that were not intended by the author. Proust was tolerant with regard to *contresens* (as the counterpart of voluntary or intended meaning) because he was convinced that the entirety of intratextual references and correspondences causes both the intended meaning and the different reading to follow the same "progression of beauty."[9] Proust's "contresens" does not exclude the "commonsense" approach, as it is sometimes called. The subtitle of Antoine Compagnon's book *Le démon de la théorie* is indeed *Littérature et sens commun*. (Literature and Common Sense). Peter Shillingsburg calls this the "more traditional" view that "the work of art is a personal communication from an author to an audience" (1997: 147). It is "common sense" because "generally speaking, people think that way about their own speech acts" (147). This formulation may suggest that "generally speaking" "people" do not know any better, but in *From Gutenberg to Google* (2006), Shillingsburg elaborates on the complexity of speech and script acts. He refers to Eco and "those who hold that the specific words, word order, and punctuation alone provide limits to possible meanings" (61), arguing that this view "seems to have common sense, but [that] it also lacks a full sense of the complexity of acts constructing meaning" (61). An awareness of this complexity, however, does not necessarily imply a rejection of the commonsense approach. The view that a work of literature is a personal communication from an author to a reader applies a notion of so-called "expository" writing (which is supposed to be straightforward and preferably unambiguous) to literature (which is usually expected to be susceptible to divergent interpretations). But as Shillingsburg argues, this distinction is quite artificial and "highly disingenuous, for it tends to absolve the critic of literary texts from any responsibility to justify interpretation as the completion of or fulfillment of complex communicative acts" (63). If it is possible at all to make a distinction between these two types of writing, they are not mutually exclusive: "expository writing has at its disposal all the tools of literary language and (. . .) literary writing is frequently intended by its authors to have expository effects" (63).

It is significant that Shillingsburg revalues the work of E. D. Hirsch, even though he does not necessarily hold the latter's point of view. Especially in the 1980s and 1990s, Hirsch was regarded as a synonym for critical conservatism, orphaned after "The Death of the Author" by Roland Barthes (1968). In the meantime, the author seems to have returned,[10] not with a vengeance, but simply like Tim Finnegan, because of the whiskey spilled at the wake. According to Hirsch, "verbal meaning necessarily has the character of a willed type" (1971: 62), and this meaning is "that which is represented by a text" (8). The literary work thus appears as Will and (often inadequate) Representation. The fact that it is impossible to read an author's mind was no reason for Hirsch to abandon authorial intention as an interpretive criterion: "I can never know another person's intended meaning with certainty because I cannot get inside his head to compare the meaning he intends with the meaning I understand. (. . .) But this obvious fact should not be allowed to sanction the overly hasty conclusion that the author's intended meaning is inaccessible and is therefore a useless object of interpretation" (1971: 17). The possibilities of revaluing the "use" of this object as an intermediary between the text and the historical context is discussed by Fotis Jannidis in *Rückkehr des Autors* (1999).

Hirsch made another distinction by insisting on the difference between "interpretation" and "criticism": "The object of interpretation is textual meaning in and for itself and may be called the *meaning* of the text. The object of criticism, on the other hand, is that meaning in its bearing on something else (standards of value, present concerns, etc.), and this object may therefore be called the *significance* of the text" (1971: 211). In *Resisting Texts*, however, Peter Shillingsburg annuls this distinction and treats both concepts as synonyms: "Criticism is interpretation" (1997: 147). Interpretations "cannot be proved or validated," he argues, but they "can be supported by evidence and argument" (147). In any case, whether one tries to "validate" or "support" an interpretation, the body of evidence to check the plausibility of one's argument may become considerably vaster when one consults the genetic dossier.

In her discussion of Beckett's developing ambiguity, Rosemary Pountney points out a "fundamental problem (. . .) about the study of an author's discarded drafts and notes" (1988: 101). She refers to the introduction of John and Beryl Fletcher's edition of *Fin de partie*, in which the editors claim that "in pruning his work Beckett undoubtedly improved it, but sometimes compressed things so drastically that the surviving statement is somewhat obscure" (Fletcher in Pountney 1988: 101). For that reason, they indicate "the original intention" in the notes. Pountney rightly argues that to pin down the original intention "may have a destructive effect on the text, unless the full evolutionary process is stressed" (102). But against Fletcher's "original intention," Pountney posits another intention:

> Precisely the reason that Beckett suppresses the specific from his later drafts, however, is (. . .) to free the plays from limiting identifications. *This* is his intention. (102)

The "fundamental problem" relates not only to the *original* intention, but to any conjecture regarding authorial intention. In "Genesis: A Fallacy Revisited," W. K. Wimsatt refers to his colleague Monroe Beardsley's statement regarding the inadequacy or even irrelevance of authorial intention in literary studies: "The objective critic's first question, when he is confronted with a new aesthetic object is not, What is this supposed to be? But, What have we got here?" (Beardsley quoted by Wimsatt 1968: 195). It is hard to argue about a text in terms of what the author wanted or did not wish to do (for example, "Beckett has no wish to . . ." [Pountney 1988: 102]); it is equally difficult to try to establish revised texts that are "as close as possible to how Beckett wanted them to be" (*TN* 1: v).[11]

Nonetheless, among the numerous possible strategies, an allocratic reading remains a valuable approach to literary studies, and to call it "reactionary" (De Graef 2001) is part of the tactics, politics, and rhetoric of criticism. The wish to know an author's intentions can be a form of empathy, a basic human quality without which literature would perhaps not even exist. As Alan Palmer argues in *Fictional Minds*, readers are interested in characters because they try to understand and follow their mental processes; characters in novels also try to find out about each other's cognitions. The author is evidently interested in these cognitions, and it is only natural that readers are, in their turn, interested in the thought processes, motives, and intentions of the author.

Evidently an interest in these intentions is no guarantee for the correctness of one's conjectures. Popper's falsifiability principle may be useful to the study of literature, but it is not applicable to "intention." It is possible to trace the source texts from which a set of notes are derived, but the intentions that made the author incorporate his notes in his drafts are much more difficult to fathom. When Beckett deletes a passage, this may reflect an intent of undoing; when he adds a passage or indicates "amplify" as in his "Analysis" of *Not I* (RUL MS 1227-7-12-1, f. 6r), this may reflect an intent of adding. Moreover, intentions are prone to change. Between the "original intention" stressed by Fletcher and the texts as Beckett "wanted them to be," various versions and numerous variants indicate a process.

This process is also an immaterial object of research, as immaterial as an author's intentions, but if there are enough material traces of this process, it is possible to reconstruct it, or at least create the impression of process the way movies create the illusion of movement by means of the quick succession of stills. From that perspective, it is important that Samuel Beckett kept his manuscripts and donated many of them to university libraries. Thanks to the preserved manuscripts of *Stirrings Still*, for instance, we can reconstruct its writing process as a set of stirring stills.

The reasons underlying Beckett's donation are difficult to fathom. *From the author's perspective*, one of the motives may have been the wish to provide his readers with the material traces of the creative process, and of his evolving intentions during that process. Confronted with the most divergent interpretations and performances of his plays, it is not inconceivable that his thoughts may indeed have been similar to what Geert Lernout formulated in his position statement: "Take away intention and context, and the only thing left to say about a text is that it can mean anything at all" (1994: 25). Intentions belong to the realm of what Hans Magnus Enzensberger called the method "from the inside," which only authors can apply to their own works. *From a reader's perspective*, the only option is the method "from the outside" (Enzensberger 1962: 62), based on inevitably "poor" material, because no memories are attached to it. But it is possible to study a work of literature as not just a text, but as "the imagined whole implied by all differing forms of a text that we conceive as representing a single literary creation" (Shillingsburg 1996: 43). When an author preserves his manuscripts, they allow us to include the drafts among the variant forms, which may have consequences for the "imagined whole" we infer from them.

Empiricism and Positivism

In a polemic in the newspaper *Le Monde* with the hermeneutic Laurent Jenny, the French genetic critic Pierre-Marc de Biasi argued that genetic criticism opens up "a formidable mine of discoveries" (1997: xii). The consequent impossibility of "closure" of the text is, according to de Biasi, what upsets hermeneutic critics such as Jenny. The polemical rhetoric tempts de Biasi into claiming that, from a hermeneutic point of view, the text is the only God and the critic his prophet. In contrast, genetic criticism is presented as an antifundamentalist approach, emphasizing that "meaning is unstable and the truth problematic" (xii).

Yet, the same Pierre-Marc de Biasi presented the methodology of genetic criticism under the programmatic title "Toward a Science of Literature," which implies a methodology that accords with the logic of scientific discovery. However, as opposed to Compagnon's use of manuscript evidence to refute a particular interpretation, Daniel Ferrer and Michael Groden suggested that "genetic documents do not authorise or forbid interpretations, but they open dizzying new ranges of potentialities" (1995: 511). Geert Lernout suggests that this presentation (characterized by remarkably liberal views that are usually not exactly associated with textual studies) may have been prompted by a fear of being lumped together with philology (2002). Especially in France, the notion of philology is associated with old-school, nineteenth-century positivism, and calling yourself a positivist in France requires a "superhuman amount of masochistic self-denial," according to Michael Werner (1987: 141). The poststructuralist environment in which genetic criticism became a major paradigm in France seems to have had a considerable influence on the way it was presented. As Geert Lernout has examined in *The French Joyce*, poststructuralist literary studies resulted in an increasingly subjective and even mystical approach. Its ostentatious breakaway from a critical tradition still complicates any attempt to admit a continuity with pre-1968 approaches. That French genetic critics are on the alert for reproaches concerning positivism is therefore not only understandable but apparently necessary, since both from the hermeneutic (Laurent Jenny) and from the sociological side (Pierre Bourdieu), genetic criticism is accused of "the most traditional positivism of literary historiography" (Bourdieu 1992: 276).

Against this background, it is also understandable that the critical voices within French genetic criticism itself question precisely the somewhat artificial insistence on the difference from traditional philology. Jean-Yves Tadié regrets that the antihistorical attitude has led to a dichotomy between a "proletariat devoted to scholarship and an aristocracy of interpretation" (1987: 292). Laurent Jenny's polemical presentation of genetic criticism as a throwback to nineteenth-century positivism, as opposed to the "sovereign" hermeneutic gesture, suggests that Tadié's observation is unfortunately all too acute. Apart from Tadié, another genetic critic who aired some internal criticism was Antoine Compagnon. In his introduction to an issue of *Romanic Review* devoted to genetic criticism, he vented three perplexities, asking (1) whether genetic criticism is a theory of criticism or "just helpful advice"; (2) whether it represents a rupture; and (3) how it relates to textual criticism and scholarly editing (1995: 394).

The last question may be regarded as a difference in focal points. Scholarly editing uses manuscript research in view of producing an edition, whereas genetic criticism concentrates on the dynamics of (usually literary) writing processes. Traditionally, it may have been taken too much for granted that manuscript research was only part of scholarly editing and textual criticism. One of genetic criticism's merits is its new approach toward manuscript research, insisting that it does not need to be exclusively at the service of editing. In this sense, genetic criticism does not represent a rupture (Compagnon's second issue), but it does constitute a new attitude. Investigating the genesis of literary works may be of help in the study of an author's poetics. The writing process turns out to be a fascinating object of research in its own right. Moreover, it may provide valuable textual information that can be useful in the interpretation of the published text. Compagnon's first question—whether genetic criticism is a theory of criticism or just helpful advice—is a matter of politics. What matters is that genetic criticism may be instrumental in bridging the gap between what Tadié called the "proletariat" of scholars and the "aristocracy" of critics.

Proliferation of Meaning

In an "era of industrial and bourgeois society, of individualism and private property," it is typical, according to Michel Foucault, that the author plays an important role (1979). But as society changes, he is convinced that the author-function will disappear. What will not disappear, however, is our fear of the proliferation of meaning. Consequently we will always need a system of constraint. The original French lecture of 22 February 1969 was published in *Bulletin de la Société de philosophie*. In 1970, Foucault presented a modified version of this paper at the University of Buffalo. In this second version, Foucault argues "that, as our society changes, at the very moment when it is in the process of changing, the author-function will disappear, and in such a manner that fiction and its polysemic texts will once again function according to another mode, *but still with a system of constraint*" (1979: 160; emphasis added).

Eco suggested self-constraint; De Graef suggested letting the aporias of the text itself determine the limits of interpretations. Whereas New Critics regarded the text as a relatively stable unit, poststructuralists and deconstructionists focused on the aporias and instabilities of texts, but "only in relation to meaning and interpretation," as Michael Groden points out (2004: 230). Structuralism, and especially structuralist poetics, as suggested by Roland Barthes and Jonathan Culler, attempted "to make explicit the underlying system which makes literary effects possible" (Culler 2002: 137). As opposed to hermeneutics and its quest for meaning, poetics takes attested meanings and effects as a starting point in order to find out *how* they are achieved. It would seem logical that this kind of research might benefit from the study of the writing process, but structuralism has focused almost exclusively on synchronic structures. Genetic criticism opens up this research focus to include the diachronic axis, drawing attention to the fact that literary texts are also structured by time.

This diachronic structure raises the question whether a text is separable from its historical context. If a text has meaning only when it is being acted upon, it may be regarded as the scene where this action takes place. A text is defined by Peter Shillingsburg as "the actual order of words and punctuation as contained in any one physical form" (1996: 46). The physical form is referred to as a "document." It can contain only one text, but it may contain more than one "version" of more than one "work"—a "work" being neither the sum of all versions, nor the published text, but "the message or experience *implied* by the authoritative versions of a literary writing" (176). If the text is the scene of literary activity, the work's implied aspect constitutes the obscene. What takes place out of the seen is the most fascinating part of literature, and obviously also the cause of the heated debates about the limits and methods of interpretation. Not unlike the thirteen-year-old Briony, literary critics are all sensitive to the off-stage with its threatening proliferation of meaning. In Samuel Beckett's first novel (posthumously published), *Dream of Fair to Middling Women*, the protagonist, Belacqua, resolves to write a book in which the experience of his reader will be "between the phrases, in the silence, communicated by the intervals, not the terms, of the statement" (1993a: 138). Toward the end of his career, Beckett had perfected this strategy. The extreme reduction of contextual information burdens each written word with a heavy load of potential meanings. Even though this method is in stark contrast with James Joyce's expansive writing method, the effect is similar. As Sam Slote remarks, the problem with *Finnegans Wake* is not that it "makes no sense, rather it makes *too much sense*" (1997: 266). This situation intensifies the pertinence of the questions of how much a critic may read (or project) into a work of literature; to what extent such a projection is avoidable; and whether a way of limiting the proliferation of meanings is desirable.

At first sight, enlarging the scene of the text by including the early versions (manuscripts, typescripts, notes, proofs) may seem to enhance the joyful proliferation of meaning. But—to play the devil's advocate—one could argue that, with reference to manuscript research, a similar mechanism may be at work as the one described by Foucault in "What Is an Author?" We tend to present the author as the opposite of his function, according to Foucault, to hide our need of a constraining principle; perhaps manuscript genetics is a similarly self-deceptive way of enlarging the scene to reduce the dimensions of the ob-scene.

A good example to investigate this hypothesis is Beckett's penultimate text, *Stirrings Still*, which contains several implicit intertextual references and allusions to his earlier works. It ends with the line: "Oh all to end." This death wish is an echo of Mercier's words "Oh but to cease!" in *Mercier and Camier*, Beckett's own translation of the first novel he originally wrote in French (in 1946). It was not published until 1970, one year after the publication of Michel Foucault's lecture "Qu'est-ce qu'un auteur?"/"What Is an Author?" Foucault opens his lecture by quoting the sentence: "Qu'importe qui parle (...)" / "What matter who's speaking, someone said what matter who's speaking." To Foucault, it mattered enough to mention Beckett as the author of this quotation, which is taken from the third of Beckett's *Textes pour rien*. According to Foucault, the sentence "Qu'importe qui parle" "nicely formulates" the indifference toward the notion of authorship that characterizes contemporary writing. But precisely in the case of Samuel Beckett, this is less unequivocal than it may seem. What Foucault interprets as indifference seems to have been the object of a permanent internal struggle throughout Beckett's career as a writer, as the examples of *Mercier et Camier* and *Stirring Still* show.

The eponymous heroes in *Mercier et Camier* have made an agreement: they will not tell each other their dreams, nor will they use quotations. At a certain moment, Camier reminds Mercier of the deal they made, whereupon

Mercier asks whether the sentence "Lo bello stilo che m'ha fatto onore" is a quotation. It is indeed a line from canto 1 in *Inferno*, where Dante recognizes Virgil as his "auctoritas": "You are my teacher, the first of all my authors, / and you alone the one from whom I took / the noble style that was to bring me honor." (lines 85–87, trans. Mark Musa). In his translation of *Mercier et Camier* into English (published in 1974), Beckett omitted the passage with the direct quotation, thus establishing the auctoritas only to obscure it again later on through the act of translation.

A similar procedure marks the genesis of the third and last section of *Stirrings Still*. In the published text, there is not a single direct reference to Dante, and yet the "maestro" is present. In the same first canto of *Inferno*, a mere twenty lines earlier, Dante describes him as a shadowy figure coming toward him, the figure of someone grown "faint" or "hoarse" (fioco): "per lungo silenzio fioco." This line recurs in the manuscripts of *Stirrings Still*.[12] The relevant passage is about a sentence "from deep within" with one crucial word the protagonist cannot "catch" because it is too "faint." The adjective "faint" seems to have reminded Beckett of the "fioco" line, which he wrote on the facing verso page of his copybook (RUL MS 2934, 9v). He then considered adding "hoarse from long silence" to the draft, but eventually decided to reinstall the original adjective "faint." So, at the surface level nothing changed, and in the published text there is indeed nothing to indicate any intertextual reference.

Without the help of the manuscripts, hardly any reader will recognize "faint" as an allusion to Dante. Why, then, would a reader care to know that it is? Because it widens the scope of possible interpretations. It adds to the "proliferation of meaning." The word "faint" can still simply mean any faint idea, but with the manuscript information it can also be read as a trace like the hole in Vermeer's painting. It indicates the ambiguous attitude of a writer toward the authority of his "maestro." In a quick movement, he refers to the moment Virgil appears to Dante and almost instantly undoes the reference again, committing a kind of patricide and simultaneously paying tribute to his master.

By donating his manuscripts to a university library, Beckett enabled his readers to follow the process of failing, trying again, and failing better. He probably knew better than anyone else that what S. E. Gontarski called "the intent of undoing" can only be conveyed if one also shows the things that have been undone to arrive at the published version. In the example of the Dante quote, the word "fioco" is not a mysterious key to the one and only correct interpretation. But it does give us a clue as to what it was that Beckett needed in order to be able to undo it. If an author preserves his manuscripts, this is not necessarily a means of making money, of streamlining the afterlife of his work, or of reinstating authorial authority; it may also be an integral part of his poetics, part of his continuous search for a form that also allows the chaos, for a scene that also accommodates the obscene.

3
Strategies and Typologies

Ratiocination inevitably takes place in what Beckett called the ivory dungeon. But more often than not, a pen and a piece of paper help materialize this thought process. Arthur Schopenhauer called this "thinking with the quill," a phenomenon he did not exactly admire. He compared it to walking with a cane. The sharpest thinking proceeds without any tools; canes and quills are a sign of aging. At first sight, the comparison seems obvious, but the question is whether it is true. In 1982, the German textual critic Siegfried Scheibe made a clear distinction between two basic types of writing methods (12–29). Some authors develop not just an idea but a whole book in their minds before putting pen to paper; these are called "mindworkers" (*Kopfarbeiter*). Others think on paper; these are referred to as "paperworkers" (*Papierarbeiter*). In spite of this manifest difference, Scheibe was of the opinion that these strategies had enough in common to draw up an "ideal" basic model of writing. This "ideal model" consisted of seven more or less distinct phases:

1. The first phase is characterized by the intention to write. This intention can materialize in the form of notes, when for instance the author looks something up in an encyclopedia and makes a few excerpts. Scheibe calls these preparatory writings *Vorarbeiten*, or paralipomena.

2. The first plan or scheme put down on paper is followed by

3. the actual writing (*eigentliche Niederschrift*), resulting in the first syntactic version that already shows some common elements with the textual structure of the work.

4. The changes made by the author on this document, with the exception of immediate corrections (*Sofortkorrekturen*, or *currente calamo*), bring about a new version. One document can thus contain several versions.

5. If the author changes a few things while copying, the (fair) copy or typescript is a new version. This process is usually repeated a number of times,

6. until the author decides his work has reached a form that is fit to be shown to the public. The publication of this version does not necessarily imply the end of the writing process.

7. Even after publication, the author continues to revise his text, thus creating one or more new versions.

Most typologies work with a model process as a kind of contrastive background against which any deviation in a concrete writing process can be highlighted. The other extreme is a typology that is so refined that one particular writing strategy of one particular author may be classified under several categories. That is the kind of typology suggested by Hanspeter Ortner, who discerns four general categories, subdivided in almost a dozen subcategories. Only one of these is referred to as mental designing. Authors working according to this method are categorized as the *Typ des Niederschreibers* because they devise both the macrostructure and the formulations on a microlevel in their minds and only have to write them down subsequently. This category corresponds to Scheibe's category of the *Kopfarbeiter*. As an example, Ortner mentions Franz Kafka, whose texts came into being during his walks and were subsequently written quite quickly, almost without corrections—as if they were "abgerufen aus dem Kopf," according to his biographer Klaus Wagenbach (Ortner 2000: 463). This classification already indicates that the "mindwork" (*Kopfarbeit*) is only one out of several writing strategies, most of which are forms of "paperwork" (*Papierarbeit*).

The most extreme form of "thinking on paper" in this typology is writing as a form of ratiocination. This is the approach of the so-called "syncretists," that is, authors who initially write separate blocks of texts that are later reshuffled and linked together. Their counterparts are authors writing "step by step" (more or less corresponding to Scheibe's "ideales Grundmodell"). It is often quite difficult to discern these two subcategories, even within one single composition process. For instance, Joyce to some extent answers to the profile of the so-called *Schritt-für-Schritt-Schreiber* (subcategory *a*). For *Finnegans Wake*, he first collected information in his notebooks and subsequently used this information to draft the different sections of his novel. But these different sections were not written in the order of the final narrative structure. In these early stages of the writing process, Joyce wrote a half dozen short vignettes, which he referred to as "active elements." Before he even had a clear structure in mind, he was confident that in due course these active elements would "begin to fuse of themselves" (*L I*: 204)—which makes him a "syncretist" in Ortner's typology.

The overabundance of strategies that can be labeled as "thinking with the quill" inevitably raises the question of why Schopenhauer considered this form of thinking inferior to ratiocination inside the skull. Many of the greatest thinkers and authors, such as Wittgenstein, Proust, and Joyce, were "paperworkers." They did indeed use pen and paper as tools to support a mental process, but the complexity of their compositions can hardly be compared to walking with a cane.

Ortner's classification may be a bit overdivided, but the importance of differentiation was recognized by other scholars as well. Whereas in 1982 Scheibe emphasized what the two categories of writing methods (*Kopf-* versus *Papierarbeit*) had in common, he later stressed their differences (1998: 168–76). The manuscripts of a mindworker are usually less chaotic than a paperworker's. As a consequence, Scheibe advised scholarly editors to choose a different type of apparatus variorum for each of the two categories. Scheibe's dichotomy is completely geared to scholarly editing, which is the focus of German *Editionswissenschaft*.

The approach of French genetic criticism is somewhat different, since its main focus is the study of the writing process, rather than the production of a scholarly edition (which may, but does not need to, be a spin-off of the genetic research). Louis Hay suggests another distinction (1984: 307–23). The two main types of writing Hay discerns are "writing according to plan" (*écriture à programme*) and writing that is open to any contingency along the way or "process writing" (*écriture à processus*). Hay's categories do not coincide with Scheibe's. They are two distinct forms of "paperwork." The category of the "mindworkers" is somewhat ignored in Hay's dichotomy, which is logical since genetic criticism examines the writing process only insofar as it can be reconstructed on the basis of extant manuscripts.

Because of this empirical dimension, it is significant that the French genetic critic Pierre-Marc de Biasi presents his basic model of the average writing process as a typology of genetic documentation (1996: 26–56). Readily admitting that this is just an abstract model and that every concrete writing process deviates from it to some degree, he divides the model process into five phases: precomposition, composition, prepublishing (or postcomposition), publication, and postpublication. His model hinges on the so-called "pass for press" moment (*bon à tirer*). It is designed as "a typological tool applicable to numerous (. . .) collections of genetic material" (31). De Biasi is well aware of the artificial nature of his undertaking and immediately notes that one needs to "take into account all sorts of ruptures, doubts, and reversals" (33). Every writing process is characterized by singularities that deviate from the general typology. De Biasi immediately adds that some collections of genetic material may prove "uninterpretable in the terms of this chronotypology" and clearly states that his model "does not claim in any way to reconstitute the norm" (51–52).

De Biasi distinguishes between three major stages in the writing process: the *avant-texte*, the text, and the so-called post-text. The first stage is divided from the next by the *bon à tirer* moment. Here, de Biasi draws a sharp line at what he calls "the decisive moment when what had been in a pliable and mobile state up to that point becomes fixed in the frozen shape of a published text" (37). The metaphor emphasizes the idea of an absolute dividing line, separating *manuscript genetics* from *textual genetics*. The latter has traditionally been the domain of textual criticism and scholarly editing. Possibly the need to profile genetic criticism as a new field of research by distinguishing it from textual criticism or philology may have contributed to this rather black-and-white dichotomy. For sometimes the step from *avant-texte* to text is a gradual transition zone. Joyce's "Work in Progress" is a case in point, for even after publication in Eugene Jolas's magazine *transition*, the sections continued to be modified, expanded, and revised.

The distinction between *avant-texte* and text is important to de Biasi because he wishes to differentiate between compositional variations (in the drafts) and postpublication modifications or textual variants (between different editions). The main argument is that the former take place in the private atmosphere of the writing, whereas the latter belong in a public sphere (1996: 40). If one regards the publication of a chapter in *transition* as a *bon à tirer* moment (because of the change from private to public domain), it is hard to argue that the numerous modifications that took place afterwards are to be treated as textual variants. If, on the other hand, one regards the first publication of *Finnegans Wake* in its entirety (4 May 1939) as the *bon à tirer* moment, it is hard to maintain the private/public argument, since three-quarters of the book had already been shown to the public in serial form. In a typology, it is of course necessary to draw clear lines, but in reality it may be useful to link the text to its *avant-texte*, rather than separating the two.

The *avant-texte* can be subdivided into a precompositional, a compositional, and a prepublishing phase. In these phases, two types of genetics interact, which de Biasi calls "exogenetics" and "endogenetics" (two terms coined by Raymonde Debray-Genette).[1] Exogenetics consists of the intake of extratextual impressions. It "designates any writing process devoted to research, selection, and incorporation, focused on information stemming from a source exterior to the writing. Handwritten or not, any documentary notes or copies, any quoted or intertextual matter, any results of inquiries or observations, any evidence of iconographic matter (. . .), and generally any written or text-image *documentation*, belongs by nature to the exogenetic category" (de Biasi 1996: 43–44). At first sight, this seems to be a clearly defined category, especially when contrasted with endogenetics, "the process by which the writer conceives of, elaborates, and transfigures pre-textual material," that is, the processing of these notes in drafts "without recourse to outside documents or information" (43). But especially this last remark is only true in theory. In practice, the border between exo- and endogenetics is usually blurred. De Biasi recognizes this phenomenon and concludes: "Logically speaking, there is no such thing as a purely exogenetic element: every exogenetic fragment bears the primitive seal of endogenetics" (47).

This is indeed true in the case of Joyce's *Finnegans Wake* notebooks. In many cases, the process of Wakean distortion already starts between the moment Joyce reads a word and the moment he writes his reading note. The notebooks also illustrate that exogenetics is not necessarily confined to the precompositional phase. Even during the prepublishing and publication phases, an author can take recourse to extratextual material. In these late phases, however, the endogenetic processing of this material will usually belong to what de Biasi calls "le scriptural" (scriptability), that is, the textualization or creation of syntactic units of text. This "scriptability" is a microgenetic phenomenon, which interacts with the macrogenetic "structuring" of the work in progress. It is understandable that when Joyce (re)read, for instance, the *Beiträge zu einer Kritik der Sprache* by Fritz Mauthner in 1938 (toward the end of the work's progress), this exogenetic reading act was almost immediately followed by an endogenetic script act. By then the whole structure of *Finnegans Wake* was in place. In contrast with this late reading of Mauthner, his earlier reading of Giambattista Vico's *Scienza nuova* obviously had more impact on the structuring process. The notes he took from his reading of Mauthner merely served as lexical material for the expansion of already existing syntactic units. When Beckett—who was helping Joyce at that time—also read Mauthner and made notes, the impact on the then thirty-two-year-old writer, who was still developing his own poetics, may have been more fundamental.

The so-called "operational functions" of the various phases of the writing process are defined by de Biasi as:

1. orienting, exploring determination of the composition project, conceiving and initial planning (= precompositional phase);

2. general structuring of the composition, researching, and textualization (= compositional phase);

3. finishing touches and preparing for publication (= prepublishing phase), followed by the *bon à tirer* moment, the first edition, subsequent editions during the author's lifetime, and posthumous editions. These operational functions correspond with different sorts of documents, such as marginalia, work plans, unfinished compositions, notebooks, documentation, previously abandoned projects, drawings, topographical sketches, chronologies, lists, rough drafts, corrected fair copies, revised pages of instalments, galleys, and page proofs.

Insofar as these documents are extant in the case of Joyce's *Finnegans Wake*, it is useful to try to find out to what extent "Work in Progress" fits into de Biasi's scheme, and to chart the instances where it does not. Evidently this scheme is only meant "to organize a virtual structure" (de Biasi 1996: 52), not to be superimposed upon a concrete composition. But in reconstructing a literary genesis, it may serve as a scaffolding that can be removed afterwards. In the next chapter, de Biasi's typology will thus be confronted with the complex composition history of *Finnegans Wake*.

PART II

Joyce's Know-How

He was not convinced of the truth of the saying [Poeta nascitur, non fit] "The poet is born, not made" but he was quite sure of the truth of this at least: [Poema fit, non nascitur] "The poem is made not born."

James Joyce, *Stephen Hero*

4

Introduction

"Work in Progress"

To prepare for the composition of the "Children's Games" episode of *Finnegans Wake* (book II, chapter 1), Joyce read a book by Kate Greenaway called *Book of Games*. One of the games explained by Greenaway is called the "Russian Scandal":

> The players sit in a circle and the leader whispers some anecdote or quotation to his left-hand neighbour, which he in turn repeats to the person next him, and so the story is whispered round the circle, the last player relating aloud what has been told him. The original is then repeated, and it is amusing to see how entirely different the two narratives are. (1987 [1889]: 24)

Any attempt to retell the narrative of *Finnegans Wake* is doomed to create the same effect. The paraphrases are legion, and transformations inevitable. One of the pioneering enterprises in genetic Joyce studies was David Hayman's 1963 edition of *A First-Draft Version of "Finnegans Wake."* In this invaluable transcription, the first drafts of each section are presented as "the complete skeleton of the *Wake* reduced to its simplest language" (4). Although Hayman is aware of the artificial nature of the classification according to the final narrative structure, there is a danger that this arrangement of early versions will be regarded as a paraphrase of *Finnegans Wake*. Hayman somehow even encourages such a reading of the first drafts by using the metaphor of the skeleton, since it had already been employed by Joseph Campbell and Henry Morton Robinson in their *Skeleton Key*. But as A. Walton Litz pointed out, no work loses more through paraphrase than *Finnegans Wake* (1966: 103).

And yet it does not seem all that inappropriate to try to rewhisper the story of *Finnegans Wake*, for this retelling is in a way what this "process verbal" is all about (*FW* 515.15). When Joyce met his Maecenas, Harriet Shaw Weaver, in the summer of 1922, he told her that his next project was going to be a history of the world (Ellmann 1983: 537). And to Sylvia Beach, he once said that "history was like that parlour game where someone whispers something to the person next to him, who repeats it not very distinctly to the next person, and so on until, by the time the last person hears it, it comes out completely transformed" (Beach 1959: 190). And indeed, if one were to summarize this 628-page book in one word, "rumors" could certainly compete in *Monty Python*'s Summarize *Finnegans Wake* Contest.[1] A crime is said to have been committed, and no matter how void the accusation may be, the word spreads like wildfire.

"On briefest glimpse" (*FW* 267.10), the book is about a Dublin family: HCE (the initials of Humphrey Chimpden Earwicker, or Here Comes Everybody, or Howth Castle and Environs, etc.), ALP (Anna Livia Plurabelle), and their three children. Issy, Shem (the penman), and Shaun (the postman) are a source of worry. At the book's close, their mother, ALP, complains especially about her two sons, the artist and the respectable citizen, because "[t]hem boys is so contrairy" (*FW* 620.12). But the narrative core of Joyce's last book is just a rumor. Apparently something must have happened in Phoenix Park, Dublin, between HCE and two girls. Three soldiers are said to have witnessed it, but the reader never clearly gets to know what HCE actually did in the park. When ALP starts defending her husband, she only makes things worse.

The book's circular structure[2] is only the most conspicuous of Joyce's techniques to disrupt traditional linear narrative. Joyce presents his history of the world as an enormous, always expanding network of hearsay. Even the title is presented as a misapprehension or a transmissional departure. As in the "Russian Scandal" game, the omitted apostrophe causes an inaudible minor transformation with major semantic effects. The circular structure and the eternal recurrence of the same anew may create the impression of indifference, but this appearance is deceptive. On the contrary, Joyce draws attention to the importance of differences, even the most minute variants, such as an omitted apostrophe. As a consequence, a textual approach to *Finnegans Wake* may be quite appropriate.

One of the major complications in the attempt to match de Biasi's typology against the composition history of *Finnegans Wake* is that on a macrogenetic level (considering "Work in Progress" as a whole), the different compositional phases and their corresponding operational functions do not follow each other in a neat chronological sequence, since Joyce usually worked on different levels simultaneously. Throughout the composition process, Joyce kept making notes. He thus compiled more than fifty notebooks between 1922 and 1940. In his catalogue of *James Joyce's Manuscripts & Letters at the University of Buffalo*, Peter Spielberg distinguished four types of notebooks:

a. VI.A, or "Scribbledehobble";

b. The B-notebooks (VI.B.19–VI.B.48) contain all sorts of notes, characterized by parataxis. Fragmentary excerpts from external sources may be the result of random reading or focused research; in both cases, they are usually reduced to a few words, and seldom quoted *in extenso*. Several clusters of notebook entries have been retraced to the most divergent external sources (articles from the *Irish Times*, the *Encyclopaedia Britannica*, books on various subjects). A transcription can be found in *The "Finnegans Wake" Notebooks at Buffalo*.

c. The C-notebooks (VI.C.01–VI.C.18): At the end of 1933, Mme France Raphael started copying—at Joyce's request—the notebooks he had already compiled, leaving out the crossed-out entries. These transcriptions were made in a very clear and large handwriting, because of the author's eye problems.

d. The D-notebooks were presumed to be lost when Spielberg compiled the catalog. In the meantime, some of them have resurfaced. As Luca Crispi has established, most of the uncrossed entries in all four *Ulysses* notebooks acquired by the National Library of Ireland in 2002 were transcribed by France Raphael into notebook VI.C.136–269, so that these four notebooks constitute what Spielberg refers to as "D.4." Thanks to Mme Raphael's transcriptions, it is possible to (partially) reconstruct seven of these "missing notebooks": D.1 corresponding with C.2: 123–97; D.2 cf. C.3: 178–242; and C.15: 177–252; D.3 cf. C.4: 220–80; and C.5: 1–91; D.4 cf. C.136–269; D.5 cf. C.8: 217–end + C.9: 1–19 and C.10: 249–end + C.16: 1–65; D.6 cf. C.11: 96–217; D.7 cf. C.16: 232–74.

According to Danis Rose's chronological survey of the notebooks in the *Textual Diaries* (1995: 25–35), five more notebooks are missing: X.1 (late Jan./early March 1923); X.2 (Dec. 1923); X.3 (summer 1923); X.4 (Nov./Dec. 1930); and X.5 (March/Aug. 1938). As the survey of these notes indicates, exogenetics are not confined to the initial phases of the writing process. Both the jotting down of the notes and their possible usage in the drafts could take place in any phase of the *avant-texte*. To a certain extent, this peculiarity is closely connected to Joyce's method of working with sections—units of text (usually not more than a few pages at the first-draft stage) that initially developed in relative isolation and were connected only in a later compositional phase.[3] This writing strategy complicates a macrogenetic study, but it is possible to analyze the *avant-texte* as a collection of microgenetic processes.

One solution would be to focus on the compositional phase, and even more specifically on the textualization process. This is the focus of David Hayman's invaluable *A First-Draft Version of "Finnegans Wake,"* which tells the story of the *Wake* by means of a transcription of the first draft of each section. However, these first drafts were not written in the order of *Finnegans Wake*'s synchronic structure (of four books, subdivided into seventeen chapters).

The following survey gives a general idea of the book's content by approaching it from a genetic perspective and highlighting narrative aspects of all the sections in the order of their composition. This chronological survey owes a debt of gratitude to the pioneering transcription of David Hayman. It is merely intended to give a general impression of the relationship between the material traces of the writing process (notebooks, manuscripts) and the final narrative structure of *Finnegans Wake*. It privileges certain aspects of the writing process (such as the first draft). What it cannot take into account is the long elaboration of the drafts. The dating of the manuscripts is based on the *James Joyce Archive* and on the invaluable *Textual Diaries*, in which Danis Rose established the notebook chronology. The dates in the survey are indications of what (at this stage in genetic *Wake* research) is thought to be the period in which Joyce was using a particular notebook.

The survey may give the impression that Joyce started taking notes in a new notebook as soon as the previous one was full. This was not always the case. For instance, the notes on volumes 1 and 2 of Fritz Mauthner's *Beiträge zu einer Kritik der Sprache* in notebook VI.B.41 were most probably written before Joyce read and jotted down notes on volume 3 of the *Beiträge* in notebook VI.B.46. Yet, in the chronological survey, VI.B.46 (early Dec. 1937–Feb. 1938) is mentioned before VI.B.41 (late Aug.–mid-Oct. 1938), because the main part of VI.B.46 was written earlier than VI.B.41. Joyce's notes in VI.B.46 are divided quite systematically into different sections, or "indexes" as Danis Rose has called them in his transcription and edition of *The Index Manuscript* (1978). Each index is preceded by a subject heading, such as "Hebrew," "East Vikings," "Chinese," or "Buddha," showing an explicit interest in (often exotic) languages. But not all indexes were equally extensive, and some pages were left blank. The Mauthner notes are probably of a later date (probably late summer 1938) than the indexes, since they were jotted down wherever Joyce found some blank space, starting on page 60 and continuing in retrograde direction on pages 54–55, 50, 49, 48, and 46, written in green ink. After having made his Mauthner notes in VI.B.41, Joyce apparently took the older notebook VI.B.46 again and filled the blank pages (in retrograde direction) with notes on the third volume of Mauthner's work. In a chronological survey, it is not always possible to take into account such overlaps or reuses, which have undoubtedly occurred more than once.[4]

In 2006, the National Library of Ireland acquired six sheets with (parts of) sketches Joyce wrote shortly after the publication of *Ulysses*. Until recently, the order of the vignettes that constitute the preparatory phase of "Work in Progress" was usually considered to be:

- Roderick O'Conor
- Tristan and Isolde
- Saint Kevin
- Saint Patrick
- Mamalujo
- Here Comes Everybody

Based on a first analysis of the newly acquired documents, Luca Crispi has come to the conclusion that, rather than a clear set of six vignettes, the early sketches constitute an amorphous cluster of texts, resulting from Joyce's active attempt to abandon avenues he had already walked.[5] For instance, apart from the "Tristan and Isolde" sketch with Isolde as a kind of 1920s flapper, the new documents show that Joyce also considered a much younger version of Isolde in a draft that explicitly refers to Saint Dympna, who was chased by her father. This draft suggests that—from a genetic perspective—the central figure in the nuclear family of *Finnegans Wake* is not the father (HCE), but the daughter. Crispi convincingly argued that it is the daughter who generated—successively—the concept of the father, the mother, and finally the brothers.

While Joyce was focusing on lives of young saints (St. Dympna, St. Kevin ["Kevineen"], St. Patrick), he also wrote a draft on the "Four Waves," which differs considerably from the "Mamalujo" vignette with the four historians (representing past, present, "absent," and future). According to Luca Crispi, it was only after Joyce had recognized that the saint vignettes were too formulaic that he discovered the idea of history and how it is misconstrued, resulting in the "Mamalujo" sketch.

The following survey is not a summary of *Finnegans Wake*. It focuses on narrative kernels in the first drafts, presented in the order in which Joyce first formulated them. The dates in square brackets give an indication of the moment or period in which Joyce worked on the respective section.

1922–1923: Joyce takes notes in VI.B.10, 3; VI.A, VI.B.25, 2, and 11; and starts drafting:

II.3, section 7B; FW 380.07–382.30: Roderick O'Conor, last king of Ireland, empties the glasses left by the guests after his last supper. [10 March 1923; L I 202]

II.4, sections 1–2; FW 383.01–398.30: "Tristan and Isolde": Tristan, a "rugger and soccer champion" (*FDV* 208), is courting Isolde, "the belle of Chapelizod" on a boat. She asks him to recite some poetry, and he answers with an iambic hexameter from *Childe Harold's Pilgrimage*: "Roll on, thou deep and darkblue ocean, roll!" The subsequent love scene is described as a soccer attack, Tristan driving "the advance messenger of love (. . .) into the goal of her gullet" (*FDV* 209), while the seaswans sing: "Three quarks for Muster Mark" (*FDV* 212) [Spring 1923]. Joyce also drafts the vignettes on "Young Isolde" and "Four Waves" (NLI 2006).

IV, section 2; FW 604.27–607.22: Saint Kevin, born on the island of Ireland in the Irish ocean, goes to Glendalough to live on an isle. On this isle is a pond with an islet. On this islet, he builds a hut and digs a cavity, which he fills with water. In the center of this pool, he places a tub filled with water, in which he seats himself and meditates on the sacrament of baptism. (The nine concentric circles are numbered by Joyce in the first draft; cf. *FDV* 273–74.) ["Summer 1923" (*JJA* 63: 33)]

IV, section 3; FW 607.23–614.18: "St. Patrick and the Druid": The archdruid "Barkeley" explains to Patrick the "illusiones of the colourful world." Everything in this phenomenal world appears under only one of the seven colors of the spectrum, that is, the one that the object cannot absorb and therefore reflects. He believes that it is possible to see "the thing as in itself it is" (*FDV* 279). But when the archdruid tries to explain his theory "in other words," he seems to contradict his own thesis, for instead of showing themselves in their true colors, all the objects he enumerates appear green. The latinizations, such as "illusiones" and "coloribus," may be regarded as the first truly Wakean linguistic distortion. [July 1923; cf. letter to Harriet Shaw Weaver, 2 August 1923; L III 79]

I.2, section 1; FW 30–34.29: "Here Comes Everybody": Humphrey Coxon Earwicker is initially presented as a respected citizen, owner of a pub, who is said to have received his name from the king himself and is first given the nickname Here Comes Everything, which is then changed into Everybody (*FDV* 63). On the other hand, it has been suggested that he suffers from a vile disease (*FDV* 63) and that he was involved in some obscure incident in the park—under the ludicrous imputation of annoying soldiers (*FDV* 63). ["August–September 1923: (*JJA* 45: 1); cf. *L III*, 23 August 1923; letter to Harriet Shaw Weaver, 10 September 1923 (*BL* Add. 57347:101–2); letter to Harriet Shaw Weaver, 17 September 1923; *L I* 205]

II.4, section 3B; FW 398.31–399.34: The "Anno Domini" poem was probably designed to follow immediately after the "Mamalujo" sketch. The verses are personalized and composed according to a scheme, which was sent to Miss Weaver on 12 October 1923 (*L I* 197). In this scheme, each of the Evangelists (Matthew, Mark, Luke, John) is connected with one of the Four Masters (Peregrine O'Clery, Michael O'Clery, Farfassa O'Mulconry, Peregrine O'Duignan, respectively), with a pronoun (thou, she, you, I, respectively), with the four provinces of Ireland (Ulster, Munster, Leinster, Connacht), with their respective evangelist symbols, with a specific Irish accent, etc. [September–October 1923; letter to Harriet Weaver, 12 October 1923, *Selected Letters I* 296–97]

II.4, sections 2–3A; FW 383.01–398.30: Mamalujo (Matthew, Mark, Luke and John) or the Four Masters/annalists/historians, metamorphosed into sea waves, listen in on Tristan and Isolde (*FDV* 213) [September 1923; cf. letter to Harriet Weaver, 17 September 1923; *L I* 205]. Recent NLI acquisitions indicate that Joyce tried to merge this sketch with the "Tristan and Isolde" sketch (Deppman 2007: 310).

I.2, section 2; FW 34.30–44.21: "Guiltless" HCE is clearly, for once he said so himself. When in Phoenix Park a cad simply asks HCE in Irish what time it is, the latter thinks it is necessary to emphasize that he has nothing to hide, that—even though certain accusations have been made against him—he is an innocent man. Judging by this overreaction, the cad obviously thinks something must be wrong and subsequently spreads the rumor (to other characters such as Treacle Tom and Frisky Shorty). The rumor also reaches the poet Hosty, who subsequently writes a ballad. [letters to Harriet Weaver, 2 November 1923 (*L III* 82), 17 November 1923; 19 November 1923 (*L III* 83)]

I.2, section 3; FW 44.22–47: "The Ballad of Persse O'Reilly" (introduced with a thunderous clapping) about HCE—once a king—who fell from the Magazine Wall like Humpty Dumpty. [November 1923; letter to Harriet Shaw Weaver, 17 December 1923; *L I* 207]

I.3, section 1; FW 48–61.27: Who caused HCE to fall? A short introduction on those who spread the rumor is followed by the cad's account of his meeting with HCE. The data are "too few to warrant certitude" (*FDV* 71), and several Dubliners are asked what they think of it. The street interview starts with three soldiers: "It was the women, they said; he showed himself a man afterwards" (*FDV* 71); the two maids, however, tell another story. [November 1923; letter to Harriet Shaw Weaver, 17 December 1923; *L I* 207]

I.3, section 2; FW 61.28–67.27: A report of HCE's flight, of the terrors he had to defy, and of an assault by a masked person. [November 1923; letter to Harriet Shaw Weaver, 17 December 1923; *L I* 207]

I.3, section 3; FW 67.28–74: Through the gate of his closed pub, HCE is jeered at by an unsolicited visitor (*FDV* 74). HCE draws up a list of all the abusive names he was called. [November 1923; letter to Harriet Shaw Weaver, 17 December 1923; *L I* 207]

I.4, section 1A; FW 75–92.05: It seems to be generally accepted that HCE is dead (*FDV* 75). Kate Strong, a widow who did all the scavenging "from good King Charles' days" (*FDV* 75), makes a statement, saying that she left a filth dump near the dogpond in the park on which bootmarks and fingerprints were found "of a very involved description" (*FDV* 75). On this spot HCE may have become the victim of another assault. A suspect called Festy King is arrested (*FDV* 76). [November 1923; letter to Harriet Shaw Weaver, 17 December 1923; *L I* 207]

I.4, section 2; FW 96.26–103: HCE has escaped from his grave or mausoleum; he appears as a fox and is hunted. All kinds of stories are going around. "Who then was the scourge of Lucalizod, it was wont to be asked" (*FDV* 80). Only in the second draft "one nearer, dearer than all" opens the apologia of HCE. [November–December 1923; letter to Harriet Shaw Weaver, 17 December 1923; *L I* 207]

I.5, section 2 >> IV, section 4: The "Revered Letter" with which ALP tries to defend her husband, HCE, against the accusations. [December 1923; letter to Harriet Weaver, 17 December 1923; *L I* 207; 16 January 1924; *L I* 208]

I.5, section 1, FW 104–113.22: The different aspects of the letter are analyzed: its composition, its author(s), the envelope, the matter of the hen (who is said to have found it on a midden heap), the handwriting, etc. [December 1923; cf. letter to Harriet Weaver, 23 December 1923 (*BL* Add. 57347–128); cf. also letter to Harriet Weaver, 16 January 1924; *L I* 208]

I.5, section 4; FW 113.23–125: A paleographical analysis of the letter, parodying Sir Edward Sullivan's introduction to the facsimile edition of the

Book of Kells. [December 1923; cf. letter to Harriet Weaver, 23 December 1923 (*BL* Add. 57347–128); cf. also letter to Harriet Weaver, 16 January 1924; *L I* 208]

I.5, section 3 >> book III: "The Delivery of the Letter": The confusion of the letter's composition is followed by the "zigzaggery" of its delivery (*FDV* 90). Apparently, the accused HCE, who is being defended in the letter, is also the one to whom this letter is delivered by his sons Iacopus Pennifera and Johannes Epistolophorus, "thereby giving him of his own" (*FDV* 90). [December 1923; cf. letter to Harriet Weaver, 23 December 1923 (*BL* Add. 57347–128); cf. also letter to Harriet Weaver, 16 January 1924; *L I* 208]

1924: Joyce takes notes in VI.B.6, 1, 16, 5, 14, D.3, and starts drafting:

I.7, section 1; FW 169–187.23: Shaun's biased portrait of the artist Shem and his plagiarist pen (*FDV* 117), which is in many ways a self-parody of Joyce, culminates in the Latin description of how he produces ink from his excrements to write his books. [January 1924; letter to Harriet Weaver, 16 January 1924; *L I* 208]

I.7, section 2; FW 187.24–195: Mercius (or Shem) is accused by Justius (or Shaun) of the so-called *Improperia* (*FDV* 120), listed in the first draft: 1. Hell (he has become "a doubter of all known gods"); 2. Progeny; 3. Prophecy; 4. Shirking (refusing to work); 5. Sin (more specifically fratricide); 6. Doles (being wasteful); and finally he is accused of forswearing his 7. Mother. Shem's only defense is that "gossipaceous" Anna Livia will speak through him. (*FDV* 122) [January 1924; letter to Harriet Weaver, 16 January 1924; *L I* 208]

I.8, section 1A; FW 196–208.26: The gossip about ALP and HCE by two washerwomen on the banks of the Liffey. [February 1923; *L I*, 7 March 1924]

I.8, section 1B; FW 208.27–216: Anna Livia, upset about all the gossip, decides to distribute presents to all of her children. "Her Pandora's box contains the ills flesh is heir to," Joyce wrote to Harriet Weaver [7 March 1924; *L I* 21]. As the night begins to fall, it becomes increasingly difficult for the two washerwomen to understand each other, and eventually they become a tree and a stone. [February 1923; *L I*, 7 March 1924]

III.1A/1D/2A/2C; FW 403–473: The questioning of Shaun (still without the "Dave the Dancekerl" passage), followed by his "long absurd and rather incestuous Lenten lecture to Izzy, his sister" [letter to Harriet Weaver, 27 June 1924; *L I* 216], after which he takes leave of her. (At this point, chapters III.1 and III.2 were still conceived as one whole.) [March 1924; cf. *L I*: 24 March 1924; *L III*: 15 March and 6 April 1924]

III.3A; FW 474–532.05: The four old men find Yawn on a midden heap and cross-examine him, about his place of origin, his language, the letter, his family; several voices of other characters speak through Yawn, for example, Treacle Tom (introduced in I.2), who gives his version of the encounter in the park. Other witnesses (Kate, Sigurdsen) are called to testify, and Issy talks to her mirror image. ["November/December 1924" (*JJA* 58: 1)]

III.3B; FW 532.06–554: Haveth Childers Everywhere: HCE delivers his self-defense, boasting of the magnificent city he founded ["November/December 1924" (*JJA* 58: 23)].

1925: Joyce takes notes in D.3, B.7, D.2, D.1, B.9, 8, 19; VI.A; B.13, and starts drafting:

III.4; FW 555–590: It is night in the house. Matt, Mark, Luke and John, located at the four bedposts, give their view of the parents' copulation in four positions. This passage is a compilation of several fragments (A-T), some of which (D, H, I, J, M, O) were written somewhat later than the others. Because of the complex nature of the first drafts, they are reproduced twice in the Archive, once arranged as in the original notebook (47482a) and once according to the final narrative structure. (Cf. *JJA* 60: 1–252). [October–November 1925; *L III*, 5 and 23 Nov. 1925]

1926: Joyce takes notes in VI.B.13, 20, 17, 12, D.5, B.15, and starts drafting:

III.2B; FW 461.33–468.19: "Dave the Dancekerl": Jaun introduces Issy to his proxy, Dave. The section is written in reaction to Wyndham Lewis's *The Art of Being Ruled* [cf. BL Add. 57348–129; 30 March 1926, Joyce mentions that he is replying to Lewis in "a most grotesque addition to /\b"]

II.2, section 8; FW 282.05–304.04: "The Triangle" or "The Muddest Thick That Was Ever Heard Dump": During the mathematics session, Dolph explains to Kev, in a lesson on Euclid, the geometry of ALP's private parts. [*L I*, 15 July 1926; see also *L I*, 25 July and 18 August 1926] At this stage, the footnotes and marginalia were not yet added.

I.1, section 1A; FW 3.01–10.23: "Overture": Introduction of Finnegan, his fall and promise of resurrection, the personification of the landscape (his sleeping body lying alongside the river Liffey) where the Willingdone Museyroom is located. During the visit to this Museyroom, the question of the crime in the park is raised. [*L I*, 24 September and 8 November 1926; *L III*, 16 October 1926]

I.1, *section 1B/D; FW 10.24–13.29/14.28–15.28*: After all the battles mentioned in the "Museyroom" episode, a gnarlybird (*FDV* 52) or hen (an incarnation of ALP) collects all the litter of the past in her "nabsack"—which is probably the one from which ALP distributes presents to her children in I.8.

I.1, *section 1C; FW 13.30–14.27*: The "Annals" passage in which the dates 566 and 1132, associated with the fall (the law of falling bodies—32 feet per second per second) and renewal, are discussed.

I.1, *section 1E; FW 15.29–18.16*: The "Mutt and Jute" dialogue, in which the invader and the native swap hats (*FDV* 55) and talk about the Battle of Clontarf.

I.1, *section 2A; FW 18.17–21.04*: The story of the development of the alphabet. ["November 1926" (*JJA* 44: 83)]

I.1, *section 2B; FW 21.05–29*: The tale of Jarl van Hoother and the Prankquean, based on Grace O'Malley, who was refused entrance at the Earl of Howth's castle when he was at dinner. She therefore presented him with a riddle and kidnapped Tristopher, one of his twin sons. The other son, Hilary, was kidnapped when the Prankquean arrived a second time. The third time, she wanted to take the earl's daughter, but at that moment a thunderclap was heard and eventually they all drank free (*FDV* 59). Finnegan wakes up, but is told to lie down again and Finn no more (*FDV* 60), for he will be replaced by HCE, the hero of the democratic period (in Vico's cyclic view on history). ["November 1926" (*JJA* 44: 83)]

I.4, *section 1B; FW 92.06–96.25*: Four judges (*FDV* 78) preside at the trial concerning the attack, for which the suspect Festy King was arrested. As the evidence is inconclusive, no one is found guilty. ["probably late 1926–early 1927" (*JJA* 46: 1)]

1927: Joyce takes notes in VI.B.15, 18, D.6, and starts drafting:

I.6, *section 1A; FW 126–149.10*: Each item of the questionnaire, as Joyce called it, discusses another cluster of characters. These are enumerated in a list of sigla preceding the first draft (BL 47473-150v; *JJA* 47: 2; cf. also BL 47473-132v; *JJA* 47: 28). The title of the book itself (represented by a square) appears among the characters, HCE, ALP, the four old men (here the four capital cities of Ireland), Sigurdsen, Kate, the twelve customers, the twenty-nine Maggies or leap-year girls, Issy, Shaun, and Shem. The last question is by far the shortest, and is preceded by the longest one, concerning Shaun. His answer to the question of whether he would help his brother in times of need is simply no, but it will take him about twenty pages or three extra sections to explain the difference between him and his brother. [*L I*, 12 and 31 May 1927, referring to the quote from *Peer Gynt* used on manuscript pages 47473-127-8 (*JJA* 47: 21-22)]

I.6, section 1B; FW 149.11–150.14: The time problem—changed in the first draft into the "dime-cash" problem—is considered from the point of view of a "spatialist" (*FDV* 99), aka Wyndham Lewis. ["June or July 1927" (*JJA* 47: 1)]

I.6, section 2; FW 150.15–152.03: Further explanation of the dime-cash problem by Professor Levis (*FDV* 100) (later Professor Jones). ["Summer 1927" (*JJA* 47: 109)]

I.6, section 3; FW 152.04–159.23: As the professor thinks his explanations will probably be too difficult to grasp (*FDV* 101), he illustrates them by means of the fable of The Moose and the Gripes (later The Mookse and the Gripes). The Mookse represents several prominent Englishmen (such as Pope Adrian IV and Henry II, who invaded Ireland in 1171); the Gripes represents, among others, St Lawrence O'Toole, bishop of Dublin during the period of the invasion. Their dispute remains unresolved when Nuvoletta, failing to attract their attention, drops rain into the Liffey ["July or August 1927" (*JJA* 47: 125); some of the content of the fable is explained by Joyce in a letter to Frank Budgen (3 September 1933; *L III* 284-85); see also letter to Sylvia Beach, 14 August 1927, in which Joyce mentions that in question 11 Shaun speaks with the voice of The Enemy]

I.6, section 4; FW 159.24–168: The "Burrus and Caseous" episode, alluding to Brutus and Cassius, who assassinated Julius Caesar. ["probably August 1927" (*JJA* 47: 143)]

1928: Joyce writes notes in VI.B.21, 22, 26, 23, and starts drafting:

III.1BC; FW 414.14–419.10: The fable of The Ondt and the Gracehoper: Shaun has been speaking to a crowd of people and is now called upon to sing a song. Instead of singing, he tells the fable of the Ondt, who works hard during the summer, building a house and collecting supplies for the winter, and the Gracehoper, who has failed to do so. The Ondt is the representative of Space, the Gracehoper represents Time. The fable roughly follows the same narrative as Aesop's fable of the ant and the grasshopper: by the time the summer is over, the Gracehoper has no choice but to beg for the Ondt's humiliating charity. The Gracehoper sings and praises the Ondt, telling him that his "Genus is worldwide" and his space is sublime, but the last line is the crucial existential question: "why can't you beat time?" (BL 47483–97; *JJA* 57: 323). [February 1928; *Selected Letters I*, 26 March 1928]

1929: Joyce takes notes in notebooks VI.B.4, 27, and 24.

1930: Joyce takes notes in notebooks VI.B.29, 28, 32, and starts drafting:

II.1, section 2; FW 222.22–236.32: The "Children's Games": Glugg (the Devil) is asked a riddle, which he fails to answer. After a second failed attempt to answer a riddle, the rainbow or flower girls dance and sing in praise of their sun hero Chuff (Shaun as Angel). The section ends with a variation on the sentence by Edgar Quinet (quoted on *FW* 281.4–13), alluding to the cyclical nature of history and the transitoriness of human civilizations. [letter to Harriet Weaver, 22 November 1930; *L I* 295; cf. also letters to Harriet Weaver 21 May, 7 June, 15 July 1926]

II.1, section 3; FW 236.33–240.04: The flower girls try to seduce sunny boy Chuff, exposing (as flowers tend to do) their genitals and turning them toward him in heliolatry (*FDV* 135). The answer to the riddles is "heliotrope," as Joyce explained to Frank Budgen (*L I* 406; end July 1939). ["probably December 1930" (*JJA* 51: 73)]

1931: Joyce takes notes in notebooks VI.B.28, 33, VI.A, B.31, and starts drafting:

II.1, section 4; FW 240.05–244.12: Glugg is jealous and threatens to reveal to the world the truth about his family, notably HCE (here with traits of Lewis Carroll and Emanuel Swedenborg) (*FDV* 136). ["probably January 1931" (*JJA* 51: 91)]

II.1, section 5; FW 244.13–246.35: Night falls and darkens the "fun nominal world" (*FDV* 137). ["probably January 1931" (*JJA* 51: 91)]

1932: Joyce takes notes in notebook VI.B.35, and starts drafting:

- *II.1, section 6; FW 246.36–257.02*: The Devil is asked a third riddle, but again fails to answer (*FDV* 139). The parents arrive and take the boys home. Issy seems to stay behind, in her capacity of the little cloud Nuvoletta (*FDV* 140). [early 1932]
- *II.2, section 4; later incorporated into section 5*: "Scribbledehobbles": The children are studying and doing their pensums (*FDV* 148). ["probably 1932" (*JJA* 52: 147)]
- *II.1, section 1; FW 219–222.21*: Since the children's games are conceived as a play, an introduction is added with the program and dramatis personae of The Mime of Mick, Nick and the Maggies. [probably mid-1932 (*JJA* 51: 5)]
- *II.1, section 7; FW 257.03–259*: As HCE shuts the door of the pub, the bang is followed by a thundering noise (another thunderword), and the noise of applause. The game played by the children appears to have been a play, which is now over; the curtain drops (*FDV* 141). [probably mid-1932 (*JJA* 51: 137)]

1933: Joyce takes notes in notebook VI.B.34 and on notesheets; France Raphael copies notes in VI.C.1–4[?])

1934: Joyce takes notes in VI.B.36 and on notesheets, and starts drafting:

- *II.2, section 1; FW 260–263.30*: The tavern is approached. ["probably 1934" (*JJA* 52: 1)]
- *II.2, section 2; FW 264–266.19*: A description of Chapelizod and environs, based on the Chapelizod entry in Thom's *Dublin Directory* (cf. *TD* 119). ["probably 1934" (*JJA* 52: 5)]
- *II.2, section 3; FW 266.20–275.02*: The children are studying grammar and history. "Jellyous Seizer" (*FDV* 143) is one of the topics. Issy is reminded of her "gramma's" advice that she should "take the dative with his oblative," but mind she's "genderous" (*FDV* 146). ["probably 1934" (*JJA* 52: 13)]
- *II.2, section 6; FW 279n*: Issy's letter (assembled primarily with notes from notebook VI.B.21 when Joyce was preoccupied with his daughter's health).

The focus is on her attempts at writing, her knowledge of life, the other twenty-eight ("octette and virginity") girls in her shade, and "the runes of the gamest game ever" (*FDV* 158). ["probably 1934" (*JJA* 52: 225)]

II.2, section 7; FW 280.01–282.04: Issy reads the Quinet sentence in French. ["probably 1934" (*JJA* 52: 239); "Summer 1933" (*TD* 119). While he was in Evian-les-Bains, Joyce asked Paul Léon to find the Quinet excerpt (in notebook VI.B.01), which he had left in Paris. Two days later, on 6 July 1933, Léon sent a transcription to Evian.]

II.2, section 9; FW 304.05–308.25: The children have to make a selection from a list of subjects, such as "Subjugation" or "the benefits of Recreation" (*FDV* 167), to write a short essay. (The night letter, from the children to their "Pep and Memmy," was added at a later stage.) ["probably 1934" (*JJA* 53: 265)]

II.2, section 5; FW 275.03–279.09: Chapter II.2, section 4 ("Scribbledehobble") integrated/elaborated in an extra fragment about the children's pensums. ["1934" (*JJA* 52: 209); possibly later: "November/December 1937" (*TD* 120)] Joyce revised and augmented the existing sections of II.2. Footnotes and marginalia were added to some of the already drafted pieces for II.2.

1935: Joyce takes notes in notebook VI.B.40 and on notesheets; France Raphael copies notes in VI.C.5–10[?]. More footnotes and marginalia are added to the already drafted pieces for II.2. ["early 1935" (*TD* 120)]

II.3, section 1; FW 309–331.36: The tale of Kersse the tailor and the Norwegian captain who orders a suit; the finished suit does not fit, and the captain reproaches Kersse for being unable to sew; the "talerman" (*FDV* 176) in his turn blames the captain for being impossible to fit. [1935, possibly "early 1936" (*TD* 122)]

1936: France Raphael copies notes in VI.C.11–18[?]; Joyce takes notes in VI.B.38, 39, and 37, and starts drafting:

II.3, section 2; FW 332.01–337.03: Kate comes in to tell HCE that ALP wants him to come to bed upstairs. ["December 1936–early 1937" (*TD* 123)]

II.3, section 3; FW 337.04–338.08: Introduction to the story of how Buckley shot the Russian General. ["probably December 1936" (*JJA* 54: 319)]

1937: Joyce takes notes in notebooks VI.B.44, 42, 46, and on notesheets, and starts drafting:

II.3, section 4; FW 338.04–354.06: On a television broadcast, Butt and Taff tell the story of Buckley and the Russian General. Buckley, an Irish soldier, is about to shoot a Russian general, hesitates when he sees him defecating, but kills him when the general wipes himself with a clod of turf. ["December 1936–early 1937" (*TD* 123)]

II.3, section 6A; FW 355.08–355.13: Closing-time ("Shutmup") is announced. At this moment in the writing process, Joyce may have planned to close II.3 here (cf. *BL* 47480-16; *JJA* 55: 31).

II.3, section 6B; FW 355.14–370.29: HCE's apology. Joyce's recombination of decomposed excerpts now proceeded in a most systematic way. From notebook VI.C.06, he took a cluster of notes copied by Madame Raphael: "and that is true / (. . .) I have just been / reading a book / + whilst / turning over the leaves etc. / on the lavatory / often when I am / I sometimes / in fact I'm // big altogether" (VI.C.06: 198–99). This cluster forms the basis of the first draft: "That is true (. . .) I have just (. . .) been reading in a book (. . .) and whilst I have been turning over the leaves (. . .) on the lamatory often when I am contemplating of myself I sometimes am cadging hapsnots of distant renations (. . .) in fact I am big altogether" (*JJA* 55: 5; *BL* 47480–83). So the apology starts with an acknowledgment ("That is true"), but soon becomes a confirmation ("I am big altogether"). This passage was systematically expanded to such an extent that it takes up four pages in the published version of *Finnegans Wake*, starting with "That is too tootrue" (*FW* 355.21) and closing with "I am big altoogooder" (*FW* 358.16). ["late 1937–early 1938" (*TD* 128)]

1938: Joyce takes notes in notebooks VI.B.46, 45, 41, 47, 30, and starts drafting:

II.3, section 5; FW 354.07–355.07: A coda, added to the dialogue between Butt and Taff, originally "two & the same person" (*JJA* 55: 129; 47480–68), who will become one and the same in the final version (*FW* 354.08). ["early 1938" (*TD* 124)]

IV, section 1A; FW 593–598.27: The sleeping giant wakes up (*FDV* 271). ["February 1938" (*TD* 129–30)]

IV, section 1B; FW 598.26–601.30: More regenerations are announced. The twenty-nine leap-year girls call for Kevin (*FDV* 272). ["Spring 1938" (*TD* 130; 132)]

IV, section 1C; FW 601.31–604.26: The old stories of HCE's indiscretion are unearthed, and the meeting in the park is echoed, with the rhyme of time and crime, when the cad asks HCE what time it is (*FDV* 273). But the question of what Kevin is doing (*FDV* 273) is insisted upon. ["Spring 1938" (*TD* 130; 132)]

II.3, section 7; FW 370.30–382.30: The customers are reminded that it is closing time. They encourage Hosty to sing a ballad. After they have finally left, HCE is alone in his pub, collecting and drinking what is left in the customers' glasses (= the integrated "Roderick O'Conor" sketch). ["probably September 1938" (*JJA* 55: 469)]

IV, section 2; FW 604.27–607.22: The "Saint Kevin" sketch (1923) is recycled and expanded with echoes of old motifs, especially HCE's indiscretion in the park. ["July 1938" (*TD* 130)]

II.4, section 2; FW 383.01–398.30: The "Tristan & Isolde" sketch (1923), integrated into the elaboration of "Mamalujo" (1923). ["July 1938" (*JJA* 56: 109); *TD* 131]

II.4, section 3A; FW 398.29–398.30: Two lines introducing the "Anno Domini" poem. ["July 1938" (*JJA* 56: 109); *TD* 131]

II.4, section 3B; FW 398.31–399.34: The "Anno Domini" poem. ["July 1938" (*JJA* 56: 109); *TD* 131]

IV, section 3; FW 603.23–614.18: In the twilight of dawn, the phenomenal world is deceptive (*FDV* 277). Muta and Juva (variants of Mutt & Jute/Shem & Shaun) introduce and watch the encounter of St. Patrick and the Archdruid. What follows is an elaboration of the "Saint Patrick" sketch (1923). After sixteen years of silence, Patrick finally answers and wipes his nose. Thus, the snotgreen island is converted, but at the same time St. Patrick seems to be converted by Ireland as well. ["Summer 1938" (*TD* 133)]

IV, section 4; FW 614.19–619.19: The Revered Letter (drafted in 1923–24), written in defense of HCE, is reincorporated, though in a rearranged and augmented form. [Summer/Fall 1938]

IV, section 5; FW 619.20–628.16: Anna Livia Plurabelle's final monologue. [Fall/Winter 1938]

1939: Joyce continues taking notes in notebook VI.B.48, VIII.C.2, and adds corrections and small alterations to the text in his unbound copy of *Finnegans Wake*, most of which ended up in a list with errata.[6]

What this general impression of the work's diachrony does not indicate is that the invention of new sections occurred in the midst of several other activities, such as fair copying, correcting, revising, proofreading, and pre-publishing. The following table therefore visualizes the interplay between Joyce's private writing activities (with the start of each section's composition on the left-hand side) and the public appearances of parts of the work as it was still in progress (the list on the right-hand side—further elaborating A. Walton Lizst's chart (Ellmann 1983: 794)—indicates the sections on which Joyce's attention was focused in terms of the "prepublishing phase" [de Biasi], parallel with the "composition" of other sections).

As the survey indicates, the final version of *Finnegans Wake* consists of relatively small textual units, which were easily publishable in installments or even as separate units. They could be regarded as a form of what Roland Barthes in *S/Z* called "lexias," but the important difference is that in the case of *S/Z*, the lexias were a division applied by the critic, whereas the sections of *Finnegans Wake* reflect the work's genesis. Barthes' notion of lexias was employed by George Landow to formulate his working definition of "hypertext": "Hypertext, as the term is used in this work, denotes text composed of blocks of text—what Barthes terms a lexia—and the electronic links that join them" (Landow 1997: 3). Although the electronic aspect is obviously not applicable to the period in which *Finnegans Wake* took shape, hypertext does offer a suitable notion to conceptualize and reconstruct the mechanics of complex geneses, such as the writing of Proust's *A la recherche du temps perdu* or Joyce's *Finnegans Wake*.

The development of each of the separate sections or lexias more or less follows the general typology suggested by de Biasi, but their protohypertextual combination into *Finnegans Wake* implies a much more complex genesis. Especially given the *Wake*'s long composition process, it is remarkable that the genetic dossier is lacking in "general sketches, chronologies, grand overarching rough models, overarching workplans," which constitute the material evidence of the "preparatory process" in de Biasi's typology (corresponding to the operational functions of conceiving and initial planning). In this respect, Joyce seems to have been a so-called "mindworker" (*Kopfarbeiter*). The rare "paperwork" (*Papierarbeit*) that testifies to large-scale planning mainly consists of what Joyce confided to people like Harriet

Table 4.1. Interaction between the Private and Public Aspects of "Work in Progress"

Start of Composition	Publication before *Finnegans Wake*
1923	
II.3, section 7; *FW* 380.07–382.30	
II.4, sections 1–2; *FW* 383.01–398.28	
IV, sections 1–2; *FW* 604.27–607.22	
IV, section 3; *FW* 607.23–614.18	
I.2, section 1; *FW* 30–34.29	
II.4, section 3B; *FW* 398.31–399.34	
II.4, sections 2–3A; *FW* 383.01–398.30	
I.2, section 2; *FW* 34.30–44.21	
I.2, section 3; *FW* 44.22–47	
I.3, section 1; *FW* 48–61.27	
I.3, section 2; *FW* 61.28–67.27	
I.3, section 3; *FW* 67.28–74	
I.4, section 1A; *FW* 75–92.05	
I.4, section 2; *FW* 96.26–103	
I.5, section 2 >> IV, section 4 (1938)	
I.5, section 1, *FW* 104–113.22	
I.5, section 4; *FW* 113.23–125	
I.5, section 3; >> Book III.	
1924	
I.7, section 1; *FW* 169–187.23	II.4 section 2, "Mamalujo":
I.7, section 2; *FW* 187.24–195	*Transatlantic Review* 1, no. 4 (Apr. 1924)
I.8, section 1A; *FW* 196–208.26	
I.8, section 1B; *FW* 208.27–216	
III.1A/1D/2A/2C; *FW* 403–473	
III.3A; *FW* 474–532.05	
III.3B; *FW* 532.06–554	
1925	
III.4; *FW* 555–590	I.2 section 1: *Contact Collection* (Contact Editions, 1925): 133–36.
	I.5: *Criterion* 3, no. 12 (July 1925): 498–510.
	I.8: *Le Navire d'Argent* 1 (Oct. 1925): 59–74.
	I.7: *This Quarter* (Nov. 1925): 108–23. [Reprinted versions in *Two Worlds* 1, nos. 1–5 (Sep. 1925–Sep. 1926)]
1926	
III.2B; *FW* 461.33–468.19	
II.2, section 8; *FW* 282.05–304.04	
I.1, section 1; *FW* 3.01–18.16	
I.1, section 2; *FW* 18.17–29	
I.4, section 1B; *FW* 92.06–96.26	

(continued)

Table 4.1—*Continued*

Start of Composition	Publication before *Finnegans Wake*
1927	
I.6, section 1A; *FW* 126–149.10	
I.6, section 1B; *FW* 149.11–150.14	
I.6, section 2; *FW* 150.15–152.03	I.1: *transition* 1 (Apr. 1927): 9–30.
I.6, section 3; *FW* 152.04–159.23	I.2: *transition* 2 (May 1927): 94–107
I.6, section 4; *FW* 159.24–168	I.3: *transition* 3 (June 1927): 32–50.
	I.4: *transition* 4 (July 1927): 46–65.
	I.5: *transition* 5 (Aug. 1927): 15–31.
	I.6: *transition* 6 (Sep. 1927): 87–106f.
	I.7: *transition* 7 (Oct. 1927): 34–56.
	I.8: *transition* 8 (Nov. 1927): 17–35.
1928	
III.1BC; *FW* 414.14–419.10	
	II.2 section 8: *transition* 11 (Feb. 1928): 7–18.
	III.1: *transition* 12 (March 1928): 7–27.
	III.2: *transition* 13 (Summer 1928): 5–32.
	I.8: *Anna Livia Plurabelle* (Crosby Gaige, Oct. 1928)
1929	
	III.3: *transition* 15 (Feb. 1929): 195–238.
	I.6 section 3; II.2 section 8; III.1C: *Tales Told of Shem and Shaun* (Black Sun Press, 1929)
	["A Muster from *Work inProgress*" in: *transition stories*, ed. Eugene Jolas and Robert Sage (1929)]
	III.4: *transition* 18 (Nov. 1929): 211–36.
1930	
II.1, section 2; *FW* 222.22–236.32	III.3B: *Haveth Childers Everywhere* (Fountain Press, 1930)
II.1, section 3; *FW* 236.33–240.04	I.8: *Anna Livia Plurabelle* (Faber and Faber, 1930)
	III.1C (fragments): *Imagist Anthology 1930*, ed. R. Aldington (Chatto and Windus, 1930), 121–22.
1931	
II.1, section 4; *FW* 240.05–244.12	III.3B: *Haveth Childers Everywhere* (Faber and Faber, 1931)
II.1, section 5; *FW* 244.13–246.35	

Start of Composition	Publication before *Finnegans Wake*

1932

II.1, section 6; *FW* 246.36–257.02
II.2, section 4 >> section 5
II.1, section 1; *FW* 219–222.21   I.6 section 3; III.1C: *Two Tales of Shem*
II.1, section 7; *FW* 257.03–259   *and Shaun* (Faber and Faber, 1932)

1933

1934

II.2, section 1; *FW* 260–263.30   II.1: *transition* 22 (Feb. 1933): 49–76.
II.2, section 2; *FW* 264–266.19
II.2, section 3; *FW* 266.20–275.02   II.1 (excerpt): *Les amis de 1914* 2, no. 40
II.2, section 6; *FW* 279n   (23 Feb. 1934)
II.2, section 7; *FW* 280.01–282.04   II.1: *The Mime of Mick, Nick and the*
II.2, section 9; *FW* 304.05–308.25   *Maggies* (Servire Press, 1934)
II.2, section 5; *FW* 275.03–279.09
Footnotes and marginalia for II.2

1935

More footnotes and marginalia for II.2   II.2 sections 1, 2, 3, and 9: *transition*
II.3, section 1; *FW* 309–331.36   23 (July 1935): 109–29.

1936

II.3, section 2; *FW* 332.01–337.03
II.3, section 3; *FW* 337.04–338.08

1937

II.3, section 4; *FW* 338.04–354.06
II.3, section 6A; *FW* 355.08–355.13
II.3, section 6B; *FW* 355.14–370.29
                                          II.3, section 1: *transition* 26 (Feb 1937): 35–52.
                                          II.2 sections 1, 2, 3, and 9: *Storiella as*
                                          She Is Syung (Corvinus Press, 1937)

1938

II.3, section 5; *FW* 354.07–355.07
IV, section 1; *FW* 593–604.26
II.3, section 7; *FW* 370.30–382.30   II.1 section 5: *Verve* 1.2 (March 1938)
IV, section 2; *FW* 604.27–607.22   II.3, sections 4–5: *transition* 27 (May
II.4, section 2; *FW* 383.01–398.28   1938): 59–78.
II.4, section 3; *FW* 398.29–399.34
IV, section 3; *FW* 603.23–614.18
IV, section 4; *FW* 614.19–619.19
IV, section 5; *FW* 619.20–628.16

1939

                                          Finnegans Wake
                                          (London: Faber and Faber; New York: Viking
                                          Press, 4 May 1939)

Shaw Weaver in his letters. Because Joyce apparently preferred to work with relatively small units of texts and to combine them only gradually, any attempt to periodize "Work in Progress" along the lines suggested by de Biasi tends to be somewhat artificial. For instance, it would be possible to impose a decimal system on the writing process and divide it into periods:

1. orienting (1922–Spring 1923)
2. exploring and conceiving (Spring–Fall 1923)
3. textualizing (Fall 1923–Spring 1924)
4. textualizing & prepublishing (Spring 1924–Spring 1926)
5. structuring (Spring 1926–Winter 1926)
6. prepublishing (1927–1930)
7. abandoning? (1930–1932)
8. recycling (1933)
9. assembling and reformatting (1934–1936)
10. reincorporating (1937–1939)

The first five periods would roughly follow de Biasi's chronotypology of operational functions, but after the first two periods, the order is already disrupted. The division could only serve as a very rough indication of the compositional focus in each period. Apart from the orienting stage, which is characterized by note taking, the other periods are marked by a combination of operational functions. Most of the precompositional material is contained in the notebooks, characterized by parataxis. The most appropriate of de Biasi's categories would be the "provisional process" (corresponding to the operational function of orienting). But in many cases—for instance, the excerpts from *Encyclopaedia Britannica* entries on cities in VI.B.29—the notes are a form of research, with a direct purpose in mind. In de Biasi's scheme, the research process is already part of the composition (rather than the precompositional) phase. So, even within one single notebook, the notes can have several operational functions. The accumulation of lexical material throughout the composition history is not limited to the so-called phase of the "provisional process." In the case of Joyce's last work, "provisional" has less to do with preliminaries than with provision in the sense of verbal supplies. Even during the most creative period in 1923–24, when Joyce focused almost exclusively on the writing of new episodes, the endogenetic textualization is continuously "fed" by exogenetic note taking. As a consequence, it seems more appropriate to study "Work in Progress" according to the "decomposition/recombination" division suggested in *Finnegans Wake*, starting with the examination of its lexical provision.

5

Decomposition

"Ex nihilo nihil fit." Joyce mentioned this line in one of his keys to explain his "Work in Progress" in a letter to Harriet Shaw Weaver (13 May 1927): "Out of nothing comes nothing" (1975b: 321). Joyce drew on hundreds of exogenetic sources to write his last work. Since genetic criticism can only work with the material traces of the reading and writing process, it is often impossible to reconstruct this early phase in the work's genesis. But Joyce's reading notes are a useful starting point to try to retrace his reading process.

One of the most powerful and effective impulses for Joyce to go on writing was negative criticism by colleagues. One colleague in particular thus unwittingly became one of Joyce's "anticollaborators" (*FW* 118.25–26): Wyndham Lewis. His "Analysis of the Mind of James Joyce" (a chapter in *Time and Western Man*, 1927) was first published in Lewis's own magazine, the *Enemy*. But this was not Lewis's first criticism of Joyce's work.[1] Lewis's book *The Art of Being Ruled*, published in early 1926, already contained some criticism of Joyce's work, which he relates to Gertrude Stein's, according to "the fashion" Samuel Beckett was to criticize a decade later in a letter to Axel Kaun:

> Perhaps the logographs of Gertrude Stein are nearer to what I have in mind. At least the texture of language has become porous. (. . .) To bring this method into relation with that of Joyce, as is the fashion, strikes me as senseless as the attempt, of which I know nothing as yet, to compare Nominalism (in the sense of the Scholastics) with Realism. (1984 [1937]: 172–73)

After this fashion, Wyndham Lewis links both Stein's "mental stutter" and Joyce's "eccentricities" (1989 [1926]: 346–47) to Mr. Jingle in Charles Dickens's *The Pickwick Papers* (346). And Joyce read this chapter on "Mr. Jingle and Mr. Bloom" toward the end of March 1926. He mentions it in a letter of 23 March to Harriet Shaw Weaver, and on 30 March he writes to her that he is replying to Lewis's criticism by means of a grotesque addition to chapter III.2. But Joyce did not only read and react to the chapter containing the criticism on "Mr. Jinglejoys" (*FW* 466.18). That he also took some interest in (at least parts of) the rest of Lewis's book can be derived from his (scattered) reading notes in notebook VI.B.20.

The notes reflect the way Joyce decomposed Lewis's argumentation. He jotted down fragments that must have seemed to him to be potentially useful for the composition of his own work in progress. Joyce shows strikingly little interest in Lewis's argumentation. More often than not, Joyce's notes refer to other works (mentioned by Lewis) or are derived from quotations cited in *The Art of Being Ruled*.

From Lewis's chapter "The Matriarchate and Feminine Ascendency" (part 7, chapter 10), Joyce excerpted a bibliographical reference to "The Dominant Sex, by Mathilde and Mathias Vaerting" (Lewis 1989 [1926]: 199; cf. Joyce's notebook VI.B.20: 49, bottom of the page). As David Hayman notes, Lewis was "adamantly opposed to all attempts to portray the inner dynamic of the mind because such attempts reproduce feminine 'flux'" (1998: 626). In part 8 ("The 'Vicious' Circle"), Lewis further elaborates on the theme of feminine ascendancy by applying it to "sex-transformation" and "sexual inversion" (209). Oscar Wilde serves as a paradigm: "He became almost a political martyr, other countries using his well-advertised agony to point to the philistinism of England" (209). In this context, Joyce's early notes (March–July 1923) derived from Frank Harris's biography of Oscar Wilde may be of interest. Sam Slote has drawn attention to a passage in this biography, mentioning the rumor about a sex scandal in which Wilde's father-in-law, Horatio Lloyd, might have been involved: "The charge against Horatio Lloyd was of a normal kind. It was for exposing himself to nursemaids in the gardens of the Temple" (Frank Harris, quoted in *FWNB* VI.B.3: 12; cf. Slote 1995: 105). Starting from this passage, Joyce jotted down a crucial note in the development of the plot of *Finnegans Wake*: "It is not true that / Pop was homosexual / he had been arrested / at the request of some / nursemaids to whom / he temporarily / exposed himself / in the Temple gardens" (VI.B.3:153).

Joyce seems to have been less interested in the issue of homosexuality than in the concept of denial as the impulse to the rumors. "In the buginning is the woid" (*FW* 378.29) around which the rumors keep whirling. That is the "vicious circle" of Joyce's project. By the time he read Lewis's chapter "The 'Vicious' Circle" (around March/April 1926), the idea of the denied accusation, combined with the Bywaters case, was already well developed in the drafts, but Joyce had not yet announced the circular structure of his book. "The book really has no beginning or end" (*L I* 246), he wrote to Harriet Shaw Weaver on 8 November 1926, a half year after he excerpted notes from the following passages in Lewis's *The Art of Being Ruled* (the highlighted words are excerpted by Joyce in notebook VI.B.20):

> A drunkard soon develops a red *nose* (...) by which people are generally repelled for some reason. The "*Nancy*ism" of the *joy-boy* or joy-man—the over-manned personality, the queer insistence on "delicate nurture," that air of assuring those met that he is a "real *lady*," (...) are to some human norm almost as central as that which resents the red nose, or the big paunch, offensive. (1989 [1926]: 210)

Joyce excerpted the highlighted words on page 50 of notebook VI.B.20. The "old portugal's nose" (*FW* 463.19), mentioned in the "Dave the Dancekerl" episode, may have been derived from this passage, although the note "nose" (VI.B.20:50) is not crossed out. It is not crossed out in France Raphael's transcription either (VI.C.3:270). The only note derived from the above passage that was deleted is "joyboy," which found its way into Jaun's lecture to his sister, mentioning his "bringing proceedings verses [versus] the joyboy" (*FW* 443.11). Joyce thus emphasizes the dichotomy between Shem and Shaun. By excerpting lexical fragments from Lewis's text in his notebook and using the notes in divergent episodes of "Work in Progress," Joyce not only decomposed and neutralized Lewis's criticism, but also scattered the decomposed particles in such a way that the Enemy's comments served as leitmotifs. In this case, Lewis's palaver about "sexual inversion" thus served as verbal material to reinforce the image of Shem as an "inversion" of Shaun.

In general, Joyce's reading notes show a preference for examples. Rather than excerpting passages that reflect Lewis's argument, Joyce wrote "T foreign sexual habits" (notebook VI.B.20: 58), corresponding to a set of passages about "*foreign habits*" (256), which Lewis quotes from Dr. Westermarck's *History of Moral Ideas*, mentioning the *ke'kcuc* ("men transformed into women") among the Koriaks; the Marshall Islanders; the *mahoos* in Tahiti, who "assume the dress, attitude, and manners of women" (256); the "transformed *shamans*" (257); and native American tribes, among a great number of which "homosexual customs have been observed" (257). "The Transformed *Shaman*" is the title of the next chapter in *The Art of Being Ruled*, opening with an account of "Chukchee inversion" on the "*tundras* and steppes" in Siberia, where great importance is attached to "rapid *eating*" and "*quick*-lunch" (260). The highlighted words form a cluster of notes on page 58 of notebook VI.B.20.

After a brief digression about the role of the shaman in summoning "a ghost to accompany the *hunters*" (cf. VI.B.20:58) of the Allocet Indians, Lewis returns to the Chukchee. Chief among the arts of their shamans is ventriloquism. Whereas Lewis employs the adjective "ventriloquial" (262), Joyce notes down "ventriloquent" (VI.B.20:59). The "soft man," or *shaman*, is typically "*bashful*" (261; VI.B.20: 59). The Chukchee apparently attribute shyness to particular diseases as well, "especially such as cannot harm man much—for instance, a cold in the head. In one of their tales, on this principle, a *cold in* the *head*, desirous of *entering* a *house* [59], lacks courage to do so" (262). By means of his sigla, Joyce applies this to Shem (VI.B.20:59).[2] The boys who shrink from making the transition to manhood are referred to as "spoilt" children, and this "*spoiled*" (VI.B.20:60) nature is linked to Shaun in Joyce's notes.

That Joyce focused on examples that Lewis took from other sources does not necessarily imply that he had no interest in Lewis's argumentation.[3] Joyce's habit of quoting from quotations was part of his encyclopedic project and the easiest way to create the impression of enormous erudition. Through his reading of Lewis, Joyce thus gathered notes from a handful of books on just one single page. The next entry on page VI.20:060 ("stone-wife") is derived from (Lewis's quotation of) a passage in Mary Czaplicka's account of Siberian customs: "The Maritime Koryak have at times ordinary stones instead of wives. A man will put clothes on such a stone, put it in his bed, and sometimes caress it as if it were living" (267).

After this reading of part 9 ("Man and Shaman"), parts 10 ("Socialist Theory") and 11 ("*Proudhon* and Rousseau") do not seem to have caught Joyce's attention in the same way as part 12 ("The 'Intellectual'") did, although he did note Proudhon's name on page VI.B.20:60. Initially, Joyce still focused on the quotations, such as the long extract Lewis quotes from the French socialist thinker François Marie Charles Fourier:

> The philosophers, accustomed to reverence everything which comes in the name and under the sanction of commerce, will (. . .) consecrate their servile powers to celebrating its (the new order's) praises. (. . .) The tenderest expressions have replaced the old language of the merchants, and it is now said, in elegant phrase, that "*sugars are languid*"—that is, are falling; that "soaps are looking up"—that is, have advanced. (331; VI.B.20:65)

The note "languid" (VI.B.20:65) was crossed out and used in Jaun's lecture to Issy,[4] in a passage about "true fiminin risirvition" (*FW* 434) and lingerie, which can be read as a metafictional reflection on the "silks apeel" (*FW*

508.29) of the "feminine fiction, stranger than the facts" (*FW* 109.32): "Sure, what is it on the whole only holes tied together, the merest and transparent washingtones to make Languid Lola's lingery longer?" (*FW* 434.21–23).

Gradually Joyce seems to take greater interest in Lewis's own words, for instance when he points out that the other French socialists Charles Péguy and Georges Sorel may claim the intellectual is "too much a *word-man*" while they were themselves "more enamoured, no doubt, of '*poesy* and the fine arts' than their socialist ticket would have allowed them to confess" (333; VI.B.20:65). When Lewis turns his attention to "Bergson's gospel of fluidity and *illiquation*" (334; VI.B.20:68), he has Joyce's full attention.

According to Lewis, many of his contemporaries focused too exclusively on time. His chapter on "The Great God Flux" (1989 [1926]: 335) starts with the question of why there is such unanimity about what he calls "bergsonism." Lewis complains about the uniformity of contemporary thought: "It is in the very *sullage* or backwash of revolution that these unanimous organisms thrive" (335; VI.B.20:69). He refers to *Le bergsonisme, ou une philosophie de la mobilité* and Julien Benda's contention that contemporary writers are the "*flunkeys*"[5] of the *idées reçues* of their epoch (335). Lewis's fulmination against Bergson's fluidity and "Heraclitus' famous *flux*" (VI.B.20:69) are particularly interesting in view of Joyce's work in progress, which already contained a quite "fluid" chapter on ALP, but had not yet been conceived as a "riverrun" in its entirety. Lewis seamlessly connects this focus on flux to "hatred of language": "Hatred of *the word* goes hand in hand with hatred of the intellect, for *the word* is, of course, its sign. Language is one of the things to be broken up—a stammer, a hiatus, an ellipsis, a syncope, a hiccup, is installed in the midst of the verb, and the mind attacked through its instrument."[6] The stammering is typical of the third of four manifestations of the "anti-intellect campaign," according to Lewis: the Child; the Amateur; the Demented; and the Pragmatic. Gertrude Stein is the prototype of the Demented, and "the various stammering, squinting, punning group who follow her" (344), as well as the worshippers of the "Great God Flux," such as "the psycho-analysts, futurists, dadas, *proustites*, etc. (344). The note "proustite" (VI.B.20:73) was not crossed out, but the whole "crowd of the Flu Flux Fans" (*FW* 464.15) does make its appearance in the "Dave the Dancekerl" episode. Lewis builds up his criticism to culminate in the chapter on "Mr. Jingle and Mr. Bloom," elaborating on the "exploitation of madness, of ticks, *blephorospasms*, and eccentricities of the mechanism of the brain" of the "abnormally wordy" Mr. Bloom" (346–47; VI.B.20:73). Again, Lewis's criticism is decomposed and employed to insert a metafictional comment on "the process verbal whereby you would sublimate your blepharospasmockical suppressions" (*FW* 515.15–17, in Yawn's cross-examination by the four old men).

To what extent this reading, notably the ideas of the vicious circle and the flux, may have contributed to the structure of *Finnegans Wake* is neither verifiable nor falsifiable on the basis of this notebook material alone. But the notes do give an insight into the way Joyce decomposed the texts he read during the composition of his last work. By 1926, he already had some experience with the decomposition of negative criticism and its recycling in his own work. Moreover, excerpting from source texts was only one form of decomposition. Joyce applied this technique to the even smaller unit of the word as well, which is the starting point of the next chapter examining Joyce's expansive method of recombination.

6

Recombination: S, M, L

SMALL: "Word Versions"

Language only gradually became the main character of "Work in Progress" as Joyce detached his lexical material from its conventional referentiality. The more words he decontextualized, the more opportunities he created for their meanings, associations, and resonances to interact, causing an energetic effect of simultaneity.[1] The most conspicuous tool he used to create this effect was the so-called portmanteau technique. Humpty Dumpty in Lewis Carroll's *Through the Looking-Glass* defined the notion of the portmanteau as "two meanings packed into one word" (1988: 678). Joyce usually packed up more than two meanings, but the principle is the same and the result all the more effective.

Each portmanteau word in *Finnegans Wake* is usually the result of several successive distortions. In textual criticism, the notion of "version" is defined as a relatively large unit of text, consisting of more or less well-formed sentences. For instance, Siegfried Scheibe distinguishes the "first version" from what precedes it by defining it as a text that "possesses the textual structure of the work (...) contain[ing] articulated, connected sentences" (1995: 196–97). But in "Work in Progress," Joyce seems to be working also with a smaller size of versions. To map out the translation of words into mature Wakese, it is necessary to retrace the different versions of single words or small word units.

B-notebooks

The first "word version" is, in most cases, a note or an excerpt derived from a source text. For instance, in notebook VI.B.06, Joyce took many notes from (mainly negative) reviews of *Ulysses*. Most of these source texts were located by Ingeborg Landuyt.[2] Joyce used several of these notes for the description of Shem the Penman. "Obscene"—it will come as no surprise—is the word that occurs in the majority of the reviews. Joyce noted it down on page 117 of notebook VI.B.06. The surrounding pages (116–19) are filled with other excerpts from almost a dozen clippings concerning *Ulysses*:

- "Aramis." "The Scandal of *Ulysses*." *Sporting Times* 34 (1 April 1922): 4.
- Arnold Bennett. "James Joyce's *Ulysses*." *Outlook* (29 April 1922): 337–39.
- Ernest Boyd. "Expressionism of James Joyce." *New York Tribune*, 28 May 1922.
- Mary M. Colum. "The Confessions of James Joyce." *Freeman* 5, no. 123 (19 July 1922): 450–52.
- James Douglas. "Beauty—and the Beast." *Sunday Express*, 28 May 1922.
- Stephen Gwynn. "Modern Irish Literature." *Manchester Guardian*, 15 March 1923.
- Margaret Maitland. "Mr. Joyce and the Catholic Tradition." *New Witness*, 20 (4 Aug. 1922): 70–71.
- John Middleton Murry. "Mr. Joyce's *Ulysses*." *Nation & Athenaeum* 31 (22 April 1922): 124–25.
- Edmund Wilson. "*Ulysses*." *New Republic* 31, no. 396 (5 July 1922): 164–66.
- Virginia Woolf. "Modern Novels." *Times Literary Supplement* 899 (10 April 1919): 189–90.

The following sample of relevant passages (presented in the order in which Joyce read and excerpted them) illustrates how these reviews were "decomposed" by Joyce in his notebook. The highlighted elements are excerpted by Joyce in his notebook.

It is remarkable that even in generally positive evaluations, Joyce extracted only the negative remarks. For instance, in Edmund Wilson's review, the "work of high genius" is ignored; only its "longueurs" are noted down. When Joyce added these negative remarks to chapter 7, he had already written a first draft in his "Guiltless" copybook (BL 47471b). The systematic addition of these review excerpts started during the composition of the second draft of the second section (in the same copybook). The first section was subsequently revised and "enriched" with these negative assessments at the third draft stage or fair copy (*BL* 47474).

Table 6.1. "Decomposition" of Reviews in Notebook VI.B.06 (Landuyt 1999)

Source texts	Notes	Chapter I.7		FW
	VI.B.06	draft 2	draft 3	
"Let us record the **atoms** as they fall upon the mind in the order in which they fall, let us trace the pattern, however disconnected and **incoherent** in appearance, which each sight or incident scores upon the consciousness." (Woolf 125)	page 116			
"(…) a work of such originality yet fails to compare (…) with *Youth* or *Jude the Obscure*. It fails, one might say simply because of the comparative **poverty of** the writer's **mind**." (Woolf 126)	116, red-deleted	47471b–72 (I.7§2)		192.10
"After a rather boresome perusal of James Joyce's *Ulysses* (…) I can realise one reason at least for Puritan America's Society for the Prevention of Vice, and can understand why the Yankee judges fined the publishers of *The Little Review* one hundred dollars for the original publication of a very **rancid** chapter of the **Joyce stuff**, which appears to have been written by a perverted lunatic who has made a speciality of the literature of the latrine." (Aramis 192)	116, red-deleted		47474–10 (I.7§1)	182.17
"For the driving impulse of this remarkable book is an immense, an uprecedented, liberation of **suppress**ions (…) of an adult man who has lived under the shadow of the Roman Catholic Church (…)." (Murry 124)	116			
"'Ulysses' is, fundamentally (though it is much besides), an immense, a prodigious, self-laceration, the tearing-away from himself, by a **half-demented** [Joyce: "Semi demented"] man of genius, of inhibitions and limitations which have grown to be flesh of his flesh." (Murry 124)	116, red-deleted		9 (I.7§1)	179.25
"The lowest **demi-mondaines** in Dublin – or, for that matter, in London, Glasgow or Cardiff – would be **revolted** by many things that Joyce writes of." (Aramis 193)	116, red-deleted		8 (I.7§1)	
"Joyce is **more than a bit like that** himself. Lenehan and Boylan are **clean little cherub**s compared with him." (Aramis 193)	116, red-deleted		8 (I.7§1)	177.14

(continued)

Table 6.1—*Continued*

Source texts	Notes	Chapter I.7		FW
"The latter extract displays Joyce in a mood of **kindergarten** delicacy." (Aramis 193)	116, red-deleted	70v (I.7§2)		191.21
"The main contents of the book are enough to make a **Hottentot sick**." (Aramis 193)	116, red-deleted	71v (I.7§2)		193.02
"I fancy that it would also have the very simple effect of an **ordinary emetic**. *Ulysses* is not alone sordidly pornographic, but it is intensely dull." (Aramis 194)	116, red-deleted	71v (I.7§2)		192.14
"The doctrinaire zeal of a coterie seems to be bent upon leaving the profoundly Irish genius of James Joyce in the possession of a **prematurely cosmopolit**an reputation, the unkind fate which has always overtaken writers isolated from the conditions of which they are a part and presented to the world **without any perspective**." (Boyd 7)	117			
"if Ireland were to accept the paternity of Joyce and his Dublin **Joyceries**, which out-rosse the rosseries of the Parisian stews, Ireland would indeed (…) degenerate into a latrine and a sewer." (Douglas 5)	117, red-deleted	68v (I.7§2)		187.35
"but I must plainly add, at the risk of **opprobrium**, that in the finest passages it is in my opinion justified …" (Bennett 339)	117, red-deleted		5 (I.7§1)	172.34
"And those who read it will profit by the **vicarious sacrifice**." (Murry 124)	117			
"Every thought that a super-subtle modern can think seems to be hidden somewhere in its **inspissated** obscurities." (Murry 125)	118, red-deleted		9 (I.7§1)	179.25
"And there are many places in which both the thing said and the motive are plain to us, where the trouble seems to be simply that Mr. Joyce has been unable to hold his hand, where he seems to have dropped the illusion of truth for the truth, the effect to truth for the fact, which is, in art, to drop the **bone** for the **shadow**." (Murry 125)	118, red-deleted		12 (I.7§1)	184.08
"Yet, for all its appalling **longueurs**, *Ulysses* is a work of high genius." (Wilson 165)	118			
"The only question now is whether Joyce will ever write a **tragic** masterpiece to set beside this comic one." (Wilson 165)	118			

Source texts	Notes	Chapter I.7	FW
"Seven hundred pages of a tome like a **Blue-book** are occupied with the events and sensations in one day of a renegade Jew" (Gwynn 301)	118, red-deleted	9 (I.7§1)	179.27
"This vision of human beings as walking **drain-pipes**, this focussing of life exclusively round the excremental and sexual mechanism, appears on the surface inexplicable in so profoundly imaginative and observant a student of humanity as Mr. Joyce." (Maitland 273)	118		
"Like Rousseau, Joyce derives everything from his own ego; he lives in a narrow world in which he himself is not only the **poles**, but the **equator** and the **parallels of latitude** and longitude" (Colum 452)	118		

Among these notes (notebook VI.B.06, page 116) are some excerpts from Virginia Woolf's essay "Modern Novels" (later revised and published as "Modern Fiction"), in which she writes:

> we seek to define the element which distinguishes the work of several young writers, among whom Mr. James Joyce is most able, from that of their predecessors. (. . .) Let us record the *atoms* as they fall upon the mind in the order in which they fall, let us trace the pattern, however disconnected and *incoherent* in appearance, which each sight or incident scores upon the consciousness. (125; emphasis added)

From this passage, Joyce excerpted and combined the words "incoherent atoms" (notebook VI.B.06:116). The other passage in Woolf's essay that caught his attention was: "A work of such originality yet fails to compare (. . .) with *Youth* or *Jude the Obscure*. It fails, one might say, simply because of the comparative *poverty of* the writer's *mind*." When he was writing the portrait of Shem the Penman in his "Guiltless" copybook, he used only the critical note, "poverty of mind" (*BL* 47471b-72). Whenever Joyce inserted a note in his drafts, he crossed it out with a colored crayon, a system he devised in order not to use any note twice. But even the undeleted entries can be of interest, as they show, for instance, what caught Joyce's attention. The undeleted entry "incoherent atoms" can shed some light on the development from *Ulysses* to *Finnegans Wake*, which is in many ways a radicalization of the atomic method observed by Virginia Woolf.

This atomic method is quite unique. Joyce's notes are extremely paratactic compared to more traditional forms of note taking, such as Virginia Woolf's own notes—for instance, the ones she made during her reading of Joyce's *Ulysses*. In "Les bibliothèques virtuelles de James Joyce et de Virginia Woolf," Daniel Ferrer analyzes the way Woolf begins a new notebook (nr. XXXI) with the heading "Order of Ulysses" and a list of seven colors: "I—Claret red / II—pale blue / III—orange / IV—dark green / V light green / VI—green / VII—dark blue." Rather than referring to some kind of impressionist division of the book, the colors are a dry bibliographic description of the numbers of the *Little Review* in which the first chapters of *Ulysses* appeared as installments. The book was not finished yet when Woolf read these installments in the first seven issues, which she had borrowed from a friend, but apparently she did not start reading *Ulysses* straight away; the heading "*Ulysses James Joyce*" only features on the second half of the page. Before embarking on this difficult literary voyage, she read an article she found in the second of the seven *Little Review* issues. From this article by May Sinclair entitled "The Novels of Dorothy Richardson," Virginia Woolf excerpted a half page of notes, starting with "Reality is thick and deep. Novelist must confine himself/to this knowledge at first hand. He must/'plunge in.'" Even though this is an abbreviated form of what May Sinclair wrote, Woolf's notes are more or less syntactic sentences. Eventually, this accidental reading concerning a completely different author would considerably color Woolf's analysis of Joyce's works. A French quotation in May Sinclair's article (from Rémy de Gourmont's *Promenades littéraires*) caught Woolf's attention: "Il y a peut-être un sentiment nouveau à créer, celui de l'amour de la vie pour la vie elle-même, abstraction faite des grandes joies qu'elle ne donne pas à tous, et qu'elle ne donne peut-être à personne" (Sinclair in Ferrer 2001: 179). Virginia Woolf simultaneously translated and extracted the elements that interested her: "The ordinary life richer than the extraordinary—the fabric of life—life itself." She also mentioned the bibliographic reference. Daniel Ferrer draws attention to the movement from emotional considerations (the possibility of creating an emotion or sensation) to a more abstract evaluation, and from a hesitant formulation ("peut-être") to a universal assertion, whereby the idea of "the love of life for life's sake" becomes "life itself." This condensed result will end up in Woolf's essay "Modern Novels": "If we want life itself, here surely we have it." "Here" refers to Joyce's work, not to Richardson's. Woolf wrote the words "Modern Novels" above the excerpts from Sinclair's article, but this title seems to have been added at a later stage. What is important, however, is that notebooks appear to be a creative space where accidental juxtapositions can lead to new insights, as Edgar Allan Poe had already claimed in "American Prose Writers": "Novel conceptions are merely unusual combinations. The mind of man can imagine nothing which does not exist" (*Broadway Journal*, 18 January 1845). Notebooks often provide the necessary information to reconstruct an author's library and to find out how s/he made use of it.

The virtual library of James Joyce is gigantic, and the ways he made use of it are often peculiar. Although not entirely inscrutable, the amalgamation of different source texts is quite thorough. A source text is "decomposed" because Joyce picks out only a few words and jots them down in his B-notebooks. Since each B-notebook is based on several source texts, it constitutes a creative environment in which a note from a newspaper can end up next to a note from, say, the *Encyclopaedia Britannica*, without any distinction. This obliteration of the original context creates opportunities for new associations.

Joyce extracts elements or "incoherent atoms" from the most diverse sources and thoroughly destroys every form of context. Unlike Virginia Woolf, he almost never mentions the bibliographic reference. He also removes the elements from the sentence and syntactic structure in which they were originally embedded. And the elements he extracts seldom summarize the content of the source text. His attention is mostly caught by lexical peculiarities, either with the composition of a specific chapter in mind or not.

In terms of the metaphors of the spider and the bee, which Jonathan Swift applied in *The Battle of the Books* to characterize the Ancients and the Moderns, Joyce's method seems to correspond to that of the bee, openly taking its pollen from diverse sources to make its honey. But in chapter 7, Joyce insists on the metaphor of digestion and its less mellifluous result. Shem's method of producing ink from his own excrements, described in Latin (*FW* 185), reads as follows in Roland McHugh's translation:

> First the artist, the eminent writer, without any shame or apology, pulled up his raincoat & undid his trousers & then drew himself close to the life-giving earth, with his buttocks bare as they were born. Weeping & groaning he relieved himself into his own hands. (. . .) he put his own dung which he called his "down-castings" into an urn (. . .) he then passed water into it happily and mellifluously (. . .) Finally, from the foul dung (. . .) he made himself an indelible ink (McHugh 1991: 185)

The ellipses contain short remarks in English, commenting on the prosy Latin style and reducing the message to what it comes down to: "(highly prosy, crap in his hand, sorry!)," "(did a piss, says he was dejected, asks to be exonerated)," "(faked O'Ryan's, the indelible ink)" (185). Although Shem is presented as a "notesnatcher" (*FW* 125.21–22), taking his inspiration from wherever he can find it, his method is not depicted as the production of honey. In Swift's fable, the bee readily acknowledges that it takes its pollen from numerous flowers, whereas the spider claims to produce her web solely from its own entrails. He may have wanted to build his own web "with [his] own hands, and the materials extracted altogether out of [his] own person," as Swift puts it (1986: 112), but the Ancients point out that the spider also feeds on insects and the "vermin of its age," and otherwise it would not be able to make its web. Joyce's masterstroke was that he used the "vermin" of his age, more specifically the vermin of his reviewers, to write the chapter on Shem, thus combining the method of the Ancients with a Modern approach. Joyce's deprecatory manner of presenting his own writing method seems to have inspired Beckett, who elaborated on it in a more radical way (see chapter 9).

In typological terms, the B-notebooks contain lexical material that can be subdivided into a few categories:

1. *Decomposition* is materialized in reading notes that are the result of either
   . random reading, or of more or less
   . focused research, with a specific section in mind.

2. *Precomposition* in the notebooks consists of extremely succinct conceptual notes, usually marked by one of the sigla, denoting either archetypal character amalgams (such as /\ for Shaun) or parts of the book (such as /\ for book III, the book of Shaun). For instance, after one page of excerpts from *Ulysses* reviews (notebook VI.B.06, top of page 117), Joyce jots down a conceptual note, thus turning his own precompositional activity into part of the narrative: "Shem puts down notes/for △" (the triangle being the sign for ALP, whose letter in defense of HCE is said to be actually written by Shem). Consequently, the "Joyceries" mentioned in James Douglas's review are immediately turned into "Shemeries" in Joyce's notes on the same page 117.

3. *Protocomposition* is rather rare in the notebooks and consists of short protodrafts, usually consisting of not more than a few sentences that contain a core or a fragment of a first draft. As a rule, the actual composition of such a first draft takes place in a copybook (especially reserved for compositional purposes) or on loose sheets.

With his system of crossing out a note with a colored crayon whenever he used it in a draft, Joyce turned each of his notebooks into a sort of distribution center. For instance, the decomposed elements in notebook VI.B.11 (compiled in the fall of 1923) are subsequently distributed over several drafts in a copybook that is preserved in the British Library (BL 47471b), containing first and second drafts of parts of chapters 2, 3, 4, 5, 7, and 8, as well as three drafts of ALP's letter and an early version of its delivery. (It opens with the word "Guiltless"; hereafter it will be referred to as the "Guiltless" copybook.) After a while, he used several B-notebooks to write his drafts by means of a "recombination" of the decomposed elements. As a result, the different distribution centers (the various B-notebooks) are in their turn subject to a further assembly. In the case of the "Guiltless" copybook, Joyce assembled or "recombined" notes from at least seven notebooks to write his drafts: notebooks VI.B.10, 3, 25, 2, 11, 6, and 1.

C-notebooks

After ten years of working in this fashion, Joyce asked France Raphael to transcribe all the undeleted notes from his old B-notebooks into new notebooks, the so-called C-notebooks. The order in which France Raphael copied the B-notebooks does not correspond with the chronology of their original compilation. For instance, notebook VI.C.01 consists of the leftovers of B-notebooks 11, 16, and 34. The first seventy-four pages of VI.C.01 are based on the undeleted notes from VI.B.16 (April–May 1924); these are followed on pages 75–208 by notes copied from VI.B.11 (September–November 1923) and on pages 209–80 by notes from VI.B.34 (first half of 1933). This random order indicates that Joyce did not object to the further amalgamation of notes originally taken in completely different periods of "Work in Progress." He even asked France Raphael to copy some of his old *Ulysses* notebooks. Among the manuscripts exhibited in 2004 at the National Library of Ireland, a few of the subject notebooks show the pencil mark "/\abcd" on the inside of the cover. These notebooks contained lexical material that was originally intended for usage in *Ulysses*, neatly organized under headings referring to the book's episodes, with some extra pages with "Eventuali." According to his customary method, Joyce struck out the entries he used in the drafts with colored crayons. More than a decade after the publication of *Ulysses*, he asked France Raphael to copy the undeleted entries from these old notebooks, together with the undeleted entries from the B-notebooks. The pencil mark /\abcd, referring to the four chapters of book III, thus came to mean "recycling." The separation of the mark into /\a, /\b, /\c, and /\d was subsequently used to indicate the redistribution of the recycled material over the four chapters. These four chapters had already been published as separate installments under the heading "Continuation of a Work in Progress" in the journal *transition*. For the further elaboration and revision of book III, Joyce devised a remarkably mechanical system.

Notesheets

The most striking aspect of this compositional phase is Joyce's sustained effort to separate the entries in the notebooks from their contextual history, that is, the original context from which they were derived. The last part of notebook VI.C.01 consists of notes copied from notebook VI.B.34.[3] According to Danis Rose's chronology, this notebook was compiled between January 1933 and the summer of that year, which is around the time (or just before) he asked France Raphael to start copying. The decision to work with notesheets was apparently made earlier than the completion of the first C-notebook. Before he gave notebook VI.B.34 to France Raphael to copy, he had already leafed through this document in retrograde direction to compile the notesheets. Apart from that, the procedure of gathering more lexical material is just as systematic as in the case of the C-notebooks. After having given VI.B.34 to France Raphael, and after she had transcribed the undeleted entries in VI.C.01, Joyce used the latter fairly quickly afterwards to compile the first set of notesheets. In other words, he culled the same material twice. For instance, when he flicked through VI.B.34 in retrograde direction, he did not judge the note "parroteys lust" (VI.B.34:007) interesting enough to transfer to the notesheets. But after France Raphael had copied it (VI.C.01:212), he reappraised it and transferred it to /\c (*BL* 47486a–43v).

Since Joyce used VI.B.34 for the notes rather quickly after he compiled this notebook, he probably remembered the entries' original context. But the fact that he leafed through the notebook in retrograde direction seems to indicate that he did not care about the original content of the sources; it may even imply that he actively tried to obliterate the contextual memory. Ian MacArthur therefore concluded that Joyce called in France Raphael on purpose to distort his own notebook material.[4] Yet, in *The Textual Diaries*, Danis Rose mentions several counterexamples and draws attention to instances where Joyce apparently remembered the source and restored the original phrasing. On the other hand, there are also examples of Raphaelian distortions which Joyce seems to have liked enough to insert them in book III, making use of his notesheets.

Consistent with the principle of teleological arrangement, the *James Joyce Archive* (the Garland facsimile edition, volume 61) organizes these notesheets according to the chapter of destination. For instance, all the notesheets for the first chapter are grouped together, but the order of the notesheets within this group is not chronological. This is what the French genetic critic Pierre-Marc de Biasi refers to as the "rangement," or "static classification," in which each folio is "identified by the official, 'external' numbering"—in this case the numbering of the British Library—and arranged according to "the teleological identification of the fragments of definitive text to which it is related" (2004: 51).

By retracing the prehistory of each word-unit, it is possible to rearrange each of the four stacks of notesheets in chronological order. This is what de Biasi refers to as the "classement," or "genetic classification": the critical endeavor to "reclassify all the rough drafts according to the operational logic proper to the writing process" (52).[5] For instance, the classification in the *James Joyce Archive* presents the folios of the first pile or group of notesheets (/\a) in the order of the British Library numbers (BL 47486a, folios 3 to 8). The chronology of the writing genesis, however, suggests a different order of *BL* 47486a folios:

- 3 (based on the first culling of VI.B.34, and the subsequent culling of VI.B.20)
- 6 (based on VI.B.17 and the first notes of VI.C.01)
- 4 (based on VI.C.01 contd.)
- 7 (based on VI.C.01 contd.)
- 7v (based on VI.C.01 contd. and VI.C.03)
- 8 (based on VI.C.03 contd. and VI.C.02)

Folio 5 is based on notes from VI.B.21, but it is more difficult to decide whether this culling of VI.B.21 happened before the compilation of folio 3 or after folio 8. Mikio Fuse's suggestion is that the notesheets based on VI.B.21 were created side by side with the four main stacks.[6]

The sequence 3, 6, 4, 7, 7v, 8 constitutes a genetic classification that can be retraced to the notebooks. The order in which the culling took place is confirmed by the analysis of the three other stacks /\a, /\b, /\c.[7] A considerable part of the so-called "first set" of notesheets (*JJA* 61) can thus be rearranged in the following "genetic classification" (see table 6.2).[8]

The page numbers marked "contd." play a crucial role in the reconstruction of the chronological sequence as they indicate the transitional moments when Joyce finished culling a notebook and started with another one, which results in the following sequence of culling: B-notebooks 34, 20, 17, followed by C-notebooks 01, 03, and 02. The six notesheets indicated in italics (218recto-verso, 219r-v, 222r-v) are classified in the *James Joyce Archive* as

Table 6.2. Genetic Classification of the Four Stacks of "Notesheets (First set)"

Notesheets, 4 stacks: Based on notebook:	/\a	/\b	/\c	/\d
VI.B.34	3r	27r	3v	57r
		27v	48r	
		28v	47r	
		28r		
		29v		
		29r		
		25r		
		25v		
		26r		
VI.B.20	3r contd.	26r contd.	47r contd.	58r
		26v	54r	59r
VI.B.17	6r	26v contd.	54r contd.	59r contd.
VI.C.01	6r contd.	26v contd.	54r contd.	59r contd.
	4r	11r	41r	60r
	7r	11v	41v	60v
	7v	10r	39v	61r
		10v	39r	61v
		30r	42r	
		30v	42v	
		31r	43r	
		31v	43v	
		34r	220r	
			220v	
VI.C.03	7v contd.	34r contd.	220v contd.	224r
	8r	34v	221r	224v
		35r	221v	
			218r	
			218v	
			219r	
			219v	
			222r	
		222v		
VI.C.02	8r contd.	35r contd.	*222v contd.*	

part of the "second set" of notesheets (*JJA* 61: 292–97), but they appear to be a continuation of the third stack of the "first set," based on notes culled from VI.C.03 and 02. These six notesheets are also marked by a large "/\c" in the top left corner.

After having culled the first two dozens of pages of notebook VI.C.02 (and distributed entries among piles /\a, /\b and /\c), Joyce started applying another system. Instead of distributing notes over four stacks, he restarted culling from the first pages of VI.C.02, transferring the usable entries to one set of notesheets on which each entry is preceded by in-line /\a-d signs.

A schematic classification gives a rough impression of the mechanical nature of this compositional system devised relatively late in the writing process. But again, the most interesting developments took place at the level of the "word versions." To examine this development in detail, it may be useful to take a sample and follow its textual adventures from source text to final version. One of the source texts Joyce used to compile notebook VI.B.16 is a book by Eugène Gallois, *La poste et les moyens de communications des peuples à travers les siècles*, a source text located by Ingeborg Landuyt (1997: 22). This is a thematically interesting source, for at least two reasons.

First of all, it illustrates the idea behind Joyce's complicated writing strategy. Each word-unit in the B-notebooks is like a letter. Some letters are posted, some are not. If a letter is posted, either it goes directly to the drafts, or it is collected by Mme Raphael. From the C-notebooks, some notes go directly to a draft, but some have to pass through yet another intermediary stage, a kind of sorting center: the notesheets. Since some of these notesheets are marked by one of the sigla /\a, /\b, /\c, and /\d, the hypothesis is that Joyce arranged them in four piles corresponding to the four chapters of book III:

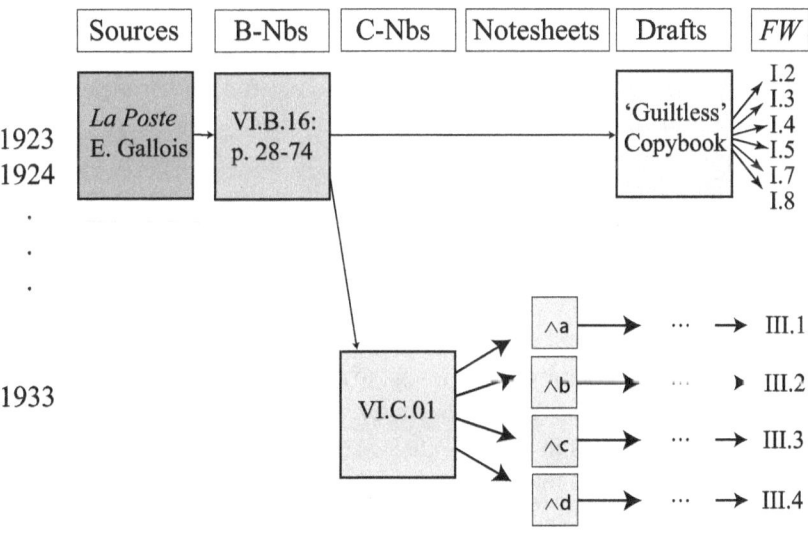

Recombination: indirect usage

Since book III is devoted to Shaun the Post, it is quite appropriate that Joyce used his old notes on *La poste* for this book, acting as a postman himself: from notebook VI.B.16, France Raphael copied the undeleted word units in notebook VI.C.01; from VI.C.01, Jim the Penman made a selection (crossing the usable entries in colored crayon), and Joyce the Postman distributed them over the four chapters, that is, the four piles of notesheets.

For instance, the crossed-out entries on one single page in notebook VI.C.01 are distributed in all directions over the four chapters. Joyce crossed out the following notes on page 11 in VI.C.01 (copied from his notebook VI.B.16, pages 30 and 31):

> entry 1: bible no graven image / of animals
> entry 7: shorthand
> entry 11: fatiguing very fatiguing
> entry 12: stadion 125 yds
> entry 14: [Shem] in Khorn terms

It is hard to find out Joyce's criteria to decide which entry had to go to which chapter. A possible suggestion could be that, given his oft-praised memory, he remembered the original context—as Danis Rose suggests in *The Textual Diaries* (1995: 176). The first deleted note on page VI.C.01:11 is based on a passage from *La poste* in which Gallois explains that according to Jewish law it was forbidden to engrave images of animals, flowers, or other representations of reality in wood or stone.[9] The second item ("shorthand") is interesting with respect to Joyce's lexical distortions. In the Middle Ages, cryptography was understandably cultivated mainly by monks and cabbalists. But in these ignorant ages it was often dangerous to correspond in a mysterious or indecipherable language. Consequently, one usually applied shorthand or *modus sine secreti suspicione scribendi* as it used to be called, the art of leading outsiders up the garden path, in the transmission of their communications.[10] The origin of the third item, "fatiguing, very fatiguing" is not certain, but the context of the notes in the C- and B-notebooks suggests that it is based on page 25 of *La poste*, where Gallois explains that among stablemen an intelligent employee was supposed to take delivery of letters carried in by a courier, hand them over to another courier, take care of the tired men and horses, and cover expenses.[11] The fourth deleted note simply refers to a parenthesis in which Gallois explains that a stadion is 125 yards and that, according to the fifth-century Greek lexicographer Suidas, a courier covered 1,500 stadions on average.[12] The last item, with the Shem siglum, seems to be a conceptual note; "in Khorn" is France Raphael's misreading of "inkhorn." Joyce seems to have been able to restore the original meaning, for in the notesheets he changed it into "inking horn" (BL 47486a–59; *JJA* 61: 186), and used it in *Finnegans Wake*, more specifically the first of the four positions of harmony, that is, Matt's view on HCE and ALP in bed, and the focus on the sleeping children.

If Joyce remembered the original context and wanted this context to be maintained in the final version of *Finnegans Wake*, it is peculiar that he apparently obliterates the historical development of Gallois' narrative by redistributing the notes:

Table 6.4. Distribution of Deleted Notes on Page VI.C.01:11, Originally Derived from Gallois' *La poste*

Notebook VI.C.01,	Notesheets for chapters			
page 11	III.1	III.2	III.3	III.4
entry 1				x
entry 7			x	
entry 11	x			
entry 12		x		
entry 14				x

There are a few instances where Joyce hesitated, creating some remarkable "forking paths" in the writing process. For instance, he apparently hesitated with reference to the distribution of the entry "fatiguing very fatiguing" (VI.C.01:11). He first decided to use it in /\b; wrote down "fatiguing, very" on notesheet 47486a–11; then changed his mind, crossed these two words out and wrote "Fatiguing, very fatiguing!" on notesheet 47486a–4, marked /\a. What made him change his mind? The final destination of this note (*FW* 409.16) suggests that he may have considered this note most appropriate for the opening pages of chapter III.1 with Shaun at rest. But there are undoubtedly other "fatiguing, very fatiguing" episodes where this note might have been suitable, for instance the opening of the chapter of Yawn, III.3, when the four old men find the exhausted postman. That the system devised for the notesheets was not binding is evident in the development of the note "bible no graven image of animals," which Joyce transferred to /\d (BL 47486a-59), but eventually decided to insert in chapter III.2 (*FW* 429.14).

The entry "shorthand" may at first sight seem an appropriate note to insert in a passage where Yawn-Shaun has to tell the four old men what happened at the wedding of HCE and ALP (III.3). But before the note reached this final stage of the text, it was transformed a few times. France Raphael copied it correctly, but when Joyce transferred it to the notesheets, he changed it into "shothand" (*BL* 47486a-41). And during the revisions, this "shothand" even became "Shotland" (*FW* 510.13). The original note has traveled a long way from Gallois almost to Scotland. If there is any connection left at all between the "sténograpie" of the source text and "Shotland," it is the *modus sine secreti suspicione scribendi*, the art of leading outsiders—critics, for instance—up the garden path in the transmission of one's communications. A crucial aspect of Joyce's history of the world is the evocation of the way history *functions*. The focus is not on the transmitted content, but on the transmission, including the transmissional departures.

A second reason why the source text *La poste* is appropriate relates to the concept of the book as a whole. Shortly after the publication of *Ulysses*, Joyce had said that his next book was going to be a history of the world; and history, according to Joyce, was comparable to the parlor game called "Russian Scandal" or—as it is called in German—"Stille Post" (silent mail). A closer look at Joyce's excerpts from *La poste* in notebook VI.B.16 sheds some light on the poetics behind this writing method. He used almost none of these notes in the drafts during the first ten years of the writing process. Then he gave the notebook to France Raphael, who often made copying mistakes. Whether Joyce counted on this copying distortion in advance or not is hard to tell, but he did use several of her copying mistakes as "active elements" in the continuous distortion process.

For instance, in *La poste*, Joyce read a remark concerning Queen Brunehaut, "qui avait gouverné deux royaumes *non sans gloire*" (who had governed two kingdoms *not without glory*) (Gallois 1894: 42; emphasis added). Joyce noted down the entry "not - glory" (VI.B.16:36[h]), the dash clearly meaning "without." In Madame Raphael's transcription (VI.C.01:14[m]), this became "net - glory"; in the notesheets, it became: "& you dreaming of net glory" (*BL* 47486a–11; *JJA* 61: 127), which is how it ended up in the published text: "and you dreaming of net glory" (*FW* 444.32).[13]

The importance of the documentary context in this process cannot be neglected. One of the effects of the intermediary stages of C-notebooks and notesheets is an increased chance that excerpts from completely different sources end up closer or next to each other. For instance, in notebook VI.B.11, Joyce took many notes from a book on children's games, *Les jeux des enfants* by Frédéric Queyrat, published in 1920. The subtitle is: "Étude sur l'imagination créatrice chez l'enfant" (A Study of Children's Creative Imagination). Joyce read and took notes (VI.B.11.38–43) until page 68; here, his reading was interrupted, and he made some eight pages of excerpts from different sources, such as an *Anthology of Irish Verse* (edited by Padraic Colum, 1922), and an article in the *Daily Mail* on names of "games old and new." Then Joyce resumed his reading of Queyrat (VI.B.11:051) and noted down—among many other things—the words: "bath[e] doll, correct it" (VI.B.11:051), derived from a passage where Queyrat tells the story of a one-year-old girl who imitated her nanny by bathing her doll, correcting it, hugging it, and so on.[14] Several notes had been crossed out and inserted in earlier draft stages. So, when Mme Raphael made her transcription in notebook VI.C.01, the note "bath doll, correct it" moved closer to one of the notes that did not derive from Queyrat: "the arts" (VI.B.11:050). When Joyce was culling France Raphael's transcription, he made an associative link between these two notes, and combined them into a conceptual note in the notesheets: "the arts [Shem's siglum]: bath doll" (*BL* 47486a–61v). The siglum for Shem the Penman links the two elements together. Thus, by means of a purely mechanical coincidence, Joyce seems to recall one of his very earliest meditations on aesthetics, the remark on the translation of Aristotle's dictum "Art imitates nature," which he wrote thirty years earlier in his Paris notebook.[15] The difference with the static imitation of nature in realism or naturalism is the dynamic way in which Joyce tries to create an artistic *process* ("Work in Progress") that is "like the natural process." Or, as he formulated it in *Stephen Hero*: "For Stephen art was neither a copy nor an imitation of nature: the artistic process was a natural process" (1991: 176). Evidently this is an artificial creation, but not much more artificial than history or, for that matter, the proliferation of rumors. Everyone has his or her own version of the facts, and this self-generative mechanism creating multiple versions is what Joyce tried to imitate, the way a one-year-old girl imitates her nanny. So in answer to the question raised in chapter 1, this example suggests that Joyce's early aesthetic statement is still applicable to his late writings. The entry "the arts [Shem's siglum]: bath doll" makes the active process of imitating into one of the central concepts underpinning his poetics, in the sense of Darwinian descent with modification. When editors take the "text version" as their basic unit, the multiple versions appear as a descent with mostly intentional modification. If we include all the "word versions" of the paralipomena (in the B-notebooks, the C-notebooks, the notesheets, etc.), it becomes clear how much unintentional modification Joyce allowed to enter his history of the world.

For instance, on page 131 of notebook VI.B.11, the word-unit "all the world was June" was incorporated without distortion in the "Guiltless" copybook (*BL* 47471b–37; chapter I.5, section 2, second draft). As opposed to this direct usage, the indirect usage involved more distortion. The undeleted notes from the same page were copied by France Raphael in 1933, but not without mistakes. Thus, the word-unit "vice supreme regent" (VI.B.11:131) became "with supreme regard" (notebook VI.C.01:183). Joyce subsequently selected this entry and added it to the /\b pile of the notesheets. It ended up in book III, chapter 2: "With supreme regards" (*FW* 461.31).

In October 1923, Joyce had told Harriet Shaw Weaver that his textual fragments were "active elements" that would gradually "begin to fuse of themselves" (*L I* 204). With reference to *Ulysses*, he had already used the same expression in another letter to Weaver (20 July 1919): "If the *Sirens* have been found so unsatisfactory I have little hope that the *Cyclops* or later the *Circe* episode will be approved of: and, moreover, it is impossible for me to write these episodes quickly. The *elements* needed will only *fuse* after a prolonged existence together" (*L I* 128; emphasis added). These "elements" refer to larger units of texts, but Daniel Ferrer duly points out that they are applicable to the notes as well. Ferrer rejects both the metaphor of pieces in a clockwork (implying that Joyce knew in advance where each element had to be inserted) and the comparison with a mosaic (implying the haphazard amalgamation of elements). Instead, he suggests that the notes are a living and evolutionary *ensemble* (2001: 193). "Life escapes" in traditional novels, Virginia Woolf had written in the essay from which Joyce extracted a few "incoherent atoms." With reference to *Ulysses*, she wrote: "If we want life itself, here surely we have it." This is probably even more applicable to *Finnegans Wake*. For good reasons, Samuel Beckett called Joyce a "biologist in words" (1929: 252), pointing out that Joyce's words are more than "polite contortions": "They are alive" (249).

The insistence of critics on the "life" of Joyce's words almost obscures the metaphorical nature of this expression. Since "life" seems to be a constant in Joyce criticism, it inevitably raises the question whether it is possible to locate the transition from inanimate matter (ink on paper) into "life itself" somewhere in the writing process. Fritz Mauthner, one of the philosophers Joyce read during the last phase of the writing process, compares the twilight zone between language and reality to the circulation of the blood, more specifically to the indefinable location of "life" between arteries and veins.[16] This consideration sheds a new light on Joyce's own description of the writing process in book IV, in which he incorporated many of his Mauthner notes. Against the background of Mauthner's *Beiträge zu einer Kritik der Sprache*, the notion of a "portal vein" becomes more important. The "vicociclometer"—according to the text of *Finnegans Wake*—is fueled and driven by "dialitically separated elements." The transition between this "decomposition" and the "subsequent recombination" is ensured by "a portal vein" (*FW* 614.27–35). A portal vein collects blood from the digestive organs and distributes it in other parts of the body through capillaries. Joyce's image is indeed an adequate organic metaphor to describe how the mechanics of the montage bring the inanimate textual material to life. A. Walton Litz points out that many critics "may insist that Joyce carried his methods of verbal elaboration beyond effective limits," but he in his turn insists that in order to be effective, Joyce needed to push these limits: "there can be no doubt that the *life* of the *Wake* lies in this elaboration" (1966: 103; emphasis added). To investigate how Joyce brought his words to life, the processing or further recombination of the notes in the drafts will be examined in the next sections by trying to retrace the writing sequence, distinguishing between intrasectional and intersectional chronology, that is, respectively the writing sequence of *Medium*-sized units (sentences and paragraphs) within one single section and the chronology of *Large* units of text (sections).

MEDIUM: Writing Sequence (Intrasectional)

The origins of Wakese can be of help in the endeavor to reconstruct Joyce's "recombination" of old notes and abandoned sections into chapters and books. Book IV, for instance, consists of both old and new sections: two early sketches written in 1923 ("Saint Kevin" and "Saint Patrick and the Druid"); the abandoned Letter, extracted from chapter 5 in 1924; and two new sections, written in 1938.

The Wakean idea of combining words from numerous languages to create a multilingual hybrid was not completely new. Apart from Lewis Carroll's idea of the "portmanteau" and Humpty Dumpty's definition of it ("two meanings packed into one word like a portmanteau" [Carroll 1988: 678]), there are foreshadowings of this technique in Joyce's own writings. In an article devoted to the "Sirens" episode of *Ulysses*, Bart Eeckhout (1992) compares some of Joyce's literary techniques to Johann Sebastian Bach's cello suites, in which the illusion of polyphony is created on an instrument that is not built to play chords. Joyce already experimented with his "portmanteau" technique in the "Sirens" episode, to create an effect of simultaneity. A good example is the word "Siopold," in which three names are merged:

Si (Simon Dedalus, father of Stephen Dedalus)
Lionel (the hero of the opera *Martha*)
Leopold (Bloom)

Joyce later fully developed this technique in his last work, *Finnegans Wake*, but not from the very start. The first sketches do not yet show the characteristics of what was to become "Wakese." The early signs of Joyce's idea to apply the portmanteau technique more systematically can be traced to the first draft of the "Saint Patrick and the Druid" sketch (July 1923), sent to Harriet Shaw Weaver on 2 August 1923 (*L III*: 79). In this sketch, the archdruid "Barkeley" explains the "illusiones of the colourful world" to Saint Patrick. The word "illusiones" is one of the several latinizations, added in the first overlay of the first draft, such as the change from reflection to "reflectionem"; "colours" suddenly appeared in their true "coloribus" and to "absorb" was given a Latin infinitive ending, "absorbere." The archbishop thus "absorbs" Saint Patrick's Latin while he is explaining his theory to him. Joyce described this sketch to Harriet Shaw Weaver as the conversion of Saint Patrick by Ireland (*L III*: 79), but while this religious-philosophical conversion is taking place, a linguistic conversion in the other direction silently occurs. Saint Patrick remained silent for almost fifteen years, until Joyce decided to recombine the piece with the "Saint Kevin" sketch and ALP's letter in book IV. In the summer of 1938, Saint Patrick finally replies, notably by wiping his nose in the name of the fire, the sun in his "halo cast" (*BL* 47488–112v; *JJA* 63: 170; *FW* 612.25–30). Joyce's concluding amen ("Onman") seems to be that none of the conversions makes any difference, for in the end no body is present which was not there before, only the order is othered and naught is nulled (*BL* 47488–113v; *JJA* 63: 172). Berkeley tries to convince Saint Patrick—along the lines of Bishop Berkeley's philosophy—that objects have no knowable existence outside of the mind that perceives them and that only the "seer" who beholds the "thing as in itself it is" can see these objects in their true colors. While he is explaining this view, the words he uses to describe each of the spectral colors turns them into shades of green, so that Saint Patrick's snotgreen response wraps up the problem in a piece of textile, woven or "textus" by James Joyce.

The latinizations added to the first (1923) draft were not the only indications of a new linguistic approach. The addition "panephiphanal" is an early portmanteau word that combines more than just the themes of the archdruid's account, suggesting that the whole hueful world is a set of epiphenomena. It also contains a hint to what Joyce may have experienced as a kind of epiphany, that is, the idea to re-create (decompose and recombine) this epiphenomenal world by means of his own version of the portmanteau technique, with the evidently unreachable nominalist aim of creating a language with a different word for each single aspect of the phenomenal world.

The unattainability of this goal seems to be hinted at in *Finnegans Wake* when the writer's pen is compared to a hare, the patient paper to the turtle: "hare and turtle pen and paper" (*FW* 118.24). One of the results of this invigorating chase is the copybook that opens with the word "Guiltless," preserved in the British Library (*BL* 47471b). This "Guiltless" copybook contains first and second drafts of parts of six chapters of *Finnegans Wake*. All these passages were composed in about five months' time (late 1923–early 1924). Unlike most of Joyce's *Finnegans Wake* notebooks, the "Guiltless" copybook does not contain loose excerpts and notes, but textual units. The fact that these texts—as opposed to the majority of later manuscripts—are preserved in the form of a copybook allows us to establish the relative chronology of the separate textual units or "sections" more accurately. Although Joyce started with the good intention to write only on the recto pages, the blank space on the verso pages seems to have had a remarkable influence on the writing process. The first and second draft of the first section in the copybook (I.2, section 2) are written on the recto pages; the blank versos were filled up with the first draft of the next section. This way, the writing process is characterized by a constant alternation between recto and verso pages, apparently guided by no other principle than the available blank space. Accordingly, Joyce did not hesitate to write in retrograde direction if need be, so that after a few pages, the sections get entangled.

It is possible to reconstruct the chronology of the writing process section per section, which already implies a certain degree of critical judgment, since it is often difficult to establish this chronology. But if one wants to indicate, for every single addition or substitution, when exactly it was added, this would imply so much more critical judgment that it seems only possible to present such a study in the form of a critical article, such as Hans Walter Gabler's essay "Explorations in Spaces of Writing." In this essay, he argues: "The spatial distribution of main-column text and arbitrarily scattered revisional matter (. . .) bears a relation to the temporal stages of the writing. The question (...) is how closely that relation is determinable. From Joyce's drafts, the writing sequences cannot on the whole be exhaustively established, nor demonstrated in every detail."[17] And yet, this has not discouraged Hans Walter Gabler to attempt to do just that, by trying "to catch the interplay of writing and revision in one continuous act of composition" in the opening paragraph of the "Nausicaa" episode of *Ulysses*. It is worth an attempt to investigate, with reference to the "Guiltless" copybook, "how disjunct writing sequences work towards a reading sequence whose very force and tension derives from the conjunction into linearity of the non-consecutive phases of the creation."

One of the central sections in the "Guiltless" copybook is the so-called Revered Letter: Anna Livia Plurabelle writes a letter in which she tries to defend her husband against all the allegations against him. The first draft of this letter is written on pages 31, 32, and 33 of the "Guiltless" copybook. The left-hand pages and the margins are the designated place for additions to the so-called "body" of the text. These additions are often marked with signs or pointers, which the author has to be able to decipher later on. Daniel Ferrer refers to this system as a "dialog between the writer and his later selves" (1998: 262). In this case, the left-hand page also serves as a margin. The location of additions in the margins or on the left-hand page can sometimes be an indication for the reconstruction of the writing sequence. So, toposensitivity can be combined with chronosensitivity, that is, "the spatial layout can be partly translated in terms of temporal succession" (263). But this is not always easy. On page 30 verso, Joyce has written a sentence that is not transcribed in *A First-Draft Version of "Finnegans Wake,"* David Hayman's invaluable transcription of all the first drafts of the different sections:

> and he always sat fornenst me most attractable when he was after his third mug or fourth making conversation about business & pleasure (*BL* 47471b–30v)

This "business & pleasure" passage is marked by a letter *N*. It is quite understandable that this isolated sentence did not find its way into the *First-Draft Version*, for there is no corresponding *N* on this page, nor on the facing recto page. If this is an addition, one has to find out where it belongs. By linking every reference mark to every corresponding reference mark, the missing *N* corresponding to the "business & pleasure" passage can be found on page 33, that is, three pages further on. This *N*-marker is attached to other additions, which makes it difficult to determine their sequence. The body of the text is this sentence:

> I am perfectly proud of Mr Earwicker (*BL* 47471b–33)

In the left margin, Joyce added:

> my once handsome husband, who is as gentle as a woman & more attractable

To the right of this addition Joyce has written two reference marks, an *M* and an *N*:

my once handsome husband, who is as gentle as a woman & more attractable M N

The *M* refers to an addition on the left-hand page, preceded by an *M*:

M & he never chained me to a chair since this island was born (*BL* 47471b–32v)

The *N* refers to the "business & pleasure" passage on page 30v:

N and he always sat fornenst me most attractable when he was after his third mug or fourth making conversation about business & pleasure (*BL* 47471b–30v)

In order to reconstruct the writing sequence, the key question is: which came first, the *M* or the *N*? The alphabetical order suggests that the *M* came first, but the *N*-addition is on page 30v, that is, five pages "earlier" than page 32v on which the *M*-addition is written.

The second draft of the letter is a great help in reconstructing the narrative sequence.[18] According to this second draft, the sequence of the *M* and *N* additions is not alphabetical: first *N*, then *M*. But this sequence does not necessarily correspond with the writing sequence; it is just the way in which Joyce, in his capacity of scribe and interpreter of his earlier drafts, translated these signs into a narrative sequence. The theoretical possibility that *M* was written before *N* cannot be excluded.

Inevitably, this raises the question: What is the importance of determining the writing sequence? This key issue of genetic criticism comes down to what Pierre-Marc de Biasi called the fourth dimension of literature: time. When Wyndham Lewis criticized his modernist contemporaries' preoccupation with time, he simultaneously exposed his own way of thinking. Lewis claims that "it matters very little to [Joyce] *what* he writes, or what idea or world-view he expresses, so long as he is trying his hand at this manner and that, and displaying his enjoyable virtuosity. Strictly speaking, he has none at all, no special point of view, or none worth mentioning" (1927b: 88). Lewis's point of view in literary matters is that the text is the result of a quest for the best representation of a preexisting idea. As opposed to this Lewisian poetics of the finished product, Joyce allowed his work to gradually take a shape of its own. Richard Ellmann reports Joyce saying: "In the writing the good things will come" (1983: 360). Joyce's manuscripts reflect the ways in which an idea gradually comes into being. Ideas are not preconceived but slowly find their expression through the ingenious manipulation of words.

The metaphor of fusion is remarkably persistent in Joyce's statements about his own work. To Ezra Pound, he wrote on 24 July 1917: "As regards *Ulysses* I write and think and write and think all day and part of the night. It goes on as it has been going these five or six years. But the ingredients will not fuse until they have reached a certain temperature" (Joyce in Ellmann 1983: 416).[19] In *Finnegans Wake*, Joyce refers to the work in progress as "smelting-works" (*FW* 614.31). Joyce's alchemy is a suitable metaphor for the chemistry that takes place in the author's mind. For no matter how open Joyce may have been to textual accidents and material coincidences, he always remained the mastermind that decided which coincidences were incorporated and which were not.

In the case of the *N* and *M*, Joyce tries to follow the process of ratiocination in the mind of his female protagonist, the supposed author of the Letter. Her mind is extremely associative. In this respect, she resembles Molly Bloom. Joyce's writing method, characterized by additions to additions to additions, is determined not just by the content of his character's thoughts, but also by the *way* she thinks. Joyce's characters take shape in a gradual way. He does not mold them on a clear, preconceived idea. In fact, the chapter on ALP (chapter 8) had not even been written yet. ALP's letter is one of the very first signs of her in the drafts. The way Joyce gives shape to this character is by allowing her thoughts to wander off ad lib. This draft of the letter by ALP can be seen as her letter of introduction to her author, who himself did not even know her yet.

This poetics of process can be illustrated by means of the first two sentences of page 33 in the "Guiltless" copybook (starting at the end of page 32), where ALP strays off and starts talking about an "experience" with a "clerical friend." These two sentences are composed on the basis of five entries taken from the back of notebook VI.B.02:

lettering you
shall now close
in the best
an experience
clerical friend

The first three entries, which thematically belong together, are derived from page 178 in notebook VI.B.02: "lettering you/shall now close/in the best"; the latter two, "an experience" and "clerical friend," are derived from the back cover recto page of notebook VI.B.02. These five entries are the skeleton of the two opening sentences of this page:

Well, revered Majesty, I tender you heartest thanks & regrets for *lettering you* and I *shall ^now^ close* hoping you are *in the best* of health. I don't care that for him and lies about *an experience* of mine ^as a girl^ with a *clerical friend*. (BL 47471b-32–3)

The first sentence ("Well . . . health.") was almost a closing formula; the second one, based on the latter two notebook entries, introduces a completely new story, something ALP apparently had not planned to tell. Most probably Joyce had not planned the digression on the experience with the clerical friend either. But while he was incorporating the entries from page 178, the entries on the back cover may have caught his eye and his openness to contingencies in the writing process gave the letter a sudden twist. This serendipitous montage resulted in one of the most unexpected turns in ALP's defense of her husband. It incriminates the defender, makes her unreliable and suspicious, and consequently does not help her husband one bit, quite the contrary.

Wyndham Lewis called Joyce's writing a "stupendous outpouring of *matter, or stuff*" (1927b: 89). To a large extent, this stuff indeed determines the course of the writing process and even the process of ratiocination. Joyce's openness to external stimuli that determined the course of the "riverrun" not only characterizes the writing process on a microlevel, it also marks the intersectional connections.

LARGE: Intersectional Chronology

It is relatively easy to disentangle the different sections in the "Guiltless" copybook, but it is more difficult to reconstruct the chronological sequence of their composition. After Joyce had written the letter, he started writing a mock bibliographical and philological commentary on this letter (*FW* 104–113–22). Hereafter, these two sections will be referred to as the Letter (I.5§2) and the Commentary (I.5§1). The question with regard to the intersectional chronology of the writing sequence is whether the first draft of the Commentary was written after the *first* or after the *second* draft of the Letter.

Hypothesis 1: The first draft of the Commentary was written after the *first* draft of the Letter. An argument in favor of this first hypothesis is that the Commentary is written more or less "around" the first draft of the Letter on every blank space that was still available.

Chronology:

1. Section I.4§2.*0: 27v, 28v, 28r (top), 29r (top)
2. [intermediary section]: 30r (bottom)
3. Letter, first draft (I.5§2.*0): 30v–31r, 31v–32r, 32v–33r
4. Commentary, first draft (I.5§1.*0): 33v, 34r (margin), 29v, 30r (top), 29r (bottom), 28v (bottom), 26v (bottom), 27r (bottom), 25v

On the verso of page 33, Joyce started writing the Commentary, writing "backwards" on every blank space he encountered, both on the left-hand and the right-hand pages. Presented in this way, it seems logical that Joyce wrote the first draft of the Commentary after the first draft of the Letter.

Hypothesis 2: The first draft of the Commentary was written after the *second* draft of the Letter. In the introduction to the "Book I, Chapters 4–5" volume of the *James Joyce Archive*, David Hayman writes that "1.*1 (. . .) follows in the notebook immediately after the second draft of the 'Letter'" (xvi). A few arguments support this hypothesis. Some marginal additions on page 33 verso, extending to page 34, suggest that page 34 was not blank when these additions were made. The additions are written in the left margin. A plausible explanation is that the body of text on page 34, which is the beginning of the second draft of section I.4§2/I.5§2 (containing the second draft of the Letter), was already written when the additions to the Commentary were added.

Another argument in favor of the second hypothesis is the addition "must now close & four crosses," mentioned in the first draft of the Commentary (*BL* 47471b-27). These four crosses refer to the four kisses at the end of ALP's Letter. But these four kisses only appear on the *second* draft of the Letter. This seems to imply that, after Joyce had written the four kisscrosses in the second draft of the Letter (on page *BL* 47471b-42), he discussed them in the Commentary on page *BL* 47471b-27, that is, fifteen pages "earlier" in the copybook.

Chronology:

1. Section I.4§2.*0
2. [intermediary section]
3. Letter, first draft (I.5§2.*0)
4. Letter, second draft (I.4§2.*1/I.5§2.*1)
5. Commentary, first draft (I.5§1.*0)

Yet, there is another complicating element: both the marginal inscriptions on page 34 and the words "must now close & four crosses" in the Commentary (*BL* 47471b-27r) are additions. As a consequence, a third hypothesis has to be taken into account.

Hypothesis 3: The first draft of the Commentary may have been written after the first draft of the Letter, but some of its additions, notably the addition "must now close & four crosses" (*BL* 47471b–27r) and the marginal inscriptions on page 34, may have been written after the second draft of the Letter. Consequently, a distinction should be made between the different layers of one single document.
Chronology:

1. Letter, first draft
2. Commentary, first draft, *first layer*
3. Letter, second draft
4. Commentary, first draft, *overlay additions*
   ("must now close & four crosses")

Moreover, judging from the available manuscript evidence, one cannot exclude another possibility:

Hypothesis 4: The first layer of the Commentary may have been written after the first draft of the Letter, after which Joyce started writing I.4§2.*1/1.5§2.*1, but not necessarily to the very end (*BL* 47471b–42). A short blank space (the equivalent of about three lines) in the middle of page 41, between "Ping!" and "That ought to make him hop it," may be an indication that the writing was interrupted at this stage. One cannot exclude the possibility that Joyce went back to the Commentary, added the "top layer" (such as the marginal inscriptions on page 34 and the addition "must now close & four crosses" [*BL* 47471b–27r]), and only then brought this into practice, that is, closed the letter with four crosses on page BL 47471b–42.
Chronology:

1. Letter, first draft
2. Commentary, first draft, first layer
3. Letter, second draft (ff. 36–41)
4. Commentary, first draft, overlay additions
   ("must now close & four crosses")
5. Letter, second draft (ff. 41–42; "xxxx")

Since the relationship between Letter and Commentary is one of primary and secondary literature, this fourth hypothesis suggests that the *secondary* literature (the Commentary) may have prompted the content of the *primary* literature (the Letter), that is, that the exegesis precedes the text. This textual situation resembles the structure of the fable of the hare and the turtle, to which Joyce compares the pen and the paper. A variation of Aesop's fable of the hare and the turtle is Zeno of Elea's paradox of Achilles and the turtle. Achilles will never catch up with the turtle, for by the time he reaches the spot where the turtle is, the turtle will have walked on to a next spot, and when the hare reaches that spot, the turtle will be gone again, and so on. The attempt to reconstruct the writing sequence shows how Joyce's "must now close" remains a good intention, a goal that is never fully reached. The Commentary tries to fix the content of the first draft of the Letter, but as soon as it has "caught up" with the letter, the subject has moved on again. Eventually the Letter was removed from chapter 5, only to be reinserted more than fourteen years later in the last part of *Finnegans Wake*. But the Commentary stayed behind: in the published text of *Finnegans Wake*, there are no "xxxx" or "kisscrosses" in the letter. Patrick McCarthy has carefully compared the Letter (in book IV) with the commentary in chapter I.5, and drawn attention to several phrases in the commentary that refer to the Letter but do not occur in its published version (1992). The published version of the letter ends as follows:

> The herewaker of our hamefame is his real namesame who will get himself up and erect, confident and heroic when but, young as of old, for my daily comfreshenall, a wee one woos.
> Alma Luvia, Pollabella. (*FW* 619.12–16)

And yet the Commentary (in the published text of *Finnegans Wake*) still mentions the crosses when the letter is described as

> a goodishsized sheet of letterpaper originating by transhipt from Boston (Mass.) of the last of the first to Dear whom it proceded to mention Maggy well & allathome's health well (. . .) how are you Maggy & hopes soon to hear well & must now close it with fondest to the twoinns with four crosskisses (*FW* 111.8–17)

The only version of the letter that features the "xxxx" is the second draft. This suggests that the document that is being discussed in the Commentary (*FW* 104–113.22) is an early draft of the letter. The numerous transformations of the letter throughout the writing process became part of the work itself. For instance, the phrases "unto life's &" and "until life's (!)" are actually variants of one of ALP's expressions in the second draft of the letter

"unto any life's end"	(Letter, 2nd draft; *BL* 47471b-40v)
"unto life's end"	(3rd draft; *BL* 47471b-22v)
"unto life's end"	(fair copy) (1923–24)
"unto loves end"	(*BL* 47488–116v) (1938)
	(= recycled version of the letter)
"unto lovesend"	(*FW* 617.07)
	(= recycled version of the letter in 1st edition)

And after the work continues (again) "a long the // riverrun" the phrase recurs as a moving plea to

"undo lives 'end"	(*FW* 011.28)
"unto life's &"	(*FW* 111.15)
"until life's (!)"	(*FW* 116.22)

A half century before the term "genetic criticism" was coined, Joyce had already pointed out that writing is a process rather than a product. In this process, the Commentary is just as important as the document it comments on. This process has the structure of a musical fugue, in which the Letter has a head start and the Commentary will never be able to catch up. A similar conclusion applies to the search for the writing sequence. From Joyce's perspective, the pen may have been a hare that could not catch up with the paper, but eventually it did reach the finish. More than sixty years later, genetic Joyce critics in their turn find themselves chasing after that patient pen (that took seventeen years to complete its route) without ever being able to catch up. But evidently, that makes the chase all the more challenging.

Post Scriptum

In the period when Joyce reincorporated ALP's letter in 1938, he got some help from Samuel Beckett. If his input is acknowledged in the *Wake*, the way most intertextual input is somehow acknowledged according to Atherton's rule of thumb, the word "Bethicket" (*FW* 112.05) is probably the most likely candidate.[20] It was added at a late stage to the galley proofs of book I (dated by the printer 12 March 1937, but only received by Harriet Shaw Weaver on 16 May 1938). It is part of a short paragraph that was inserted toward the end of chapter I.5§1, close to the place where the original version of ALP's letter was extracted, immediately after the comment: "the farther back we manage to wiggle the more we need the loan of a lens to see as much as the hen saw. Tip" (*FW* 112.01–02).

In the second week of December, Giorgio Joyce and Beckett corrected proofs of books I and III of *Finnegans Wake*, while Joyce was writing book II. On 18 December 1937, Paul Léon wrote to Harriet Shaw Weaver: "I am seeing Mr. Joyce rather rarely now and then only for work. My part of it seems to be done but it takes some five or six other people to check the corrections, verify the additions and read the proofs. Himself, he does the composing part quite alone" (*L III* 409). In a letter to Mary Manning (preserved at the HRHRC), Beckett suggests that his dire financial situation is the only reason why he has allowed himself to be employed by Joyce. He explicitly asks Mary Manning to keep this to herself. It is clear that he was extremely well aware of the dangers this renewed contact with Joyce entailed in terms of his own independence as a writer. He realized it was necessary for him to break down the association with Joyce, but he simply needed the 250 francs Joyce paid him for the job. To Thomas MacGreevy he confided that Joyce supplemented the payment with an old overcoat and a few ties. In the meantime, Beckett started writing an essay on Joyce's work for the homage number of the *Nouvelle Revue Française*, but around 22 December he already felt like dropping it and resolved not to write any more accompanying side-pieces whenever the work would appear in book form, even if this might have meant a break.

This perhaps overanxious attitude of independence changed after dining with Joyce shortly after Christmas and on 4 January 1938 (Norburn 2004: 180). On 5 January, he wrote to Thomas MacGreevy: "I don't feel the danger of the association any more. He is just a very lovable human being" (Beckett in Knowlson 1996: 290). The next day (in the night of 6–7 January), Beckett was stabbed on the Avenue d'Orléans in Paris and hospitalized. Joyce was a daily visitor and genuinely cared about Beckett's well-being (Pilling 2006: 73; Knowlson 1996: 282–83). The anxiety of influence indeed seems to have subsided around this period, and when Beckett was discharged from the hospital, he was regularly taken into Joyce's confidence regarding his worries about his daughter's condition. Toward the end of April, they discussed her lettrines and *Storiella as She Is Syung* (Pilling 2006: 78). Both Beckett and Joyce made notes on Fritz Mauthner's *Beiträge zu einer Kritik der Sprache* (1923) and Heinrich Zimmer's *Maya: Der indische Mythos* (1936). Especially in the latter case, Beckett's notes (on three pages that were preserved inside Joyce's copy of *Maya*; see Connolly 1978: 45–47) are clearly a form of scouting. Each excerpt or entry on the notesheets is preceded by the corresponding page and paragraph number in Zimmer's *Maya*.

When Samuel Beckett made the notes on *Maya* for Joyce (probably October–November 1938), he reencountered the old metaphor of the veil, which he knew from his reading of Schopenhauer and Mauthner. In his typed Mauthner notes preserved at Trinity College Dublin (*TCD* MS 10971/5), Beckett focused on a passage in which Mauthner mentions (among other things) the ancient Indian philosophy of Maya, which he links to metaphorical mental processes.[21] The veil of Maya is in itself a persistent metaphor. It occurs, for instance, in *Molloy* when Moran confides: "It is lying down, in the warmth, in the gloom, that I best pierce the outer turmoil's veil" (1955–58: 110). Beckett employed the veil metaphor in his (German) letter to Axel Kaun in July 1937: "wie ein Schleier kommt mir meine Sprache vor, den man zerreissen muss, um an die dahinterliegenden Dinge (oder das dahinterliegende Nichts) zu kommen" (my own language appears to me like a veil that must be torn apart in order to get at the things (or the Nothingness) behind it) (1984: 52; 171; translated by Martin Esslin). The "-ness" in Martin Esslin's translation (or the capital *N* in the original "Nichts") indicates an interesting point with reference to what the then thirty-one-year-old Beckett expected to find behind that veil. When he writes his aim is to "bore one hole after another," he again expresses his openness to whatever might lurk behind, "be it something or nothing." The seeming similarity between "nothing" and "Nothingness" is comparable to the homophony of "hole" and "whole," which was a favorite pun of both Joyce and Beckett. In *Finnegans Wake*, Joyce writes: "Sure, what is it on the whole only holes tied together" (*FW* 434.21–22). In Beckett's trilogy, after having run over Lousse's dog with his bicycle, Molloy is expected to bury the animal: "But what was my contribution to this burial? It was she dug the hole, put in the dog, filled up the hole. On the whole I was a mere spectator, I contributed my presence" (Beckett 1955–58: 36).

The interaction of presence and absence, the correlation between holes and wholes, the processes of digging, boring, writing, and decomposing, is concentrated in a crucial question, formulated by Theodor Adorno in his marginalia and notes on Beckett's *L'Innommable*:

> Ist das Nichts gleich nichts? Darum geht bei B[eckett] alles. Absolutes Wegwerfen, weil Hoffnung nur dort ist wo nichts zurückbehalten wird. Die Fülle des Nichts. (1994: 73)

> [Is nothingness the same thing as nothing? That is what everything is about with B[eckett]. Absolute throwing away, because hope is only where nothing is retained. The fullness of nothingness.]

Beckett actively looked for ways to deal with this question. With reference to drama, the general tendencies in Beckett's writing are analyzed in extensive studies by Rosemary Pountney and S. E. Gontarski. The main tendency is concisely summarized in the title of Gontarski's invaluable book *The Intent of Undoing*. Pountney formulates the main tendency in terms of the effect of this undoing: a tendency toward "increasing ambiguity" (195):

> The process of drafting each play, moreover, may be seen as a microcosm of the development of Beckett's oeuvre as a whole, a refining and scaling down of the text. A meticulous craftsmanship of both structure and language has been evident throughout the drafts. A tendency for the text to develop, as the drafts progress, from the concrete and comparatively straightforward to the indefinite and more complex has been observed. Such a development is part of the refining process and increasing ambiguity becomes as much the *signature* of a study of Beckett's drafts as a circular motif is characteristic of his structure. (195; emphasis added)

The idea that a particular writing method may be as authenticating as a "signature" is formulated by Joyce in chapter 5 of *Finnegans Wake* with reference to ALP's Letter and its philological analysis: "So why, pray, sign anything as long as every word, letter, penstroke, paperspace is a perfect signature of its own?" (*FW* 115.6–8).

But if the "progression towards ambiguity" (Pountney 1988: 86) is defined as a development "from the concrete and comparatively straightforward to the indefinite and more complex" and if it is as much a signature "as a circular motif is characteristic of his structure," Beckett's signature does seem to have some aspects in common with Joyce's *Work in Progress*. If Joyce may be regarded as an exemplary author for genetic criticism,[22] Beckett's writing method—in spite of all its differences—proves to be equally relevant and paradigmatic for manuscript genetics, as will be examined in part 3.

PART III

Beckett's Nohow

[T]he mere increase of size is not progress. If it were, elephantiasis which causes a man's legs to become as large as tree-trunks would be a sort of progress too.

Joseph Conrad, "Certain Aspects of the Admirable Inquiry into the Loss of the *Titanic*"

7

Introduction

"Work in Regress"

"In the beginning was the pun. And so on" (Beckett 1957: 65).[1] By the time this sentence was finally published as part of Beckett's novel *Murphy*, James Joyce was still working on *Finnegans Wake*. His version of the opening words of the fourth Gospel had not yet been written: "In the buginning is the woid, in the muddle is the sounddance and thereinofter you're in the unbewised again" (*FW* 378.29–30). This passage was added to the revised typescript of the "Roderick O'Conor" sketch when Joyce inserted it in chapter II.3 in the summer and fall of 1938. On a verso, Joyce added a long passage of about twenty lines, inspired by his notes on Fritz Mauthner's *Beiträge zu einer Kritik der Sprache*. The relatively short period between this reading and the publication of the *Wake* had no impact on the degree of linguistic distortion. For instance, the entry about the development of children's *speech* being an *abbr*eviation of *hist*ory in general[2] (notebook VI.B.41:236; based on the first volume of the *Beiträge*), ended up in *Finnegans Wake* as "speech obstruct hostery" (*FW* 378.32). The published version of the twenty-line addition opens with the words: "Or ledn us alones of your lungorge, parsonifier propounde of our edelweissed idol worts!" (*FW* 378.23–24), derived from Mauthner's contention that science is a form of idolatry with *personified words* and *fetish words* (VI.B.41:236; Mauthner 1923: 1: 160). By replacing "fetish" with "idol," Joyce effectively emphasizes Mauthner's point about the idleness of language, but he also plays with Mauthner's elaborateness and the thousands of idle words (three bulky volumes) the linguistic sceptic needs to make his point. The only way to become one with "*Vernichtung*" is by means of the so-called "Nichtwort."

"SILENCE" (FW 501.07)

is not good enough, for "silence is still a word": "Zum höchsten Einssein der Vernichtung gelangt man durch das Nichtwort. Schweigen ist noch ein Wort." (Mauthner 1923: 1: 83) So Joyce coined his own "Nichtwort": the "woid" (*FW* 378.29), noting in his copybook that "in the word/was no beginning" (VI.B.41: 269).

About a year earlier, Beckett famously formulated his developing poetics in terms of a "Literatur des Unworts" (in his letter to Axel Kaun of 9 July 1937). And on the way to this "literature of the unword," he thought "some form of Nominalist irony might be a necessary stage" (1984: 53–54; 173).

Self-Portrait against Contrastive Background

Beckett repeatedly insisted on the differences between his writing method and Joyce's, and it is useful to consider a few of these statements. S. E. Gontarski quotes Israel Shenker's "A Portrait of Samuel Beckett, the Author of the Puzzling *Waiting for Godot*," not without caution, because of the account's "unidentified and unverified sources" and because "Beckett considers the material misleading" (Gontarski 1985: 6). According to Shenker, Beckett stated, with reference to Joyce:

> the difference is that Joyce was a superb manipulator of material, perhaps the greatest. He was making words do the absolute maximum of work. There isn't a syllable that's superfluous. The kind of work I do is one in which I am not master of my material. The more Joyce knew the more he could. His tendency is toward omniscience and omnipotence as an artist. I'm working with impotence, ignorance. I don't think that impotence has been exploited in the past. There seems to be a kind of aesthetic axiom that expression is an achievement—must be an achievement. My little exploration is that whole zone of being that has always been set aside by artists as something unusable—as something by definition incompatible with art.[3]

In the endnotes to his indispensable biography, James Knowlson remarks that Beckett reconfirmed this statement, when on 27 October 1989, toward the end of his life, Beckett summarized his writing method by contrasting it to Joyce's:

> I realised that Joyce had gone as far as one could in the direction of knowing more, [being] in control of one's material. He was always adding to it; you only have to look at his proofs to see that. I realised that my own way was in impoverishment, in lack of knowledge and in taking away, in subtracting rather than in adding. (1996: 352)

Several similar contrastive descriptions have been reported. Charles Juliet mentions Beckett's talking, on 14 November 1975, "about Joyce and Proust, both of whom aimed to create a *whole* world, reproducing it in all its infinite richness. You have only to look at their manuscripts and their proof corrections, he says. They never stopped adding and elaborating, while he [Beckett] himself proceeds in the opposite direction, towards nothingness, making his text ever more compact" (Juliet 1995: 158; emphasis added). Around the same period, Beckett told Martin Esslin:

> The difference between Joyce and myself is that Joyce was a synthesiser. He tried to pack the *whole* world into a book, in as much detail as possible, and I am an analyser, I try to take as much of the detail away as possible.[4]

Rosemary Pountney quotes this passage (1988: 156) to illustrate the way in which "the original statement is obscured" as the writing proceeds, "until the final text has become a balancing of possibilities in the scales of ambiguity" (155). This procedure and its effect (ambiguity) are presented as opposite to Joyce's, but Beckett was referring only to the procedure. The effect is surprisingly similar. Juliet's oft-quoted report is followed by his suggestion that in spite of the "poverty" of Beckett's universe, "everything essential is expressed," to which Beckett reacted with a smile: "Smiling, he agrees that, somehow or other, the two approaches should come together" (1995: 158).

This enumeration of Beckett's statements about Joyce in relation to his own writing method is not exhaustive, but it indicates the insistence with which Beckett continued to emphasize the dichotomy. The insistence somehow affects this image. Instead of unquestioningly absorbing Beckett's view on his own poetics, S. E. Gontarski makes the important observation that "the counterimpulse, a vestige of paternal Joycean aesthetics, persists in their pattern of fastidious revision, which suggests Beckett's fundamental desire to *control* his expression and to 'say something' precisely, and even in his becoming a theatrical director to try to *control* as much as he can of the theatrical performance" (1985: 7; emphasis added). The repetition of the word "control" contrasts sharply with Beckett's statement "I am not master of my material" in Israel Shenker's account.

In *Die Entstehung eines Gedichts*, the German poet Hans Magnus Enzensberger describes two methods of studying a writing process (see chapter 2). The method "from the inside" can only be applied by the author (in such works as Thomas Mann's *Die Entstehung des Doktor Faustus*). But memory tends to distort the past, and authors may have all kinds of reasons why they wish to present the genesis of their works in a specific way, emphasizing particular aspects and downplaying or concealing others. The other method, reconstructing the genesis "from the outside," is inevitably the method of genetic critics. The material they have to work with is "poor," according to Enzensberger, because no memories are attached to it; but this has the advantage that the researcher can take a distance from it in order to examine the writing process.

With reference to Beckett, S. E. Gontarski has summarized the "broadly predictable lines" this process of composition usually follows:

> after the initial image or incident is recorded (often straight from memory or the unconscious) what follows is a shaping process that includes: (1) deleting detail, explanation, and often connection, that is, the creation of absences; (2) rejecting, consciously destroying the systems of chronology and causality; and (3) creating an alternative arrangement or internal relationship that will emphasize *pattern* if not *order*. (17)

The emphasis on "pattern" and "order" counterbalances and nuances Beckett's (over)emphasis on not being in control of his material. As Mary Pountney demonstrates with reference to *Lessness*, Beckett had to create a strict pattern in order to accommodate the aleatory. "It is the shape that matters," Beckett told Harold Hobson in 1956; and five years later he stressed the importance of form, specifying to Tom Driver that the "new form" he was looking for "admits the chaos and does not try to say that the chaos is really something else. (...) To find a form that accommodates the mess, that is the task of the artist now."[5] Beckett's "nohow" as a writer implied the know-how to create and carefully refine his composition in order to admit the decomposition to become part of it.

But in this respect, Beckett's nohow is not that different from Joyce's know-how. The idea to integrate decomposition in the composition process is inherent in "Work in Progress" and repeatedly mentioned in *Finnegans Wake*. Joyce's plan was to write a history of the world. "But the world, mind, is, was and will be writing its own wrunes for ever" (*FW* 19.35–36). Joyce is exceptionally sparse with puns in this passage and thus draws attention to the only portmanteau word: "wrunes," alliterating with "writing" and comprising both runes and ruins.

In a brilliant essay on the "definitive exegenesis of HCE," Sam Slote analyses the entry "w of b of j's f's w/describe - f" in Joyce's *Finnegans Wake* notebook VI.B.15 (page 99): "One could characterize this notebook fragment with the Old Irish word rún which means secret, if only for the illegibility of the ancient tomb markings it names. The cipher as *rune* is the illegible fragmentary remains from antiquity" (1998: 104). In his attempt to decipher these runes, Slote employs other notes from the same notebook, referring to HCE as a "storycarrier" (63, 65), who "falls - pieces" (67). If the runes can be deciphered as "w[riting] of b[ook] of j[oyce]'s f[innegan]'s w[ake]," the next entry, "describe - f," might not just entail a description of Finnegan (f) or his Fall (-f), but also the endeavor to eff "what has so happily been called the unutterable or ineffable" (Beckett 1981 [1953]: 61). The history of the world is the de-scription of the storycarrier and his stories, by means of which he builds "buildung supra buildung" (*FW* 4.26–27), each history carrying its own ruin, each building providing the dung for the one that will be built on top of it. "The great fall of the offwall entailed at such short notice the pftjschute of Finnegan" (*FW* 3.18–19), but also the fall of the wall; the "offwall" accommodates the mess of its own offal.

Beckett's *Bildung*—for instance, his study of Dante—provided the dung for a lifetime of writing wrunes. Images such as the appearance of Virgil's figure were elements to fall back on in an impasse. Throughout Beckett's life, the fragment "chi per lungo silenzio parea fioco" was part of the "offwall" that provided the means to go on whenever he arrived at a dead wall in the writing process.

Toward the end of his career, the writing process increasingly became an integral part of his works. The composition history of these works shows a fascination with dead ends. Especially in the manuscripts of his later works, Beckett seems to actively seek out dead ends that stimulate the ingenuity to find a way out. Time and again he writes himself into a deadlock situation, *and yet* he goes on with greater resolve, only to "fail better" again. For instance, among the manuscripts of Beckett's penultimate work, *Stirrings Still*, there is a version that ends with the words: "against a wall. So far" (*RUL MS 2935/3/2*). The protagonist arrives at a wall and he cannot go on: "so far" and not farther. The situation is not unlike the ultimate situation of Bartleby in Melville's story "Bartleby, the Scrivener." During his employment at the narrator's office, he is already facing a "dead brick wall" (2003: 1098), and in the end he dies, "huddled" like a fetus, in front of a "dead-wall" (1110).[6] But in Beckett's manuscript of *Stirrings Still*, when the protagonist finds himself against a wall and the manuscript version ends with the words "so far," this phrase is quite ambiguous and simultaneously emphasizes the provisional character of the situation, as in the expression "so far so good."

The ambiguous situation between "so far so good" and "so far and not farther" reflects Beckett's ambiguous attitude toward modernity in general, criticizing in particular the autokinetic movement for the sake of greater movement that characterizes modernity. As opposed to the "grand narrative" of Progress, Beckett seems to be failing deliberately. This raises the question of to what degree this attitude differs from Beckett's immediate examples, Proust and Joyce.

The image of Beckett proceeding in the opposite direction from Joyce and Proust is to an important extent construed by the author himself. According to Kevin J. H. Dettmar, "Joyce criticism has yet to shake off the 'omniscient, omnipotent' Joyce of Beckett's own creation—a straw man erected in response to Beckett's own artistic need" (1999: 87). Evidently one cannot deny the obvious differences, but perhaps the authorized image has somewhat obscured a fundamental correspondence. Beckett does indeed work in the opposite direction from Joyce and Proust, but he starts from a similar nominalist concern. He seems to purposely write toward lessness, but starting from particular situations. "All these demented particulars" (1957: 13), "the straws, flotsam, etc." (German Diaries 4, 15 January 1937; Knowlson 1996: 244) were an early interest and continued to be so until the end of his career. For example, in the early manuscripts of *Stirrings Still*, the initial situation was a room with a bed, a small heart-shaped plastic chamber pot, and a nightlight (*RUL* MS 2935/1/2). In the course of the writing process, the bed and the chamber pot were removed, and the nightlight was abstracted into a nondescript light, the source of which is impossible to retrace. Accordingly, Beckett's writing method will be analyzed (in the following chapters) as a two-movement process: the recollection of particulars and their subsequent decomposition. Before embarking on this investigation, it is useful to examine to what extent a modernist preoccupation with time may have been instrumental in refining a nominalist sensibility and the mark it left on Samuel Beckett's writings.

Beckett already drew attention to a nominalist concern for the particular in his early essay on Joyce. He illustrates Joyce's work in progress by means of the phrase "in twosome twiminds" to express the abstract notion of "doubt" in a particular situation. In this way, Joyce defamiliarizes the habitual generalization and creates a neologism that is employed only once. He describes the phenomenon "doubt" as an epiphenomenon and treats it as if he encountered this situation for the first time. Not unlike the hundreds of river names in the ALP chapter, he tries to transform the abstract notion into what it stands for. The words "perform" their content. One concept is replaced by two words, representing two minds that cannot be made up. In "Dante...Bruno.Vico..Joyce," Beckett discusses the "inability to abstract the general from the particular" (1929: 247) in the most primitive forms of language. Unlike metaphysics, which are "concerned with universals," poetry focuses on "particulars" (246).

If Joyce can be said to proceed from the abstract toward the concrete, Beckett seems to be applying an opposite writing method. This, however, raises the inevitable question of whether the nominalist concern can be reconciled with the notion of the "abstractor"—as Beckett is called, for instance by Pascale Casanova in *Beckett l'abstracteur*. When Beckett explained to Charles Juliet how both Joyce and Proust aimed to create a whole world, reproducing it in all its infinite richness, he duly pointed out that they "never stopped adding and elaborating," while Beckett himself "proceeds in the opposite direction, towards nothingness, making his text ever more compact" (Juliet 1995: 158). The important nuance is that Beckett does not simply present his writing as the complete opposite of Proust or Joyce's work, but he talks about proceeding in a direction, a movement *toward* nothingness. In *Waiting for Godot*, for instance, Vladimir says: "There's nothing" (*CDW* 81). But he immediately has to modify this observation:

> Vladimir: [*Looking round.*] It's indescribable. It's like nothing. There's nothing. There's a tree. (*CDW* 81; omitted in the revised text, Beckett 1994: 78)

Arboreal Nominalism

The tree is more than just part of the setting of *En attendant Godot*. It is almost a character, arguably even the most important character on stage. Of all the characters in this play, the tree perhaps expresses Beckett's "nominalist irony" in the most effective way. The tree may serve as an example to illustrate linguistic skepticism, the way it does in Fritz Mauthner's *Beiträge zu einer Kritik der Sprache*. Beckett's interest in this work is evidenced by the long passages he excerpted in the so-called "Whoroscope" notebook (*RUL* MS 3000), notably the discussion of "pure and consistent nominalism" in the third volume of Mauthner's work (3: 615–16).[7] In the same volume, Mauthner compares language to a military uniform. From a distance it looks impeccable, but a closer inspection of every individual soldier will inevitably show that in many cases the uniform does not quite fit after all. Similarly, all trees in a forest are called "trees," but none of them is the same:

"If the notion 'tree' were created by comparing for instance all the trees I have ever seen and subtracting, abstracting, or leaving out all the elements that are typical of each individual tree, (. . .) nothing but emptiness would remain behind the label 'tree'" (1923: 3: 277).

Against this background, the passages in *Waiting for Godot* regarding the tree are particularly telling. When Estragon asks Vladimir whether he is sure they are waiting on the right spot, Vladimir confirms:

Vladimir: He said by the tree. (*They look at the tree.*)
Do you see any others?
Estragon: What is it?
Vladimir: I don't know. A willow.[8]
Estragon: Where are the leaves?
Vladimir: It must be dead.
Estragon: No more weeping. (*CDW* 15)

The phenomenal world seems to interest Estragon only to the extent that he can classify and conceptualize it. To a certain extent this suggests some form of interest in particulars, but somehow the nomenclature seems more important to him than what the names stand for. Toward the end of the play, when Vladimir concludes that "Everything's dead but the tree," Estragon repeats his question:

Estragon: [*Looking at the tree*] What is it?
Vladimir: It's the tree.
Estragon: Yes, but what kind? (*CDW* 87)

Not surprisingly, it is Vladimir who notices in the second act that the tree has changed:

Vladimir: (. . .) things have changed here since yesterday.
Estragon: Everything oozes.
Vladimir: Look at the tree.
Estragon: It's never the same pus from one second to the next.
Vladimir: The tree, look at the tree.
[*Estragon looks at the tree.*]
Estragon: Was it not there yesterday?
Vladimir: Yes of course it was there. Do you not remember? We nearly hanged ourselves from it. But you wouldn't. Do you not remember?
Estragon: You dreamt it. (*CDW* 56)

Vladimir repeatedly refers to the concrete tree. As the empiricist of the tandem, he urges Estragon to use his senses. Estragon in his turn insistently refers to leaves as a simile to describe the noise of "the dead voices"—not unlike the voice mentioned in *Texts for Nothing*, and the trace it wants to leave, "like air leaves among the leaves" (*CSP* 152). In quite a different way from Joyce and yet starting from a similar nominalist concern, Beckett makes use of homophony as a potentially defamiliarizing tool to draw attention to the undue reduction of complexity in uniform concepts. Estragon sees all the differences, and he suggests all the variant "readings" of the dead voices (comparing their noise to wings, sand, feathers, ashes), whereas Estragon insists on the *in*variant idea of undifferentiated "leaves." Without Vladimir, Estragon probably would not even have noticed the palpable leaves on the tree:

Estragon: The tree?
Vladimir: Do you not remember?
Estragon: I'm tired.
Vladimir: Look at it.
 [*They look at the tree.*]
Estragon: I see nothing.
Vladimir: But yesterday evening it was all black and bare. And now it's covered with leaves.
Estragon: Leaves? (*CDW* 61)

From a genetic perspective, the dialogues between Didi and Gogo not only reflect George Berkeley's *Three Dialogues*, but also thematize a textual issue that may shed new light on Beckett's writings as a work in regress. Estragon tries to immobilize the ever-changing material world in a system and situate it by means of the name of a class or family of trees, the way a work of literature is given a title. If a work can be defined as the "message or experience implied by the authoritative versions of a literary writing" (Shillingsburg 1996: 176), the work is neither the sum of its versions, nor a single copy of the published text. A reader never reads a work, but always an instantiation of a work. "Usually the variant forms have the same name," Peter Shillingsburg points out (176). In the case of Beckett's bilingual works, the double nature of this "same name" is the first indication of his "nominalist irony." A reference to *Waiting for Godot* is not necessarily a reference to *En attendant Godot*. The famous difference between the French and the English versions with respect to the number of leaves is a good example. In the beginning of the second act, the French stage directions indicate that the tree has "a few leaves" ("L'arbre porte quelques feuilles"). In the English self-translation, it has "four or five leaves" (*CDW* 53). But this is only one of several variations. The genesis of the work continues even after its publication, resulting in more versions (or "instantiations"). When Beckett staged his own play at the Schiller-Theater in Berlin, he reduced the number of leaves. "The tree has three leaves," according to the revised text (1994: 50), based on Beckett's revisions and production notebook. As the General Editor's Note indicates: "The texts are now as close as possible to how Beckett wanted them to be" (*TN* 1: v). But the case of the number of leaves raises the question of which authorial intention at what stage in the work's genesis this text represents. For shortly after his own direction of the play, his intention had already changed. On the last page of his production notebook, he wrote a note under the title *TREE*:

> Was not right (3 branches).
> Two branches only, two leaves
> 3rd couple. (*TN* 1: 393)

Consequently, even the text revised according to the modifications of the authorial direction cannot be considered as the definitive establishment of Beckett's final intention. The editors of the revised text add a note referring to this jotting in Beckett's theater notebook, but they also note that "in the San Quentin production, it [the tree] (...) still had three branches, probably because with two it would have resembled too explicitly a cross. It has also tended to have three leaves, one on each branch." (*TN* 1: 89)

Still, there must have been a moment, probably shortly after the Schiller-Theater performance, when Beckett considered the possibility of a tree with only two leaves, representing a third couple apart from Vladimir and Estragon, and Pozzo and Lucky. The text, therefore, "goes on" and the work continues to be in regress. The textual condition thus interestingly reflects the *condition humaine*. Similarly, the tree has all the qualities of the Beckettian character par excellence: it is silent, it does not go anywhere, and yet it goes "on," that is, it goes on growing (old, and so on). Especially when the two men try to "do the tree," standing on one leg, "abstracting" the other one, they create a more abstract version of themselves, a caricature of the one-legged "I." If the self is merely an abstraction, a universal, instantiated by all its particular, ever-changing individual versions, the search for it is doomed to fail. "For, as all abstraction consists in mere thinking away, the farther we continue it, the less we have left," Schopenhauer concluded (1969: 2: 64).

Less Universals

The short text *Lessness* (1969) expresses this situation concisely. Beckett created a rigid framework within which he allows chance to be a major structuring principle. As Ruby Cohn (2001: 305) and Rosemary Pountney (1987) show, its 120 sentences are in fact only 60 sentences, repeated in different order. Beckett wrote each sentence on a piece of paper, mixed them in a container, and picked them out in random order twice. Beckett's own "key" to this text, preserved in the Yale University Library, explains that *Lessness* is "composed of 6 statement groups each containing 10 sentences, i.e. 60 sentences in all. These 60 are first given in a certain order and paragraph structure, then repeated in a different order and different paragraph structure. The whole consists therefore of 2 x 60 = 120 sentences arranged and rearranged in 2 x 12 = 24 paragraphs."[9] The rigidity of this grid is a comment in itself. Beckett's structuring tools correspond with the conventions to systematize time. But Beckett infuses this rigid grid of human systematization with chance, arbitrariness, and randomness.

The vain attempt to fix what is stirring, evolving, or fleeting is expressed more poignantly in the English title than in the French original. The difference between *Sans* and *Lessness* caused by the suffix "-ness" indicates how consciously this addition must have been made. The suffix "-ness" is the easiest way to create a universal. Proust has pointed this out by means of a pun: Swann's love, the particular version of the Odette he fell in love with, is the one who once made him a nice cup of tea, the Odette "du bon thé" (Proust 1987–89: 1: 218). When Swann recognizes he will never be able to grasp all her changing aspects, he marries her and thus makes her "generalizable" (Goodkin 1991: 77), so that she becomes "une Odette de bonté" (Proust 1987–89 1: 309), an Odette of kind*ness*. The suffix "-ness" in *Lessness* thus indicates the extreme ambiguity of Beckett's nominalist irony. *Lessness* is, on the one hand, a universal, but, at the same time, it is a call for more "tea" and less "kindness," less universals, less "-ness."

This principle of "less-ness" applies to Beckett's works in that each of them—for instance, *Krapp's Last Tape*—can be regarded, not just as a monolithic text but also as a fluid succession of particular versions, the way Beckett regarded Krapp or any other individual as a "succession of individuals." This unique combination of existential and (inter)textual recollection is the subject of the next chapter.

8

Recollection

1. Existential Recollection: "Life Scenes"

In his essay "Dante . . . Bruno . Vico . . Joyce," Beckett described poetry as "the first operation of the human mind": "Barbarians, incapable of analysis and abstraction, must use their fantasy to explain what their reasons cannot comprehend. Before articulation comes song; before abstract terms, metaphors" (1929: 246). But before it becomes "successful composition," a few other operations of the human mind are required, at least according to William Wordsworth:

> Poetry is the spontaneous overflow of powerful feelings: it takes its origin from emotion recollected in tranquillity: the emotion is contemplated till by a species of reaction the tranquillity gradually disappears, and an emotion, kindred to that which was before the subject of contemplation, is gradually produced, and does itself actually exist in the mind. In this mood successful composition generally begins. (Wordsworth, 1802 version)

Composition and recollection preoccupy the eponymous character in *Krapp's Last Tape* when he listens to the tape on which he recorded his memory of "the vision." In the early drafts, he mentions a "turning-point." In the third corrected typescript, Beckett changed this turning-point into a "vision" (*HRHRC* 4.2, Ts. 3), thus giving it a more pompous air. As Philip Laubach-Kiani (2005) has pointed out, the impact of Romantic discourse on the genesis of *Krapp's Last Tape* is subtle but clearly noticeable. For instance, the choice of the verb "to recollect" in the sentence "One dark young beauty I recollect particularly" (*CDW* 219) is carefully introduced in the second typescript. Originally, the verb was "to remember." In the second typescript (*HRHRC* 4.2, Ts 2, f. 3r), it was first changed into "recall" and subsequently into "recollect." In the third typescript, Beckett happened to arrive at the end of the page in the middle of this sentence. He entered a new sheet of paper in his typewriter and continued typing the rest of the sentence: "remember particularly, all white and starch, splendid bosom, with a" (*HRHRC* 4.2, Ts 2, f. 4v). After "with a" Beckett stopped abruptly, pulled out the sheet from the typewriter, and started again on the other side, again replacing "remember" by "recollect" (*HRHRC* 4.2, Ts 3, f. 4r).

The introduction of this verb is not accidental; it has a history in Beckett's work. The most conspicuous occurrence is the parodic reference to Wordsworth's definition in the story "The Expelled": "Recollecting these emotions, with the celebrated advantage of tranquillity, it seems to me he did nothing else, all that day, but turn about his lodging" (*CSP* 58). The same futile circular motion was hinted at in the original title of Beckett's almost contemporaneous first novel in French, *Voyage de Mercier et Camier autour du pot dans les Bosquets de Bondy*. In the same period shortly after the war, in July 1947, Beckett wrote in his first *Molloy* notebook:

(...) c'est dans la tranquillité de
la décomposition que je me rappelle
cette longue ~~émotion~~ ^[~~commotion~~]^ ^émotion^ confuse que
fut mon existence, et que [je le]
juge, comme il est dit que Dieu
nous jugera, et avec autant
d'impertinence. Décomposer
c'est aussi vivre, je le sais, je
le sais, ~~xx~~ ^ne^ me [fatiguez] pas, mais
[on] n'y est pas toujours [tout] entier.
D'ailleurs de cette vie-là ^aussi^ j'aurai
peut-être ~~un jour~~ la bonté de vous
entretenir, un jour, (...)

(*HRHRC* Beckett 4.5, Nb. 1: 123)

The manuscript shows some commotion about "emotion," but apart from the change from "existence" to "vie," the passage remained almost unaltered in the published version, and Beckett made no attempt to obscure the allusion to Wordsworth in the English translation.[1]

The parodic strain in this passage may give the impression that Beckett simply pokes fun at Romantic poetics. A portion of ridicule is undeniably involved, but Beckett's relationship to Romanticism seems to be more complex than that.

In "Proust," for instance, he appreciates the author of *A la recherche du temps perdu* because "[h]e is a Romantic in his anxiety to accomplish his mission, to be a good and faithful servant. He does not seek to evade the implications of his art such as it has been revealed to him. He will write as he has lived—in Time" (1999a [1931]: 81). Beckett contrasts this type of writer with the classical artist, who "assumes omniscience and omnipotence" (81). The latter are two qualities Beckett attributed to Joyce, in opposition to his own approach. This evidently does not necessarily imply a Romantic strain in Beckett's work by analogy—"the danger is in the neatness of identifications" (1929: 242). But the idea of writing "in Time" is quite applicable.

Succession of Individuals

In "Proust," Beckett describes how, after the death of Albertine, the narrator has to forget not just one, but innumerable Albertines. "And not only 'I,' but the many 'I's" (1999a [1931]: 60). This multiplicity of *Is* was clearly important to Beckett in the early 1930s, as the title of his and Alfred Péron's translation of Joyce's "Anna Livia Plurabelle" chapter indicates: "Anna Lyvia Pluratself."[2] "O, tell me all," Joyce wrote in chapter 8 of *Finnegans Wake*: "Tell us in franca langua. ^And call a spate a spate^" (*JJA* 48: 286).[3] In July 1930, Samuel Beckett and Alfred Péron (Aubert 1985: 417) translated this part of the "Anna Livia Plurabelle" chapter as follows:

> Traduis en franca lingua. Et appelle une crue une crue. (Joyce 1985 [1930]: 419)

Their translation (originally intended for publication in the avant-garde journal *Bifur*) was modified by Joyce with the help of others (Paul Léon, Philippe Soupault, Ivan Goll, Eugene Jolas, and Adrienne Monnier), but the sentence "Et appelle une crue une crue" remained unaltered. The translators did not only have to deal with a spade but also with a cat, since the French equivalent expression is "appeler un chat un chat." The semihomophony of spade and spate was hard to equal in French. Only a year before did Beckett write the famous sentence: "Here form *is* content, content *is* form" (1929: 248). In the original 1929 publication of "Dante. . .Bruno.Vico..Joyce" in *transition*, this line was followed a few sentences further on by the statement that in "Work in Progress," Joyce "is not writing about something: he is writing something" (248). If Beckett and Péron had focused solely on the form, they might have come up with a near-homophony, such as "appeler un Schah un Schah"; if the content had prevailed, the connotation of "a spate of words"—"un flux de paroles"—might have resulted in "appeler un flux un flux." But form and content had to be linked, so the translators settled for a short, monosyllabic word starting with a *c* that adequately conveys the meaning of "spate": *une crue*.

What they could not know was that the "spade" had a history. In Joyce's earliest reading notes, probably made during the last years at Belvedere College in preparation of the matriculation exam, the word "spade" occurs among his excerpts from Dante's *Inferno* (preserved at the National Library of Ireland). On page 19 verso of these Dante notes, there are three drawings of a hoe, a spade, and a shovel, each identified respectively with its Italian name: "zappa," "vanga," and "pala." This may be seen as a most visual proof of Joyce's consistent effort to find *le mot juste* and to call a spade a spade. But of course it also invites more thorough digging—both "philological spade-work"[4] and interpretive excavation.

The question of why Joyce called a *spate* a *spate* implies the negative question why he *didn't* call a *spade* a *spade*. The question is more or less answered in Arthur Power's conversations with Joyce. When Power told Joyce he preferred the classical style, Joyce replied that the classical style is inadequate when it has to deal with "the secret currents of life (. . .) for life is a complicated problem": "We believe that it is in the abnormal that we approach closer to reality" (Joyce in Power 1974: 74). In their translation, Beckett and Péron made a fair effort to respect that deviation from the normal, habitual manner of speaking. According to Beckett, Joyce's last work was "purgatorial" in the sense of an absence:

> In what sense, then is Mr. Joyce's work purgatorial? In the absolute absence of the Absolute. Hell is the static lifelessness of unrelieved viciousness. Paradise the static lifelessness of unrelieved immaculation. Purgatory a *flood* of movement and vitality released by the conjunction of these two elements." (1929: 253; emphasis added)

Against the background of this "flood," the translation "appeler une crue une crue" was quite appropriate. Another sense in which Joyce's work was purgatorial is the way in which "it purges from our inward sight the film of familiarity which obscures from us the wonder of our being" (P. Shelley 2002: 533). A century after Shelley's *Defence of Poetry*, Joyce applied this statement to prose. Beckett in his turn was not unfamiliar with this idea, especially since he was reading Proust.[5] Around the time he was making the translation with Péron in July 1930, he was reading *A la recherche du temps perdu*.[6] In his essay "Proust," he came to a similar conclusion as in his essay on Joyce: Proust "makes no attempt to dissociate form from content" (1999 [1931]: 88).

Joyce also referred to Proust in the same conversation with Arthur Power, explaining that he believed he could approach closer to reality in "the abnormal":

> Our object is to create a new fusion between the exterior world and our contemporary selves, and also to enlarge our vocabulary of the subconscious as Proust has done. (. . .) When we are living a normal life we are living a conventional one, following a pattern which has been laid out by other people in another generation. (Joyce in Power 1974: 74)

In Beckett's "Proust," the effort to counteract convention and defamiliarize habitual views through language is linked to "Habit" in general: "Life is habit. Or rather life is a succession of habits, since the individual is a *succession of individuals*; the world being a projection of the individual's consciousness (an objectivation of the individual's will, Schopenhauer would say), the pact must be continually renewed, the letter of safe-conduct brought up to date" (1999a [1931]: 19; emphasis added). Later on, this "succession of individuals" became thematic in many of Beckett's own works, notably *Krapp's Last Tape*. The scene Krapp "recollect[s] particularly" is the dark young beauty with her "splendid"—in later versions "incomparable"—bosom and "a big black hooded perambulator, most funereal thing" (*CDW* 219). This is only one of numerous reminiscences that characterize Beckett's later works. In his synopsis of *Not I*, Beckett called these kinds of recollections "life scenes" (*RUL* MS 1227/7/12/10).

I and Not I

One of these life scenes is "the one time she cried" in *Not I*. The image of the female protagonist sitting and looking at her hand is prepared in the top margin of the "Addenda" page (*RUL* MS 1227/7/12/1 f. 5v) by means of two clusters of quick jottings:

> sitting looking at her hand
> palm down on a [xx]
> suddenly saw tears on it
> could only have been hers
> all over in a second
> watched them dry
>
> dull roar like falls
> ~~the one time she cried~~

~~[since] she [could]~~ could remember
~~all over~~
~~all over in a second~~

The scene is subsequently incorporated in the first of the addenda, and refined in several versions.

> ... the one time she cried ... since she could remember ... sitting old woman already ... sitting looking at her hand ... palm [down] ^upward^ in her lap ... ~~suddenly tears [on]~~ ^in^ ~~it ... could only have been hers ... [xx xx]~~ ^no one for miles ...^ ^suddenly wet ... tears presumably ... hers presumably ... no one else for miles ...^ all over in a second ... sat and watched them dry ... (*RUL* MS 1227/7/12/1 f. 5v)

The dynamics of the writing process thus reflect a dynamic process in the mind. Not just Beckett's, but the human mind in general. The textual genesis performs an imaginative reconstruction of the way memory works. This could be called genetic mimesis. The genesis of the work becomes functional and is employed to depict the process of remembering.

Five of these scenes are part of the protagonist's attempts to deny the I, or "posit" a non-I, as a sort of counterpoint to Johann Gottlieb Fichte's theory that the I "posits" or "poses" itself.

Beckett had already encountered the notion of the "not-I" while he was writing *Dream of Fair to Middling Women* and reading Max Nordau's *Degeneration*. In Beckett's *Dream* notebook, edited by John Pilling, a series of entries (nrs. 664–7) is derived from a passage on "coenaesthesis" in Nordau's book:

> Coenaesthesis, the organic dimly-conscious "I," rises into the clear consciousness of the "Ego," by excitations of the second order, reaching the brain from the nerves and muscles. (. . .) If consciousness has adopted the habit of causality, it seeks a cause in all its perceptions, and can no longer imagine a perception without a cause. The cause of muscular perceptions—that is, of movements consciously willed—it finds in itself. The cause of nervous perceptions—that is, the information reported by the nervous system concerning the excitations which it experiences—it does not find in itself. But the latter must have a cause. Where is it? As it is not in consciousness, it must necessarily exist somewhere else; there must then be something else outside consciousness, and so consciousness comes, through the habit of causal

> thought, to assume the existence of something outside itself, of a "not-I," of an external world. (1993 [1892]: 249)

The Fichtean idea that "the I poses itself and opposes itself to the not-I" plays an important role in the development of the "stream of consciousness" technique, as Richard Ellmann notes (1983: 126). According to Ellmann, Fichte served as a starting point for Dujardin, and "what could not fail to draw [Joyce's] attention was a philosophical act of self-creation on the part of Dujardin's hero, who on the first page invokes himself into being" (126). In "The Stream of Consciousness," William James also examines this issue:

> One great splitting of the whole universe into two halves is made by each of us; and for each of us almost all of the interest attaches to one of the halves; but we all draw the line of division between them in a different place. When I say that we all call the two halves by the same names, and that those names are "*me*" and "*not-me*" respectively, it will at once be seen what I mean. (190)

James immediately adds that "[n]o mind can take the same interest in his neighbor's *me* as in his own" (190). Nonetheless, Beckett tries to approach this fundamental dichotomy from the opposite perspective. The "I" tries to act as a detached observer of its own will. Whereas Fichte's "I" needed a "non-I" as a form of resistance to overcome and thus thrive, Beckett first needed an "I" in order to be able to decompose it and compose *Not I*.

In the published version of this play, there is no mention of "I" apart from the title. In the first layer of the first version, Beckett employed the third-person singular: "she found herself in the dark" (*RUL* MS 1227/7/12/1, f. 1r). But he subsequently crossed it out and replaced it by the first-person singular: "~~she~~ ^I^ found ~~her~~^my^self in the dark" (*RUL* MS 1227/7/12/1, f. 1r). On the second page, this replacement already becomes part of the text's subject matter: "she found herself in the ... what? ... I? ... no ... no! ... she ... found herself in the dark ..." (2r). The text thus thematizes the attempt to undo the earlier replacement. In the third version, the "I" is effectively crossed out: "she found herself in the ... what? ... ~~I?~~^who?^ ... what?^...^no... ~~no~~ ^NO^! ... she ..." (*RUL* MS 1227/7/12/3, f. 1r). And finally the passage becomes: "she found herself in the - ... what? .. who? .. no! .. she" (*CDW* 377).

S. E. Gontarski notes that Beckett used the hesitation between the third- and the first-person singular in the first version to compose the rest. Beckett transformed this hesitation in a conflict that was to become characteristic of the whole play, the conflict between revealing and concealing

(Gontarski 1985: 145). The play actually starts before the curtain rises, with the voice of MOUTH unintelligibly ad-libbing before "birth," the first word of the first version. The first layer of the text opens with: "birth into the world... this world... of a small baby," as if it were the opening of a peaceful Christmas story. But in the sixth version, birth is replaced by "out": "out .. into this world" (*RUL* MS 1227/7/12/6, f. 1r). Instead of reading as a welcome to this world, the opening now reads as an expulsion from Paradise: out. In the first version of the French translation, this expulsion is characterized by a certain bestiality, as it opens with the words: "bas .. mis bas .. ici bas .. petit bout de rien" (*RUL* MS 1396/4/25, f. 1r).

The verb "mettre bas" (to have young/puppies/kittens) is usually only used for animals. In the second version of the translation, Beckett puts these words between brackets and adds the alternative "au monde .. mis au monde .. ce monde" (*RUL* MS 1396/4/26, f. 1r). In the third version, the original "birth" is replaced by the "world": "- monde... mis au monde ... ce monde" (*RUL* MS 1396/4/27, f. 2r). But this world is preceded by a dash, a *trait d'union*. In the manuscripts of his last work, however, Beckett referred to this punctuation mark as a "trait de *dis*union" (*RUL* MS 3316/1, f. 2v). In the case of *Not I*, the *trait de (dis)union* separates the "life scene" from what preceded it; it separates the scene from the ob-scene. According to James Knowlson, Beckett claimed he had prenatal recollections of scenes inside his mother's womb (Knowlson 1996: 2). In its connecting capacity of a *trait d'union*, this interesting punctuation mark simultaneously indicates that "within each personal consciousness, thought is sensibly continuous," as William James describes the sense of union between past selves that seems to characterize even MOUTH's consciousness—in spite of its "vehement refusal to relinquish third person" (*CDW* 375). "The first and foremost concrete fact," according to James, "is the fact that *consciousness of some sort goes on*" (171; original emphasis): "If we could say in English 'it thinks,' as we say 'it rains' or 'it blows,' we should be stating the fact most simply and with the minimum of assumption. As we cannot, we must simply say that *thought goes on*" (172), by which James means the "stream of consciousness" or succession of states of mind, all of which are different: "*no state once gone can recur and be identical with what it was before*. Now we are seeing, now hearing; now reasoning, now willing; now recollecting" (173).

Recollecting a "Community of Self"

The activity of recollecting enhances the sense of what James calls a "community of self," which "the time-gap cannot break in twain" (177). Whether this community is really good company is questioned in Beckett's later works. *Company* (1979) consists of fifty-nine paragraphs. With its implicit reference to the almost, but not quite full circle of the clock (seconds per minute, minutes per hour), these fifty-nine paragraphs may be regarded as a comment on the human conventions to systematize time. A quarter of these paragraphs (fifteen) are recollections of life scenes, apparently from the protagonist's past. The opening paragraph reads: "A voice comes to one in the dark. Imagine." The second paragraph recapitulates the narratological situation: "That then is the proposition. To one on his back in the dark a voice tells of a past." Apart from the "voice" and the hearer—who would employ the first-person pronoun if he could speak—there is also an "other": "Use of the second person marks the voice. That of the third that cankerous other" (Beckett 1993b: 2, par. 3). In the middle of the text (the opening lines of paragraph 30), this "cankerous other" is described as the "Deviser of the voice and of its hearer and of himself. Deviser of himself for company" (16).

James's "community of self" thus becomes somewhat more problematic and echoes Hamm's suggestion in *Endgame*: "Then babble, babble, words, like the solitary child who turns himself into children, two, three, so as to be together, and whisper together, in the dark" (*CDW* 126). The last paragraph of *Company* is a single word ("Alone.") with the same matter-of-fact harshness as the last sentence of Beckett's story "Dante and the Lobster" when the protagonist tries to soothe himself with the thought that being boiled alive is a quick death: "It is not."

Of the fifteen recollections, one paragraph deals with the birth of "you," seven with his early childhood, two with adulthood, four with old age, and one (the penultimate paragraph) has no specific age indication. Especially the first reminiscence (paragraph 7) seems to have made a deep impression: "A small boy you come out of Connolly's Stores holding your mother by the hand" (1993b: 4). The small boy looks up at the blue sky and asks his mother if the sky is not in reality much more distant than it appears. His mother does not answer, and some hundred paces later he asks the same question again. For some reason his mother's reaction is inordinately vehement. She shakes off his little hand and makes a "cutting retort you have never forgotten" (4). This scene corresponds with the recollection in *Malone Dies* when Malone remembers the same "life scene": "One day we were walking along the road, up a hill of extraordinary steepness, near home I imagine, my memory is full of steep hills, I get them confused. I said, The sky is further away than you think, is it not, mama? It was without malice, I was simply thinking of all the leagues that separated me from it. She replied, to me her son, It is precisely as far away as it appears to be. She was right. But at the time I was aghast" (Beckett 1955–58: 268). But the "devised deviser" in *Company* is not Malone; he is alone *tout court*, even when he tells himself to call the hearer "M" and "himself some other character. W." (30, paragraph 41)[7] As the thirteenth letter of the alphabet, the omnipresent *M* (linked to Beckett's birthday, Good Friday, 13 April 1906) emphasizes the suffering of Christ on the cross, referred to in the fifty-fourth paragraph: "You first saw the light and cried at the close of the day when in darkness Christ at the ninth hour cried and died" (38).[8]

Most of the recollections may have had their origin in Beckett's own life, but the text—insisting on the homophony of "lying" (supine/untruthful)—constantly undermines their "verisimilitude" (14, par. 27) and suggests that they are all lies: "as he lies the craving for company revives. In which to escape from his own" (38, par. 54). As in *Not I*, the "unthinkable last of all" is "Unnamable. Last person. I. Quick leave him" (16, par. 28). No matter how many elements from Beckett's life this text may contain, the third-person narrative constantly interrupts the autobiographical second-person narrative. Beckett presents the act of recollection as an endless process of revision. As Molloy says:

> I misjudged the distance separating me from the other world, and often I stretched out my hand for what was far beyond my reach, and often I knocked against obstacles scarcely visible on the horizon. But I was like that even when I had my two eyes, it seems to me, but perhaps not, for it is long since that era of my life, and my recollection of it is more than imperfect." (1955–58: 50)

The anecdotes in *Company* are only "figments," and the attempts to arrive at some Proustian notion of "le temps retrouvé" are doomed to fail. But the importance of this failure is that it charts the ways in which the "self" is constantly being rewritten. Porter Abbott's coinage "autography" thus involves all kinds of self-constructions and reconstructions with hindsight, in a mind that is "unstillable" (14, par. 26). The "stirrings still" or the "unformulable gropings of the mind" already foreshadow Beckett's last prose work, *Stirrings Still*. This reverberation between works within Beckett's oeuvre reflects the existential dimension of Beckett's poetics of regress implied in *Company*. The successive imaginations and mental constructions constantly change and expand like a cancer, "that cankerous other" (2, par. 3).

The penultimate paragraph of *Company* implicitly refers to "the old lutist"

Belacqua, "waiting to be purged" in Dante's *Divina commedia*. In the same manner, "you" is sitting "huddled in the dark" in fetal position:

> Huddled thus you find yourself imagining you are not alone while knowing full well that nothing has occurred to make this possible. The process continues none the less lapped as it were in its meaninglessness. You do not murmur in so many words, I know this doomed to fail and yet persist. (44, par. 58)

Many aspects of Beckett's writing come together in this passage: the insight, formulated in *Watt*, that every attempt to utter or eff "what has so happily been called the unutterable or ineffable" (Beckett 1981 [1953]: 61) is doomed to fail; the idea, formulated in *Endgame*, that "the end is in the beginning and yet you go on" (*CDW* 126); and especially the inexplicable urge to continue "none the less," in spite of the obvious meaninglessness of the process.

Beckett wrote *Company* in English, translated it into French (*Compagnie*, published by Minuit in 1980), and then adapted the English original again. As Charles Krance points out in the introduction to his bilingual variorum edition of *Company/Compagnie*, the English version shows traces of the translation. For instance, the word "trait" in the sentence "Another trait its repetitiousness" was originally "characteristic"; Beckett then changed it into "peculiarity"; and only after having translated the phrase as "Autre trait le rabâchage" did he decide to employ "trait" in the English version as well. The translation has an impact on its source text, thus creating a form of interdependence in both directions that reflects the imaginative and retrospective constructions by the "crawling creator" (paragraph 51), the "devised deviser devising it all for company" (paragraph 44).

Genetic Variants

The genesis of *Company* (started in May 1977) roughly coincided with the writing of *A Piece of Monologue*. Beckett was working on *Company* when, in August 1977, David Warrilow asked him if he wanted to write a play for him. As a central theme, Beckett suggested in a letter to Warrilow (1 October 1977): "My birth was my death" (Knowlson 1996: 649). The next day, 2 October 1977, he indeed started elaborating on the "old chestnut" of birth as the start of the decomposition process called life, originally under the title *GONE*:

> My birth was my death. Or put it another way. My birth was the death of me. Let me say that again. Words are scarce. My birth was my death.

Or put it another way. My birth was the death of me. (*RUL* MS 2068, f. 1r)

On the verso, Beckett wrote another version, deleting the opening "My":

My birth was my death. Or Put it another way. The death of me. Let *him* say that again. Words are few. (RUL MS 2068, f. 1v; emphasis added)

In the upper left corner of the first page, Beckett then added the note "all 3rd." In the first typescript, after a false start ("Birth was my death"), Beckett pulled the sheet of paper out of the typewriter and started again on the back. The most notable genetic variants are indeed the changes from the first-person singular by the third.

In the meantime, Beckett continued writing *Company*. On 17 May 1978, one year after he started writing *Company*, he considered the possibility of inserting a piece of the play in his prose text, as paragraph 54. This resulted in another set of genetic variants, chief among which is the second-person singular:

54

Birth was the death of *you*. At close of day. Sun sunk behind the larches. Needles turning green. Light dying in the room. Soon none left to die. No. No such thing as no light. Till on to dawn & never die[d]. Slowly in the dark a faint hand. It holds high a lighted spill. In light of spill faintly the [frame] & milkwhite globe. Second hand. In light of spill. It lifts off globe & disappears. Reappears empty. Lifts off chimney. Two hands & chimney in light of spill. Spill to wick. Chimney back on. (*RUL* MS 1822, f. 29r; cf. Beckett 1993b: 111–12; emphasis added)

The whole paragraph was subsequently canceled with a large St. Andrew's cross in black ink.

Matthijs Engelberts has devoted a fascinating section in his book *Défis du récit scénique* to the interplay between genres, focusing on this passage. This generic interaction has some interesting consequences, also from a textual perspective. In a special case like this, it is useful to distinguish transmissional variants (between editions) not only from genetic variants (between manuscript version), but also from generic variants (between genres).

Generic Variants

As Matthijs Engelberts indicates, Beckett's writing slightly differs depending on the genre. The "généricité" (208) of the manuscripts is most conspicuous with regard to the theme of the eyes. The emphasis on visual elements in *A Piece of Monologue* is stronger than in *Company*. This is even true in descriptive passages, as the following comparison between the second manuscript of *A Piece of Monologue* and the deleted prose version for *Company* shows. Apart from the stress on the eyes, the number of demonstratives is also higher in the dramatic piece:

DRAMA (*A Piece of Monologue*)

Birth was the death of me. (. . .) A window. ~~Looking~~ ^Facing^ west. Sun long sunk behind the larches. Light dying out. Soon none left to die. No. No such thing no light. Starless moonless heaven. Dies on to dawn & never dies. Out of the dark that window. Night slowly falling. Eyes to pane gaze out at that first night. Turn from it in the end to face the ~~glooming~~ ^darkening^ room. There in the end slowly a faint hand. (*RUL* MS 2072)

PROSE (*Company*)

Birth was the death of you. At close of day. Sun sunk behind the larches. Needles turning green. Light dying in the room. Soon none left to die. No. No such thing as no light. Till on to dawn & never die[d]. Slowly in the dark a faint hand. (*RUL* MS 1822, f. 29r)

When Beckett considered using the piece of monologue for the fifty-fourth paragraph of *Company*, this transgeneric operation involved several genetic variants. Apart from the personal pronouns, the change from "Light dying out" to "Light dying in the room" can be considered as a normal genetic variant. But some of the variants in the dramatic version may be due to the genre, such as the four highlighted word groups, all of which enhance the visual quality of the scene. Eventually, Beckett decided to stop the generic crossover operation and extracted the piece again, to develop *A Piece of Monologue* and *Company* as two separate works.

Translation Variants

Apart from genetic and generic variants, the interesting translation variants intensify the content of the work in that they persist in what, according to the text, is doomed to fail: "The process continues none the less lapped as it were in its meaninglessness" (Beckett 1993b: par. 53). Especially given the exceptional order in which the "original" and the self-translation were published, the method according to which this process continued textually can be described as "tentatives de fuite et de poursuite"—to use a phrase from the early versions of *Stirrings Still* (*RUL* MS 2933/1, f. 2r): the original follows the translation which follows the original, until it is no longer clear which is in pursuit of which. This fugal dynamics becomes effective from the very start: "Birth was the death of him. Again. Words are few. Dying too. Birth was the death of him." (Beckett 1993b: 48) In the French version, Beckett left out the repetition and reduced this passage to: "Sa naissance fut sa perte. (Beckett 1993b: 49) By leaving out the repetition, Beckett limited the message to the stony recollection of birth as the moment decomposition sets in.

2. (Inter)textual Recollection: "Bits of Pipe"

Personal reminiscences are not the only form of recollection that shaped Beckett's compositional method.[9] Reading (and rereading) was at least as important. Sometimes both forms of recollection coincided. On 30 June 1975, Beckett wrote to Jocelyn Herbert: "Only reading Dante again with memories of student reading."[10]

Recollecting implies collecting. In the 1920s, Beckett discovered Dante and thoroughly studied the *Divina commedia*.[11] His reading notes generally reflect a disciplined method of reading, summarizing, and making notes. In terms of reading notes, two types of collectors can be distinguished. Daniel Ferrer calls them respectively "marginalists" and "extractors" (2004: 7). In general, Beckett belonged to the second category (Van Hulle 2004c: 327), although he did sometimes write marginalia or marked passages in his books. In the early 1930s, under the influence of James Joyce, Beckett started jotting down peculiar phrases, in a way that resembles the *Finnegans Wake* notebooks. The best example of this method is the so-called *Dream* notebook. The notes on Homer and Shakespeare illustrate this practice. In the course of the 1930s, Beckett's excerpts became longer again, as Matthew Feldman demonstrates in his fascinating study on these Interwar Notes (Feldman 2006).

In the case of *Dream of Fair to Middling Women*, the processing of the notes was fairly direct. Many of the notes were incorporated in the text shortly after Beckett jotted them down in the *Dream* notebook (*RUL* MS 5000), edited and annotated by John Pilling (Pilling 1999). But later on, the transition between note taking and incorporation usually proceeded less directly. This indirect usage differs from Joyce's recycling of notes in his C-notebooks and notesheets. Beckett recollected his notes in various ways, ranging from recurrences of particular phrases in notebooks to quoting phrases from memory.[12]

Gradually, the number of explicit intertextual references in his writings subsided, but some phrases kept recurring throughout his career. Especially phrases from Dante's *Divina commedia* are among the most persistent intertextual figures. When Mercier asks Camier whether "lo bello stilo che m'ha fatto honore [sic]" is a quotation, the *h* in "honore" (in the manuscript of *Mercier et Camier*) indicates that Beckett is probably quoting from memory.

"I suppose all is reminiscence from womb to tomb"[13]

Another persistent line is the phrase "never been properly born," whose recurrence in Beckett's works is acutely examined by Davyd Melnyk (2005). The third of Carl Gustav Jung's lectures at the Tavistock Institute in London, which Beckett attended on 2 October 1935 (Knowlson 1996: 176) mentioned "a little girl of ten who had some amazing dreams": "Her father consulted me about these dreams. I could not tell him what I thought because they contained an uncanny prognosis. The little girl died a year later of an infectious disease. She had never been born entirely" (Jung 1966–79: 95–96). Melnyk convincingly demonstrates that "Beckett showed little sign of interest in the theories themselves, rewriting phrase and incident for his own very different purposes" (2005: 361). In *All That Fall*, Mrs. Rooney remembers "attending a lecture by one of these new mind doctors," more specifically his story of a little unhappy girl whom he was unable to treat successfully, concluding that, "The trouble with her was she had never really been born!" (*CDW* 195–96).

On 24 October 1968, in one of his conversations with Charles Juliet, Beckett recollected the story about this lecture, concluding: "Au fond, elle n'étais jamais née" (Juliet 1999: 15). And he added that he himself always had the feeling he had never been born either. In *Footfalls* (1975), "the old home" is mentioned, "the same where she- [*Pause.*] The same where she began. [*Pause.*] Where it began. [*Pause.*] It all began" (*CDW* 401). The hyphen is a self-interruption, as Beckett explained to actress Charlotte Joeres: "she was going to say . . . 'the same where she was *born*.' But that is wrong, she hasn't been born. She just began. It began. There is a difference. She was never born" (Knowlson and Pilling 1979: 222).

Against this background, a simple cancellation in one of the drafts of *Not I* appears to be a reenactment of this persistent phrase. In the five earliest versions of *Not I*, the text opens with "birth . . . into this world" (*RUL* MS 1227/7/12/1–5), until, in the sixth version, Beckett crossed out "birth" and replaced it by "out": . . . "~~birth~~ ^out^ . . into this world" (*RUL* MS 1227/7/12/6, f. 1r).

In the Addenda of *Watt*, the phrase "never been properly born" (248) appears without any context—again slightly distorted. Not unlike the parlor game "Russian Scandal," the sentence is never "properly" delivered.

The idea of never having been properly delivered recurs in many guises, and often it is to be understood in a physical sense. As Matthew Feldman points out (2005: 83), the recurrent motif of the hat in Beckett's text might be based on a note from Otto Rank's *Trauma of Birth*, which links the "modern hat" to the "embryonal caul" (*TCD* MS 1097/8/35). In both *Watt* and *Mercier et Camier*, the text explicitly mentions that the protagonists are sitting with their backs to the engine, which according to Otto Rank is to be linked to the "separation from the mother" as an explanation for many dreams of traveling. Among his notes on the *Trauma of Birth*, Beckett wrote: "disinclination of many persons to travel with their backs to the engine & *sortir les pieds en devant*" (*TCD* MS 10971/8/35). In the same vein, the eponymous hero in *The Expelled* appears to be trying to redo (or undo) his birth "properly" by leaving by the window, "head first," noting "the tufts of grass on which I pulled with both hands, in my effort to extricate myself" (*CSP* 59).

The title of S. E. Gontarski's book on Beckett's writing method, *The Intent of Undoing*, acquires an extra connotation against the backdrop of the Rank notes: "Whole circle of human creation equals an attempt to materialize primal situation, i.e., to undo primal trauma" (*TCD* MS 10971/8/35). But while manuscript research provides us with enough proof that Beckett read Rank, it is more difficult to assess his de- or appreciation of what he read. Even though he made a series of excerpts, his attitude toward the trauma of birth theory may have been quite ironic. A rare interjection in Beckett's notes certainly indicates Beckett's alertness to the jocose potential of this trauma theory, for instance when Rank writes about man's "inestimable advantage" over woman because he is able to go "back into the mother by means of the penis which stands—*ha! ha!*—for the child" (*TCD* MS 10971/8/35; emphasis added).

A similar attitude marks the Addenda of *Watt*. As Chris Ackerley points out, the Addenda are based on passages from the drafts that did not make it into the text: "they can neither be taken seriously nor yet be quite denied" (2005: 205). The most interesting aspect of the phrase "never been properly born" is that it occurs in the Addenda. By presenting the text of *Watt* in counterpoint with its *avant-texte*, Beckett indicates his concern about the fugal relationship between composition and decomposition.

Fuga Mortis

In his so-called "Super conquérant" notebook (*RUL* MS 2934), Beckett wrote on the inside of the cover: "fuire/poursuivre." This note corresponds to the line "Était-ce donc bien (. . .) le même qui (. . .) n'avait pas toujours échoué dans ses tentatives ~~de fuir et de~~ de fuite et de poursuite?"—written on a sheet of squared paper (*RUL* MS 2933/1 f. 2r, torn from a spiral notebook). The correspondence with the note "fuire/poursuivre" suggests that it may at one point have been the opening page of the spiral "Super conquérant" notebook.

The fugal structure that is hinted at in the manuscripts of *Stirrings Still* characterizes many of Beckett's texts, notably his script for *Film*, with O[bject] constantly being followed and watched by E[ye], only to eventually realize that all the time he has been chased by himself.

This fugal condition even applies to the level of the word, whenever Beckett brings his homophones into action. For instance, the "scene" in *Worstward Ho* where the skull is described as "the scene and seer of all" (Beckett 1992a: 112). With its iconic quality, the homophony resembles the object it denotes, the content of the skull. With the utmost economy of words, Beckett thus applies George Berkeley's dictum *esse est percipi* (to be is to be perceived) to human consciousness, which is constantly being watched by self-consciousness.

One of Beckett's favorite structures to analyze consciousness and self-consciousness is a variant of the fugue. The contrapuntal relationship between "self and second self his own" (*CSP* 261) is schematically represented in the tables of Arrivals and Departures, which Beckett drew up in notebook *HRHRC* Beckett 6.1 (f. 1v) to draft the opening scene of *Mercier et Camier*:

	A.	D.	A.	D.	A.	D.	A	
Mercier	9.5	9.10	9.25	9.30	9.40		9.45	9.50[14]
Camier	9.15	9.20	9.35	9.40	9.50			

On the facing recto, Beckett developed the fugue:

Camier arriva le premier au rendez-vous. C'est à dire qu'à son arrivée Mercier n'y était pas. En réalité Mercier l'avait devancé ~~d'un bon quart d'heure~~ ^de 10 bonnes minutes^. Ce fut donc Mercier, ~~qui arri~~ et non

Camier, qui arriva le premier au rendez-vous. Ayant patienté pendant [cin] ^dix^ ^5^ minutes, en [scrutant] les diverses voies d'accès que pourrait emprunter son ami, il partit faire un tour, qui dura un quart d'heure. Camier à son tour, ne voyant pas venir son camarade, partit au bout de [dix] cinq minutes faire un petit tour. (*HRHRC* Beckett 6.1, f. 2r)

The insistence on the word "tour" ("faire un tour [. . .] à son tour [. . .] faire un tour") echoes the second part of the original title: *Voyage de Mercier et Camier autour du pot dans les Bosquets de Bondy*. Implicitly, it also alludes to Leopold Bloom's journey in *Ulysses*, which Beckett contrasted with "Work in Progress" by focusing on teleology. In March 1937, he noted in his German Diaries that he suddenly realized

> how *Work in Progress* is the only possible development from *Ulysses*, the heroic attempt to [erasure] make literature accomplish what belongs to music—the miteinander & the simultaneous. *Ulysses* falsifies the unconscious, or the "monologue intérieur," in so far as it is obliged to express it as a teleology. (GD 26/3/37, Munich; Knowlson 1996: 258)

The "teleology" may refer to the concept of the Odyssean homecoming that underlies *Ulysses*. Mercier and Camier make a journey and return. The first sentence they exchange is: "Let us go home" (1974: 11). They meet "Helen" and spend a nice time with her, but they cannot stay: "Men less tenacious might not have withstood the temptation to leave it at that. But the following afternoon found them in the street again, with no other thought than the *goal* they had assigned themselves" (71; emphasis added). Unfortunately, the reader will never know what this goal is. At a certain moment, in a bar, they drink a toast,

> both saying, at the same instant or almost, Here's to you. Camier added, And to the success of our—. But this was a toast he could not complete. Help me, he said.
> I can think of no word, said Mercier, nor of any set of words, to express what we imagine we are trying to do. (83)

Somewhat later, while they are walking up and down a so-called "fatal alley," Camier asks Mercier: "Do you not know where we are going?" To which

Mercier replies: "What does it matter (. . .) where we are going? We are going, that's enough" (90).

The notion of "teleology," to which Beckett objected with regard to *Ulysses*, becomes highly problematic in *Mercier et Camier*. The original title of the voyage "autour du pot" already indicated the vicious circle that characterized the eponymous characters' voyage, thus clearly distinguishing it from other famous journeys, such as Dante's *Divina commedia*, which is frequently alluded to in *Mercier et Camier*.

Although Camier reminds Mercier of their agreement not to use quotations, Mercier asks Camier whether "lo bello stilo che m'ha fatto onore" is a quotation. Camier does not recognize it, but he replies that it certainly sounds like a quotation.[15] The line from Dante's *Inferno* refers to Virgil's style, which has brought him honor.

The style that brought Beckett honor is exemplified most succinctly in the homophony of the phrase "Nohow on," simultaneously indicating an impasse and implying the inexplicable urge and "know-how" to go on nonetheless. This stylistic feature reflects the content of Beckett's works in that it raises the key question why Beckett tends not to allow his characters to kill themselves whenever he puts them in a dead-end situation. Such a dead-end situation is presented as the only truly serious philosophical problem, according to Albert Camus in the opening sentences of *Le mythe de Sisyphe*: "Il n'y a qu'un problème philosophique vraiment sérieux: c'est le suicide" (1942: 17), that is, the question whether life is worth living or not. Not unlike Ulysses in the proximity of the Sirens, Beckett's characters are well aware of the constant threat of death, but at the same time they are attracted by it.

In *Mercier et Camier*, for instance, Mercier exclaims: "Oh but to cease!" (1974: 32), which is echoed in the last line of *Stirrings Still*: "Oh all to end" (*CSP* 265). And yet, Beckett does not grant his characters the chance to give in to that death wish. As his favorite philosopher argued in paragraph 69 of *The World as Will and Representation*, suicide "differs most widely from the denial of the will-to-live"; it is even "a phenomenon of the will's strong affirmation" (Schopenhauer 1969: 1: 398):

> The vehemence with which [the individual] wills life and revolts against what hinders it, namely suffering, brings it to the point of destroying itself, so that the individual will by an act of will eliminates the body that is merely the will's own becoming visible, rather than that suffering should break the will. Just because the suicide cannot cease willing, he ceases to live; and the will affirms itself here even

through the cessation of its own phenomenon, because it can no longer affirm itself otherwise. (1: 399)

Hence Schopenhauer's plea for the denial of the will, not by eliminating desire, but by enhancing the awareness that the will is an "unquenchable thirst" and by observing one's own "constant striving without aim and without rest" in a detached way, from a distance (1: 311–12).

Beckett's characters always somehow feel the need to go "on," which is probably the most important word in Beckett's writings. It is the most concise expression of his highly ambiguous attitude toward modernity's faith in Progress and the resulting movement for the sake of mere movement. Peter Sloterdijk called this the kinetic utopia of modernity, for which he chose the ateleological motto from Beckett's play *Endgame*: HAMM: "What's happening?"—CLOV: "Something is taking its course" (Beckett in Sloterdijk 1989: 266). From Beckett's point of view, "on" is not more positive than its reverse, "no." And "no" is not exclusively negative: it holds out the prospect of interrupting the empty movement for the sake of greater movement.

The homophony of "no" and "know" is repeatedly exploited by both Joyce and Beckett. While Joyce displays his knowledge in *Finnegans Wake*, Beckett closes *Ill Seen Ill Said* with "Know happiness" (Beckett 1992a: 97), and *Worstward Ho* with the words "Said nohow on" (1992a: 128). The homophony simultaneously creates and undoes the impasse. Even though Beckett claimed that the writing was over after *Nohow on*, he did know how on—which he proved by writing *Stirrings Still*.

The matter of the *Miteinander* and the simultaneous thus appears to be much more than a technical issue. The homophonous *Miteinander* of "no" and "know" summarizes the whole paradox: time and again Beckett's protagonists find themselves in a deadlock situation, and yet, time and again they somehow seem to "no" how to go on, nonetheless. The paradoxical simultaneity of these contradictory concepts hints at a central theme in Beckett's work: the inexplicable urge to go on, which Arthur Schopenhauer called the Will: "just as we know our walking to be only a constantly prevented falling, so is the life of our body only a constantly prevented dying, an ever-deferred death" (1969: 1: 311). This *fuga mortis*, as Schopenhauer calls it, "comes simply and solely from the blind *will*, with which every living thing is filled. But, as already mentioned, this *fuga mortis* is essential to it, just because it is the will-to-live, whose whole inner nature consists in a craving for life and existence" (2: 468).

Schopenhauer's *fuga mortis* principle crystallizes in Beckett's work. This work is not in progress in a teleological sense; nor is it a simple regress in terms of an undoing of the primal trauma, since that would imply a teleology as well. It is—not unlike *Finnegans Wake*—a circular journey, a never-ending "voyage (. . .) autour du pot."

Dante Notes and Figures of Script

When Beckett started writing the *Voyage de Mercier et Camier autour du pot dans les Bosquets de Bondy*, the "pot" around which he made his protagonists journey may have been less abstract than the French idiom suggests at first sight. During the war, Beckett had been writing *Watt*, including the fascinating passage about Watt finding himself "in the midst of things which, if they consented to be named, did so as it were with reluctance":

> Looking at a pot, for example, or thinking of a pot, at one of Mr. Knott's pots, of one of Mr. Knott's pots, it was in vain that Watt said, Pot, pot. Well, perhaps not quite in vain, but very nearly. For it was not a pot, the more he looked, the more he reflected, the more he felt sure of that, that it was not a pot at all. It resembled a pot, it was almost a pot, but it was not a pot of which one could say, Pot, pot, and be comforted. (1981 [1953]: 78)

This exercise in linguistic skepticism summarizes the difficulty that is formulated in Fritz Mauthner's introduction to his *Beiträge zu einer Kritik der Sprache*. Mauthner is fully aware of the paradoxical nature of his project and "die Selbsttäuschung, ein Buch zu schreiben gegen die Sprache" [Mauthner 1923: 1: 2] (the self-deception of writing a book against language). To utter his critique of language, he was forced to make use of language.

The linguistic skeptic inevitably became the subject of his own skepticism. "Experiments often test the experimenter more than the subject," J. G. Ballard notes in *The Atrocity Exhibition*: "One remembers the old joke about the laboratory rat who said: 'I have that scientist trained—every time I press this lever he gives me a pellet of food'" (2001: 36). Bruno Clément[16] has drawn attention to this situation (also formulated by Sartre as "L'expérimentateur fait partie du système expérimental") in connection with another passage from *Watt*, in which the figure (as a character) can be linked to the figure (of speech): "Watt was beginning to tire of running his eyes up and down this highway, when a figure, human apparently, advancing along its crown, arrested, and revived, his attention" (1981 [1953]: 224). The description of the figure corresponds with the way the figure of Watt himself is described on the opening pages of the novel, when the tram stops and subsequently moves on, "disclosing, on the pavement, motionless, a solitary figure, lit less and less by the receding lights, until it was scarcely to be distinguished from the dim wall behind it. Tetty was not sure whether it was a man or a woman" (14). One of the characteristics of the figure that appears toward the end of the novel is that "Watt was unable to say whether this figure was that of a man, or of a woman" (224). What follows is a long description that serves as a way to talk around the subject and almost literally "autour du pot," for on its head the figure is wearing "the likeness of a depressed inverted chamber-pot, yellow with age, to put it politely" (225). The pot as a hat serves as a strong image for Watt's "need of semantic succour" (Beckett 1981 [1953]: 79) and his efforts of "trying names on things, and on himself, almost as a woman hats" (80).

As an allusion to the first appearance of Virgil in canto 1 of Dante's *Divina commedia*, the passage on the "figure" arresting Watt's attention echoes a famous ambiguity that has puzzled several Dante scholars. The relevant passage reads:

Mentre ch'i' rovinava in basso loco,
dinanzi a li occhi mi si fu offerto
chi per lungo silenzio parea fioco. (canto 1, lines 85–87)

While I was fleeing to a lower place,
Before my eyes a figure showed,
Faint, in the wide silence. (Dante 2000: 7)

The line "chi per lungo silenzio parea fioco" can be interpreted in both a visual and an aural sense. The subject "chi" (one who) is a relative pronoun that can operate without a referent, which makes it a sort of linguistic equivalent of a reverse Schlemihl, a shadow without a man. The "one who" presents himself to Dante appears to be "fioco." Because this adjective is preceded by "per lungo silenzio" (from long silence), which suggests an aural impression, it is usually translated as "hoarse." But the previous line mentions explicitly that the figure appeared "to the eyes" ("a li occhi").

In their translation, based on Gino Casagrande's interpretation of this line, Robert and Jean Hollander choose the word "faint" to stress the visual aspect of the appearance. Robert Hollander concisely formulates the problem in his notes to the translation: "How can one *see* that a 'silence' is of long duration?" (Dante 2000: 18). According to Hollander, "*fioco* is to be taken as visual rather than aural; *silenzio* is understood as deriving from the Virgilian sense of the silence of the dead shades" (Dante 2000: 18).

Translation involves tough choices, and as such it may serve as a tool to throw a text's aporias into relief and show how the text proceeds in a similar way as the Unnamable: "By aporia pure and simple?" (Beckett 1955–58: 291). In "Dante and the Lobster," Beckett's fascination with such aporias is explicitly related to translation. When Belacqua mentions the "superb pun" in the line "qui vive la pietà quando è ben morta" (here piety lives when pity is quite dead), he asks the "charming and remarkable" Signorina Adriana Ottolenghi: "I wonder how you could translate that?" First, she says nothing, and after a while she murmurs: "Do you think (...) it is absolutely necessary to translate it?" (Beckett 1970b: 18). The counterquestion is left unanswered, and no attempt is made to translate the sentence. Yet, the fascination for the untranslatability of the homophone "pietà" in this "great phrase" (18) is a key to Beckett's later decision to translate his own texts. In his Dante notes in notebook *TCD MS 10966*, Beckett double-underlined the word "pietà" in his excerpt of Inferno, canto 4, line 21:

> *L'angoscia de le genti*
> *che son qua giù, nel viso mi dipigne*
> *quella* pietà *che tu per tema senti.* (*TCD MS 10966*, f. 7r)

When Dante and Virgil arrive at an abyss, the guide invites Dante to follow him. But Dante is somewhat alarmed because Virgil has suddenly gone pale. To reassure him, the guide explains that he is not pale because of fear but out of pity (*pieta*) on the patriarchs and pagans in Limbo. No matter how illustrious they may have been, their place is in hell because they are not baptized. Hence Beckett's note:

> Compassion legitimate in Limbo, but not among the damned proper .. "qui vive la pietà quando è ben morta." Furthermore, Virgil is referring to his companions, which he cannot do, even in the // Purgatory, without distress. Note also association of Dante's compassion with fear. (*TCD MS 10966*, f. 7r-7v)

Beckett refers to *Inferno*, canto 20, where it is no longer appropriate to feel the same pity with regard to the Soothsayers as with regard to the pagans and patriarchs in Limbo. Here (in the fourth Bolgia), the only way to give evidence of piety is to feel no pity for the justly condemned.

Ottolenghi's unanswered counterquestion of whether it is absolutely necessary to translate the superb pun, suggests the inevitability of failure. But instead of resignation, Beckett's attitude seems to be one of resolve to fail. Through the failure of translation, the full power of the aporia comes to the fore. The greatness of the phrase also hides in the "contresens" the superb pun potentially invites. Although the context clearly suggests the translation "here piety lives when pity is quite dead," the syntax does not exclude the reverse interpretation, "here pity lives when piety is quite dead." Why not feel pity even for the "justly" condemned? Or as Belacqua puts it: "Why not piety and pity both, even down below?" (Beckett 1970b: 20). Belacqua's attempt to translate the superb pun may be doomed to fail, but it is thanks to this failure that the composition turns out to contain its own decomposition.

The failure to translate the superb pun is an early indication of Beckett's "nohow" in terms of his writing method. Apart from the revelation, which "happened to me, summer 1945, in my mother's little house, named New Place" (Knowlson 1996: 772 n. 55), Beckett also mentioned a "Dante revelation." This important moment took place when Beckett was twenty years old, and his professors at Trinity College Dublin were not involved in it, as Beckett clearly pointed out: "This I seem to have managed on my own, with the help of my Italian teacher, Bianca Esposito" (Knowlson 1996: 715 n. 35).

The act of failing to translate has creative potential, and this potential becomes apparent in the passage where Virgil appears for the first time. The iconicity of this appearance may be regarded as a key in Beckett's Dante revelation. In his notes, Beckett shows he is fully aware of the problem:

> *chi per lungo silenzio parea fioco* But V. had not yet spoken. Difficulty not overcome by taking *per lungo silenzio* with *parea* & not with *fioco*, since Dante calls to him as soon as he sees him & is immediately answered. (*TCD* MS 10966, f. 1r)

Beckett's "nohow" consisted in exploiting the creative potential of this iconic moment. The text performs its content: since Virgil only appears as a set of words, his visual appearance coincides with the aural impression. In the "figure" scene in *Watt* mentioned above, the link between the visual image and the figure of speech becomes explicit in the interjected sentence: "Watt felt them suddenly glow in the dark place, and go out, the words, *The only cure is diet*" (Beckett 1981 [1953]: 225).[17]

The dark place may be another reference to the "selva oscura" in *Inferno*, canto 1, which Beckett summarized as follows in his notebook:

> Dante, wandering aimlessly / in a dark wood, comes to / the foot of a steep hill / and commences to climb it./

> But his path is barred by / three wild beasts, a panther, / a lion and a wolf. The / poet is compelled to return / to the wood, where he meets / Virgil, who promises to save / him from the present danger, / to lead him through Inferno, / and then to entrust him to / the charge of Beatrice if he / would ascend through / Purgatory to Paradise. Dante / follows him. (*TCD* MS 10963, f. 2r)

This summary is followed by the "Allegory of Canto I," based—as Daniella Caselli has demonstrated—on the popular Salani edition (Firenze), edited with comments by Enrico Bianchi. The first item listed under the title "Allegory of Canto I" explains what the dark wood stands for:

> *Selva Oscura* Morally, vice and sin; it is "oscura" because it clogs and overcasts the mind. (*TCD* MS 10963, f. 2r–3r)

The list of items under the title "Allegory of Canto I" is based on Bianchi's notes. These notes do not contain a separate entry for "Virgilio," yet Beckett does include him in his list:

> *Virgilio* Reason, which had / been dead & dumb in / Dante for so long that / 'per lungo silenzio parea fioco.' (*TCD* MS 10963, f. 3r)

Beckett does not translate the crucial phrase, which was to recur so frequently in his work later on. In *Le Calmant/The Calmative* (1946), Beckett applies the phrase to the narrator, who tries to speak to a young boy, opens his mouth, but only hears "speechlessness due to long silence, as in the wood that darkens the mouth of hell" (1995: 66). The "rattle" he utters is "unintelligible even to me who knew what was intended" (62).

The explicit mention of authorial intention in connection with the unintelligible result may be related to Beckett's line "Qu'importe qui parle"/ "What matter who's speaking," which Michel Foucault quoted in the opening paragraph of his essay "Qu'est-ce qu'un auteur?": "In this indifference appears one of the fundamental ethical principles of contemporary writing (*écriture*)." (141) Whether Beckett's phrase expresses "indifference" toward the notion of authorial intention, as Foucault suggests, is not unequivocal. It is paradoxically necessary to find out who is speaking in order to be able to examine whether it matters or not. The phrase "chi per lungo silenzio parea fioco" applies to Virgil. But as Beckett rightly noted in his copybook, "V. had not yet spoken," and yet his figure is "fioco" from long silence. A few lines further on, Dante recognizes Virgil as his "master" and his "author":

> Tu se' lo mio maestro e 'l mio autore;
> tu se' solo colui da cu' io tolsi
> lo bello stilo che m'ha fatto onore.
>
> (*Inferno*, canto 1: 85–87)

The "bello stilo" makes its first appearance as an isolated *figure de style* on a verso page in the French draft of *Mercier et Camier*: "Lo bello stilo che m'a ^m'ha^ fatto onore / pas de citations" (*HRHRC* SB 6.1, f. 40v). Beckett encircled this loose jotting, but it took him another thirty-six pages to incorporate it into the text:

> Tu n'ignores pas cependant ce que nous avons arrêté à ce sujet: pas de récits de rêves, sous aucun prétexte. (. . .) Un principe analogue nous interdit les citations.
> Lo bello stilo che m'ha fatto honore[sic], dit Mercier. Est-ce une citation.
> Lo bello comment? dit Camier.
> Lo bello stilo che m'ha fatto honore[sic], dit Mercier.
> Comment veux-tu que je sache? dit Camier. Ça m'en a tout l'air. En cas de doute, abstenir. Pourquoi. (. . .)
> Ce sont des mots qui me bruissent dans la tête depuis hier, dit Mercier, et me brûlent les lèvres.
> C'est certainement une réminiscence d'*un texte quelconque* dit Camier. Il s'en faut de peu que je ne sois complètement dégoûté. Nous prenons certaines précautions, afin d'être le mieux possible, le moins mal possible, et c'est exactement comme si on fonçait à la légère, la tête baissée. Il se leva. (*HRHRC* SB 6.1, f. 76r-77r; cf. Beckett 1970a: 99–100; emphasis added)

This version comes close to the published text, but the sentence "C'est certainement une réminiscence d'un texte quelconque" was omitted during the writing process. In the first version, the *Divina commedia* is presented as a random text ("un texte quelconque"), which it clearly was not in Beckett's case. Dante has been such an important guide throughout Beckett's career that the elimination of this passage in the English translation is not inconsiderable:

> And yet you know our covenant: no communication on dreams on any account. The same holds for quotes. No dreams or quotes at any price. He got up. (1974: 61–62)

In the English version, the "réminiscence d'un texte quelconque" is omitted; the intertextual recollection is effectively decomposed.

As Daniela Caselli has convincingly argued, "Virgil's role as an *auctoritas* within Dante's text fashions Dante as an *auctoritas* within Beckett's text" (2005: 113–14). By means of the quotation's omission in the English version "the relationship between the two texts is under the author's control. Camier's words comment on the absence of Dante while reinforcing the presence of the author" (115).

This inscription and deletion of authorities implies the "maestro" is in the vicinity whenever the "fioco" phrase recurs in Beckett's works. In *Comment c'est/How It Is* (1961), the "fioco" phrase is applied to Pim, whose words the narrator tries to discern; he wonders "what he has said" or what he has heard "of that voice ruined from such long silence," "cette voix ruinée de s'être si longtemps tue" (2001: 118–19).

Beckett applied the "fioco" phrase not only to his characters or narrators, but also to himself as an "autore"—and implicitly also as a "maestro." After completing *Fin de partie*, he wrote to Nancy Cunard on 6 June 1956: "have just succeeded in grinding out of my gritty old maw 'per lungo silenzio . . . fioco' the one-act howl for Marseille and am not a pretty sight as a result" (Beckett in Knowlson 1996: 426). The ellipsis is telling, for the omitted "parea" is the missing link that relates the aural to the visual appearance. It is also a crucial element in the description of the figure in *Watt*, linking it to the opening sentence of Schopenhauer's magnum opus—"Die Welt ist meine Vorstellung":

> He did not know why he cared, what it was, coming along the road. (. . .) It seemed to him that, quite apart from any question of personal feeling of grief or satisfaction, it was greatly to be deplored, that he cared what it was, coming along the road, profoundly to be deplored. (. . .) For Watt's concern, deep as it appeared, was not after all with what the figure was, in reality, but with what the figure appeared to be, in reality. (Beckett 1981 [1953]: 225–26)

Watt's wondering "why he cared, what it was, coming along the road" can inform a study of the dynamics of the writing process. In connection with Virgil's appearance in *Inferno*, Watt's concern with what the figure "appeared to be" emphasizes the importance of the verb "parea" ("chi per lungo silenzio *parea* fioco") that enables the mixture of the visual and the aural "appearance." This combination is a key element in Beckett's writing method, and culminates in Beckett's penultimate work, *Stirrings Still*. After having found the first sentence, he wrote to Avigdor and Anne Arikha (27 April 1984) that in spite of his "expiring cells," he was writing a last attempt to eff the "ineffable departure":

> A last chance at last, I'll try. "From where he sat with his head in his hands he saw himself rise and disappear." Ineffable departure. Nothing left but try—eff it. (Beckett in Knowlson 1996: 697)

In the early drafts of this work's first section, the protagonist "sees himself rise & go" (*RUL* MS 2934, f. 1r). This appearance is repeated:

> So slow that only change of place to show he went. As when he *disappeared* only to *reappear* again ~~at another place~~ later at another place. x Then *disappeared* again only to *reappear* again later at another place ~~again~~ ^again^. So again & again *disappeared* disappeared again only to *reappear* again at another place ^again^. (RUL MS 2934, f. 4r; emphasis added)

Not unlike the figure that suddenly appears in *Watt* (224ff.) this "second self his own" (*RUL* MS 2935, f. 5r) always seems to remain at the same remove. In *Watt*, this peculiarity is a cause of puzzlement:

> What so agitated Watt was this, that in the ten minutes or half an hour that had elapsed, since he first became aware of this figure, striding along, on the crest of the road, towards the station, the figure had gained nothing in height, in breadth or in distinctness. Pressing forward all this time, with no abatement of its foundered precipitation, towards the station, it had made no more headway, than if it had been a millstone. (227)

And then "the figure, without any interruption of its motions, grew fainter and fainter, and finally disappeared," (227), as "fioco" as Virgil appeared to Dante.

The issue of the unvarying distance was the first impulse to write *Stirrings Still*. The first line of the first (eventually abandoned section) reads: "Tout ~~tout le temps~~ ^toujours^ à la même distance comme c'est comment dire?" (*RUL* MS 2933/1, f. 1r). On the same page, Beckett also wrote an English version: "All always at the same remove (. . .)" (*RUL* MS 2933/1, f. 1r). This sentence indicates to what degree Virgil's appearance has left its mark on Beckett's writing. The appearance of the figure becomes more than a figure of speech; it becomes a figure of script.

This figure of script can function as a way of getting started and overcoming the intimidation of the white page. On another white page, Beckett started again with the same figure of script, this time in English: "All ^always^ at the same remove" (*RUL* MS 2933/1, f. 2r). After the first paragraph in English, Beckett continued, or started again, in French: "Revenu à lui ^ou^ à ce ~~qui passait~~ ^qui jadis avait passé^ pour tel (...) son premier mouvement fut de se demander s'il l'était vraiment." The figure of script appears as a form of recovering consciousness, coming to one's senses; it appears as "*Virgilio*," i.e. "Reason, which had / been dead & dumb in / Dante for so long that / 'per lungo silenzio parea fioco'" (*TCD* MS 10963: 3r).

As an important element in Beckett's 1926 "Dante revelation," the appearance of Virgil's figure as the emergence of Reason from dumbness has had a lasting impact on Beckett's writing method. Its ambiguous combination of aural and visual impressions proved to be a creative impulse for more than half a century.

The last appearance of the "fioco" passage occurs in Beckett's "Super conquérant" copybook (*RUL* MS 2934, f. 9v). In the final section of *Stirrings Still*, the attempt to "eff" the "ineffable departure" is thematized by means of a figure of script. A sentence "from deep within" makes its appearance to the protagonist, but he is unable to catch the crucial word: "So on till stayed when to his ears from deep within oh how and here a word he could not catch it were to end where never till then" (*CSP* 264). After a pause, the sentence recurs. Again the protagonist fails to catch the crucial word because the verbal figure is too "faint." The word "faint" is deleted in the fifth draft, on a recto page (10r) in the "Super conquérant" notebook. On the facing verso, Virgil's appearance becomes a figure of script: Beckett writes down the Italian phrase "per lungo silenzio fioco" and subsequently translates it. An open variant marks the translator's hesitation: "faint / hoarse from long silence" (*RUL* MS 2934, f. 9v). He adds "hoarse from long silence" to the text on the recto, but eventually crosses it out and decides to replace it by "faint" again (without the specification "from long silence"):

Stirrings Still Section 3, Version 05 (MS 2934 f. 10r)

Pause then as time ~~dragged on~~ ^went by^ from ~~next to none [before] again~~ not long till again to so long that perhaps never again and then again ~~[faint]~~ ^hoarse from long silence^ ^faint^ from far within oh how & here again that missing word it were to end where never till then. ~~But though [but] is not the word but where then as he stood there all bowed down and to his ears from far within again & again how something it would be~~ ^were^ ~~to end where never till then where~~

~~then ^already^ if not ^[xx]^ where never till then. This [boundless] void waste~~

The "boundless void" or "waste" is already too explicit. Beckett goes as far as he can, but as soon as he starts attaching empty labels to the "unthinkable" beyond, he calls himself back. All he can say is that the protagonist has never been there, and the word to eff the ineffable departure is "missing."

"Further One Cannot"

The figure of script can be a persistent intertextual reference or—as Mercier put it—"des mots qui me bruissent dans la tête (...) et me brûlent les lèvres" (Beckett 1970a: 99–100). But it can also be a phrase that captures a strong image, a form of realization or "coming to," as Beckett called it in his late text *Ceiling*. In the early versions of this text (written in 1981), Beckett already started from the idea of "coming to": "~~On coming to himself his first sight was of white~~" (*HRHRC* Lake 17.1, f. 1r). This is the closest the manuscripts allow us to approach the moment of creative initiative. Beckett allows the words to perform the act of coming to. The verbal figure—in the form of this single sentence—appears in much the same way as Virgil did: "Reason" appears and is confronted with the whiteness of the ceiling, the way the figure of script encounters the whiteness of the page. After its first appearance, the isolated sentence is crossed out and thus vanishes, "only to reappear again later at another place again." This time the sentence creates the momentum for a more sustained writing session: "On ^his^ coming to ~~himself~~ ^~~himself~~^ his first ^sight^ was of white." The explicit mention of "himself" is first deleted, then added again above the line, and eventually crossed out yet again. Apparently this figure of script seemed a viable incipit, and a comment urges the writer to elaborate on it: "~~Thus the germ.~~ ^Develop^." In the next line, the germ is indeed developed:

> Some time after ^his^ coming to ^~~himself~~^ his first sight was of ~~dim~~ ^dull^ white.
> For some time after his coming to his eyes remained closed. When finally they opened they were met by ^this^ ~~dim~~ ^dull^ white. (*HRHRC* Lake 17.1, f. 1r)

After a dozen lines, the elements are summed up: "Here so far four. ~~One~~ the coming to. ~~Two~~ the consciousness thereof. ~~Three~~ the eyes. ~~Four~~ the white." With these elements, Beckett develops the germ. The reflexive nature of number two is specified and described by means of the adjective that originally qualified the whiteness: "dim consciousness of dim consciousness" (*HRHRC* Lake 17.1, f. 1r). On page 3v, this "dim consciousness" is described as follows:

> Dim consciousness at first alone. Of mind alone come partly to. T̶h̶e̶n̶ ^Till^ at the sight of this [d̶i̶m̶ ̶w̶h̶a̶t̶] dim white of body too. Of body to come partly too. When the eyes forbidden opened. Partly opened. Feebly forbidden partly opened to this dull white. *Further one cannot.*
> *On.*
> Forbidden yes but bidden to. By this dull white. Then worse come the body to. Partly to. When the eyes u̶n̶b̶i̶d̶ forbidden opened. Partly opened. Feebly forbidden partly opened. Bidden by this dull white. *Further one -*
> *On.*
> Something then of some mind come to. Of some body come to. [S̶o̶m̶e̶h̶o̶] Somewhere to. Somehow to. Some why to. First consciousness alone. Dim consciousness. Of dim consciousness. Then eyes [u̶n̶b̶i̶] unbidden opened. Forbidden opened. Feebly forbidden half ^partly^ opened. Bidden by this dull white. To this dull white. *Further -*
> *On.*
> A̶ ̶p̶^P^atch of ceiling. D̶u̶l̶l̶e̶d̶ ̶b̶y̶ ̶e̶n̶d̶l̶e̶s̶s̶ ^Dull with endless^ breath. Endless ending breath. [B̶i̶d̶d̶i̶n̶g̶ ̶o̶p̶e̶n̶.̶ ̶G̶e̶n̶t̶l̶y̶ ̶b̶i̶d̶d̶i̶n̶g̶] For that last l̶o̶o̶k̶.̶ sight. Last best of sights. (*HRHRC* Lake 17.1, f. 3v; emphasis added)

The paradox of composing by means of decomposing is concisely formulated in the sequence of paragraph endings:

> Further one cannot.
> On.
> Further one -
> On.
> Further -
> On.

With this structure, Beckett found a way of saying "This is the worst" and taking it back. Even the attempt to unsay Shakespeare's line from *King Lear*– "The worst is not / So long as one can say, This is the worst"—inevitably proved to confirm it. Taking back one's words can be a form of going on.

Ruby Cohn points out that the writing process of *Ceiling* was preceded by a short poetic jotting: "*Ceiling* / lid eye bid / bye bye" (dated 9 April 1981). This jotting can be found on folio 15r of the so-called Sottisier notebook (*RUL* MS 2901), and is preceded by another English *mirlitonnade* on the facing verso: "There / the life late led / down there / all done unsaid / 23.3.81" (*RUL* MS 2901, f. 14v). By unsaying his own words "one cannot" in *Ceiling* Beckett was able to go "on" and "further." He also applied this method of unsaying to other people's words, in this case to the line "Where is the life that late I led? (Petruchio IV.1)" from Shakespeare's *The Taming of the Shrew*, which Beckett jotted down on the same page.

In another notebook (*RUL* MS 2934), Beckett unsaid Shakespeare in a different way. Apart from the early drafts of *Stirrings Still*, this notebook also contains a few abandoned dramatic fragments. One of the fragments is a dialogue about the last words of Shakespeare's sonnet CXVI:

> ~~I remember the last wo~~
> The last words come back to me
> ~~What?~~ What were they?
> ~~"Ever loved."~~ ". . . ever loved."
>
> (*RUL* MS 2934, f. 1v)

On the facing recto, an early version of *Stirrings Still* is followed by another dialogue, this time about the opening lines of two Shakespeare sonnets: Sonnet LXXI ("No longer mourn for me when I am dead") and Sonnet CXVI ("Let me not to the marriage of true minds / Admit impediments (. . .) If this be error and upon me proved, / I never writ, nor no man ever loved"). Shakespeare's *auctoritas* is first invoked and subsequently unsaid by crossing out his name:

> Where are you?
> Here. (P.) At the window. (P.) The snow has ceased.
> The what?
> The snow.
> P.
> Come & read to me.
> What?
> That ~~Shakespeare~~ sonnet we ~~once so~~ ^used to^ ~~loved~~.

The first fragment describes the act of (at least partially) successful recollection. In the second fragment, composition is a form of decomposition, in which the failing recollection becomes thematic:

> Yes. 'Let me not to -' How did it go on? (. . .)
> P.
> I ~~can't remember.~~ ^have forgotten.^
> We used to know it by heart. One would say the first quatrain, then the other the second. Then the one the ~~first . . . what do you call it.~~ third. Then the other the geegee (*RUL* MS 2934, f. 2r)

"Fuck the Author"

A recollection of the "last words" in combination with "undoing" the author is the core of the undated, unpublished fragment "Last Soliloquy" (*RUL* MS 2937/1–3).[18] The fragment is presented as a dialogue between an actor *A* and a prompter *P*, who constantly has to draw *A*'s attention to what the way he is supposed to perform his last soliloquy and the final act of committing suicide ("I have done. [. . .] All man can. Save with myself away.") by drinking a goblet with the "fatal potion": "You enter with the goblet in your hand, say your piece, (quaff,) ~~collapse~~ drop dead." *A* immediately starts swooning, to which *P* reacts:

> P. Too soon. You swoon too soon. Can't swoon here. Not ripe.
> A. And if I did? (. . .) Who'd ~~be the wiser~~ ^know^?
> P. The author.
> A. Fuck the author. Fuck all authors. (*RUL* MS 2937/2r)

Apart from the religious connotations—the author as a god forbidding man to leave the vale of tears before his time—the self-reflexive element in this dialogue is interesting as well. The immediate context suggests that *A* stands for Actor, but Author might be another possibility, as in Beckett's suggestion to Joseph Chaikin for the staging of *Textes pour rien*. When Chaikin asked permission to stage these texts in 1980, Beckett advised him to concentrate on just one of the thirteen texts and start as follows: "Curtain up on speechless author (A)" (Beckett in Gontarski 1995: xvi). The author only starts speaking when he is prompted by "voice (V)," which could be *A*'s voice, but "not necessarily." In a letter to Chaikin, Beckett explained: "The idea was to caricature the labour of composition" (Beckett in Gontarski 1995: xvi). The idea of an author needing a prompting *V* in order to put something into words is an instantiation of the figure of script, an aural equivalent to the appearance of Virgil as a set of words, as a *V* that is both faint and hoarse from long silence.

This prompting appearance is a persistent theme in Beckett's works, and yet it is the most difficult moment to pinpoint in the reconstruction of a composition process, if it is a moment at all—for usually it is a coincidence of circumstances, accidental readings, etc. By donating many of his manuscripts to university libraries, Beckett has created the conditions for his readers to "take a peep behind the scenes" (Poe 1986: 481). In this respect, he is on the same wavelength as Edgar Allan Poe, who writes in his "Philosophy of Composition":

> Most writers—poets in especial—prefer having it understood that they compose by a species of fine frenzy—an ecstatic intuition—and would positively shudder at letting the public take a peep behind the scenes, at the elaborate and vacillating crudities of thought—at the true purposes seized only at the last moment—at the innumerable glimpses of idea that arrived not at the maturity of full view—at the fully matured fancies discarded in despair as unmanageable—at the cautious selections and rejections—at the painful erasures and interpolations—in a word, at the wheels and pinions—the tackle for scene-shifting—the step-ladders and demon-traps—the cock's feathers, the red paint and the black patches, which, in ninety-nine cases out of the hundred, constitute the properties of the literary *histrio*. (1986: 481)

But before Poe starts analyzing the composition of his own poem "The Raven," he writes: "Let us dismiss, as irrelevant to the poem, *per se*, the circumstance—or say the necessity—which, in the first place, gave rise to the intention of composing a poem" (482).

Nonetheless, this moment of the "necessity" has been one of Beckett's major preoccupations throughout his career. If there is "nothing to express," the question where the so-called "obligation to express" comes from becomes all the more pressing. As an author, Poe advised to dismiss the necessity that prompted the act of composing, but in Beckett's case it was the author himself who never stopped looking for the sources of this necessity. He did not have or give an explanation for this necessity, but he did have an image for it, which he had found in Dante's *Inferno* when he had his "Dante revelation," just before the start of his career as a writer. This image takes up a central place in Beckett's bilingual works because of the untranslatable coincidence of the visual appearance and the aural impression. It is not simply important as a trace of a particular source text, but especially as a trace of the way Beckett visualized the more general and more fundamental "necessity—which, in the first place, gave rise to the intention" not just "of composing a poem" but of decomposing *tout court*, that is, of finding a way to accommodate decomposition in his composition.

9

Decomposition: L, M, S

The task of finding a form that could accommodate chaos is defined by Evelyne Grossman as "[é]crire la décomposition pour se fondre enfin dans la poussière des mots" (1998: 46). The "dust of the words" is more or less what Beckett entered in the margin of the bilingual (English/German) edition of *Eh Joe* used by Rick Cluchey: "Den[n] du bist Erde und sollst zu Erde werden (Luther)" (*RUL* MS 3626),[1] related to the line "Mud thou art." The German equivalent, "Dreck bist du," is followed by a note indicating the source: "Genesis III 19" (*RUL* MS 3626). The King James Version of the Bible reads: "for dust thou art, and unto dust shalt thou return." The semantic complex of "dust," "mud," and "Dreck" (including the connotation of excrements à la Shem the Penman) is Beckett's version of the stuff that men are made of. By means of a small change to this key motto (*memento, homo, quia pulvis es, et in pulverem reverteris*) used on Ash Wednesday to remind Christians of their mortality, Beckett draws attention to the creative potential of decomposition.

LARGE: "World Stuff"

The question of creation, which is so central in Beckett's work, is related not only to Genesis, but also to the key issue of pre-Socratic philosophy. As the early philosophy notes on the pre-Socratics[2] illustrate, Beckett's "work in regress" started from the big picture: the "cosmic matter," or the "Weltstoff," as Wilhelm Windelband called it: "Fundamental question of science: *What is the Weltstoff?* That this single cosmic matter lies at the basis of the entire process of nature was a self-evident presupposition of Ionic School" (*TCD* MS 10967/5). Among the ideas of one of these Ionic philosophers, Beckett found a variation on the "dust thou art" motif by Anaximander: "All things must in equity again decline into that whence they have their origin" (*TCD* MS 10967/7). The "world stuff" (10967/9), according to Anaximander, was "infinity": "Character of 'infinity' formulated by Anaximander as indispensable to weltstoff, as a finite weltstoff would exhaust itself in ceaseless succession of productions" (10967/7). This ceaseless process was crucial in Heraclitus's idea of the "world stuff": "not substance or matter, but motion, the cosmic process, *Becoming* itself" (10967/24v).

The lasting effect of these ideas on Beckett's career as a writer would become apparent a half century later when he wrote the short text *The Way* (1981), consisting of two sections, respectively preceded by a Möbius strip or infinity sign in two different positions (8 ∞):

> The way wound up from foot to top and thence on down another way. On back down. The ways crossed midway more and less. (...) the one way back was on an on was always back.

To the first draft, Beckett has added the note: "The two ways were one way" (HRHRC), which reads as an echo of an aphorism by Heraclitus, paraphrased by John Burnet (*Greek Philosophy, Part I: Thales to Plato*, 1914) and excerpted by Beckett in his philosophy notes: "The 'way up' (earth - water - fire) and 'way down' (fire - water - earth) are one and the same" (TCD MS 10967/26v).[3] Beckett's fascination for the "primacy of flux" (10967/24r) would make him another "proustite," or worshipper of the "Great God Flux," according to Wyndham Lewis.

Beckett's interest in the pre-Socratics is undoubtedly related to their quest for the *Weltstoff*, but it is important to note his interest in the philosophers who combined different substances and had a more complex idea of the primal matter. The problem with the early pre-Socratics' philosophical methods is their reductive approach. Gradually the pre-Socratics realized that the world's genesis could not be reduced to a single primal substance. By analogy, the Beckettian universe cannot be reduced to a basic set of source texts, and genetic criticism is not limited to source hunting. Beckett has collected, recollected, and combined these notes with other reading notes, and in order to study the dynamics of the writing process, it is not enough to follow it upstream to discover a few sources; it is also necessary to follow the "flux" downstream.

The pre-Socratics reappear in 1935 in a set of notes on the *Trauma of Birth* by Otto Rank—another thinker who tended to reduce the complexity of the (psychic) world to one single source. Rank suggests that human creativity, for instance in the form of literature, is an attempt to undo the original situation or "primal trauma" ("die Ursituation, d.h. zur Rückgängigmachung des Urtraumas"; Rank 1924: 99; *TCD* MS 10971/8/35). In his chapter on "philosophical speculation" Rank links this primal situation to pre-Socratic philosophy: "Die griechische Philosophie beginnt bekanntlich mit dem Satz des Thales, dass das Wasser der Ursprung und *Mutterschoss* aller Dinge sei" (161; emphasis added). Rank does not speak of a *Weltstoff* but reduces everything to the womb. Beckett ignores most of what Rank writes about pre-Socratic philosophy, but he does make a note on the philosopher who marked the end of this period in the history of philosophy. According to Otto Rank, "Socrates (...) was the first who succeeded in intellectually overcoming the birth trauma," and Beckett added: "had to pay the price by drinking hemlock" (*TCD* MS 10971/8/35). Hemlock is one of the herbs in the ditch into which Watt rolls himself before arriving at the house of Mr Knott. Watt is feeling weak, sits down on the path, and rolls himself over into the ditch, in which he originally (in the early drafts) encountered a mysterious sign.[4] Watt reads it from the bottom backwards. The warning "Danger this ditch is poisoned" is no longer present in the published version of the text, but Watt's face is buried in the hyssop (referring to Christ on the cross) and poisonous hemlock (referring to Socrates' death by poison):

> he rolled himself over into the ditch, and lay there, on his face, half buried in the wild long grass, the foxgloves, the hyssop, the pretty nettles, the high pounting *hemlock*, and other ditch weeds and flowers. (Beckett 1953a: 32; emphasis added)

The way Beckett recollects his notes and subsequently decomposes them is nicely illustrated in this passage. The reference to the poisonous hemlock that Socrates had to drink is recollected here, and later on decomposed to be used again at another instance, for example when the goblet with the fatal potion is mentioned in the fragment "Last Soliloquy" (*RUL* MS 2937/1-3). The recollection coincides with other intertextual recollections, because the reference to Socrates' poisoning by hemlock is at the same time an allusion to Goethe's Faust, who tries to kill himself by drinking a goblet containing poison.

Beckett read Goethe's *Faust* in August and September 1936 and recorded excerpts of it in two notebooks (*RUL* MS 5004 and 5005). These excerpts are interesting with regard to the question of why Beckett usually does not allow his characters to commit suicide (cf. chapter 8). For instance, Beckett excerpted a series of lines from the night scene, when Faust is on the verge of committing suicide, greeting the phial ("Ich grüsse dich, du einzige Phiole") filled with poison ("Du Inbegriff der holden Schlummersäfte, / Du Auszug aller tödlich feinen Kräfte"):

Ich sehe dich, es wird der Schmerz gelindert,
Ich fasse dich, das Streben wird gemindert

(Goethe 1986: 1: 696–97; *RUL* MS 5004, f. 30r)

When he puts the bowl to his lips, the Easter bells and choral songs prevent him from drinking the poison. Beckett did not excerpt any line from this mixed choir, but confined himself to the concluding one-liner: "Die Träne quillt, die Erde hat mich wieder!" (I.784; *RUL* MS 5004, f. 30r).

In *Watt*, this scene is alluded to when Watt, immediately after the passage with the hemlock in the ditch, hears a mixed choir:

And it was to him lying thus that there came, with great distinctness, from afar, from without, yes, really it seemed from without, the voices, indifferent in quality, of a *mixed choir* (1981 [1953]: 32; emphasis added)

The subsequent canon for four voices starts with the subject and countersubjects greatgranma, granma, mama, Miss Magrew, and the contrapuntal states of blooming, withering, drooping, forgotten. Two hundred pages further on, during his "coenaesthetic" experience "without thought or sensation" on the seat in the railway station, Watt hears "in his skull the voices whispering their canon (. . .) like a patter of mice, a flurry of little grey paws in the *dust*" (1981 [1953]: 231; emphasis added). In the Addenda, at the back of the novel, Faust's "die Erde hat mich wieder" is distorted into "die Merde hat mich wieder" (251)—again insisting on the link between dust, mud and "Dreck."

In this context, one of the variants between the Grove and Calder editions (in the "figure" passage discussed in chapter 8) suddenly becomes more than just a meaningless textual departure:

He did not know whether *this* was a good thing, or a bad thing (1953a [Grove]: 226; emphasis added)

He did not know whether *shit* was a good thing, or a bad thing (1981 [Calder]: 225; emphasis added)

Whether good or bad, the "shit" in this passage draws attention to the textual dimension of the figure's appearance.[5] The word "shit" is a textual variant. The Grove text simply reads: "whether this was a good thing." As Chris

Ackerley notes, "This was changed without comment by Beckett when he prepared that text for the French translation" (2005: 194). Watt's concern, "not after all with what the figure was, in reality, but with what the figure appeared to be, in reality," applies to this passage's textual appearance as well. A small variant is enough to indicate that the relevance of multiple versions in Beckett's writings is not restricted to matters of editorial concern, but has an existential dimension as the palpable appearance of this "beschissenes Dasein," to quote the closing lines of one of Beckett's earliest publications, "Sedendo et Quiescendo" (March 1932):

> Hello. Great to be here. Grand to be here. Same old Wohnung. Wonderful to be here. Prosit. God bless. Lav on the left. Won't be a sec. Mind the bike. Mind the skis. Beschissenes Dasein beschissenes Dasein Augenblick bitte beschissenes Dasein Augenblickchen bitte beschissenes. (*CSP* 16)

The textual turd ("this/shit") draws attention to the inevitability of textual variance. Whether "shit" is a good thing or a bad thing, it is just as undeniably "there" as the "small heart-shaped plastic pot" in the manuscripts of *Stirrings Still* is "there," even though it was omitted at a later stage of the writing process—"For improbable as he may be he is not so improbable as not to must needs from time to time relieve himself" (*RUL* MS 2935-1-2, f. 1r). The idea of "must needs" puts the oft-quoted line from the *Three Dialogues with Georges Duthuit* about the "obligation to express"[6] into perspective. By emphasizing the excremental aspect of writing, Beckett places his work in a long tradition, which notably finds its (Latin) expression in Joyce's chapter on Shem the Penman (*FW* 185; see chapter 6). The irreverent attitude toward both life and letters reflects Beckett's wish to find a form to accommodate the "wordshit" uttered by the "head and its anus, the mouth" (*CSP* 137; 141).

Beckett's reading of some of the great masters shows a remarkable pattern. It is generally strikingly disciplined and the reading notes are quite extensive, but when the finale is in sight, the excerpts start showing signs of rebellion and are suddenly interrupted. While Joyce's system of decomposition for the purpose of subsequent recombination roughly corresponds with the distinction between exo- and endogenetics, this analogy would be too neat in Beckett's case, for the decomposition already takes place during the recollection. For instance, as soon as Beckett approached the goal of the teleological progress in Dante's *Divina commedia*, he stopped reading. In canto 25 of *Paradiso*, when St. James gives Dante a viva on Hope, Beckett laconically notes he is "sorry to notice that our poet sucks up to the examiner in a most disgusting fashion" (*TCD* MS 10964: 19). In the next canto, Dante "again sucks up to the examiner" (*TCD* MS 10964: 20), and in canto 28, Beckett loses his patience: "[Don't understand a word of this]" (*TCD* MS 10964: 22). After carefully summarizing ninety-four cantos and following the teleological narrative that urged him to experience the climax and go on, Beckett preferred not to.

A similar scenario recurred ten years later, when Beckett was reading Goethe's *Faust*.[7] He excerpted extensive passages from Robert Petsch's editorial introduction, notably a section about the mother of all *M*s, the "Meaning of Life": "Dieser Sinn aber ist für Goethe kein anderer als der des unablässigen Tätigseins u. Tüchtigseins, d.h. des Vorwärtsstrebens" (According to Goethe, this meaning is no other than the meaning of being busy and zealous incessantly, that is, of striving forward) (*RUL* MS 5004, f. 18r). Beckett also excerpted numerous lines from both the first and the second part of the tragedy, but his silent comment on this "striving forward" was his decision not to read on after the "Klassische Walpurgisnacht."

Homuncules and Goethe's "Closed Space"

From a genetic perspective, it is interesting that the last excerpt in Beckett's *Faust* notes is the passage about the genesis of the homunculus:

> Es [homunculus] fragt um Rat u. möchte gern entstehen.
> Er ist, wie ich
> Gar wundersam *nur halb zur Welt gekommen*.
> Ihm fehlt es nicht an geistigen Eigenschaften,
> Doch gar zu sehr am greiflich *Tüchtighaften*.
> Bis jetzt gibt ihm das Glas allein Gewicht,
> Doch wär' er gern zunächst verkörperlicht.
>
> (Thales) (*RUL* MS 5005: 20r; Goethe 1986: 2: 104, line 8246; emphasis added)

The "Tüchtighaften" echoes the "Tüchtigsein" (zeal) mentioned in the editor's introduction. In the scene preceding the "Klassische Walpurgisnacht," Wagner manages to create a homunculus. It is not quite a human being, to which it relates in much the same way as Beckett's "dramaticules" relate to the longer plays.

In his summary of Beckett's process of composition, S. E. Gontarski focuses on what happens "*after* the initial image or incident is recorded (often straight from memory or the unconscious)" (17; emphasis added). These initial images can be studied only insofar as they are recorded—usually on paper. The transformation of an "initial image" into text can be elucidated by means of the creation of the homunculus as it is reported by Wagner in Goethe's *Faust II*:

> Das Glas *erklingt* von lieblicher Gewalt,
> Es trübt, es klärt sich; also muss es werden!
> Ich *sehe* in zierlicher Gestalt
> Ein artig Männlein sich gebärden.
> Was wollen wir, was will die Welt nun mehr?
> Denn das Geheimnis liegt am Tage.
> Gebt diesem Laute nur *Gehör*,
> *Er wird zur Stimme, wird zur Sprache.*
>
>   (Goethe 1986: 2: 66, lines 6872–78; emphasis added)

As in Dante's scene of Virgil's appearance, the coincidence of aural and visual impressions results in a figure of script, a homunculus who "turns into a voice, turns into language."

To examine the motif of the homunculus in view of Beckett's own creative method, the line "nur halb zur Welt gekommen" (*RUL MS 5005/20r*) in the final excerpt of his *Faust* notes is an interesting starting point. Since these notes are taken in the summer of 1936, it is not inconceivable that the line "nur halb zur Welt gekommen" (only half-born) may have reminded Beckett of that "little girl of ten" years old who had "never been properly born," which Jung had mentioned in his third Tavistock lecture on 2 October 1935 (Knowlson 1996: 176), that is, only ten months before he read *Faust*. The original "never been born entirely" (rather than "properly"; Jung 1966–79: 95–96; cf. Melnyk 2005: 361) comes even closer to the situation of the "only half-born" homunculus—"nur halb zur Welt gekommen."

The homunculus addresses his "father" with a diminutive. His first words are: "Nun, Väterchen!" (*Faust II*, line 6879). And he immediately draws attention to the glass of the phial without which it cannot live: "Das ist die Eigenschaft der Dinge: / Natürlichem genügt das Weltall kaum, / Was künstlich ist, verlangt geschlossenen Raum" [lines 6882–84] (the universe hardly suffices for whatever is natural, whereas whatever is artificial needs a closed space). The last line sums up the difficulty of finding a form that accommodates chaos. Goethe's cylindrical "geschlossenen Raum" is a plausible model of Beckett's "closed space" texts of the 1960s and 1970s. Beckett ends his notes with an excerpt that expresses the homunculus's wish to obtain corporeality. But simply breaking the glass of the phial would be a form of suicide for the homunculus.

When Beckett refers to the "homuncule" in *Malone Dies*, no mention is made of the phial:

> And if I tell of me and of that other who is my little one, it is as always for want of love, well I'll be buggered, I wasn't expecting that, want of a homuncule, I can't stop. (. . .) I shall go on doing as I have always done, not knowing what it is I do, nor who I am, nor where I am, nor if I am. Yes, a little creature, I shall try and make a little creature, to hold in my arms, a little creature in my image, no matter what I say (1955–58: 225–26)

Apart from the "homuncule," there are some other implicit references to Goethe's *Faust* that are subtly linked to the notion of decomposition. "What I mean," says Moran, "is possibly this, that the noises of the world, so various in themselves and which I used to be so clever at distinguishing from one another, had been dinning at me for so long, always the same old noises, as gradually to have merged into a single noise, so that all I heard was one vast continuous buzzing. The volume of sound perceived remained no doubt the same, I had simply lost the faculty of *decomposing* it" (207; emphasis added).[8] But then he does discern a "mixed choir," and he wonders: "Can it be Easter Week? (. . .) If it can, could not this song (. . .) have simply been to the honour and glory of him who was the first to rise from the dead, to him who saved me, twenty centuries in advance?" (208). The next moment Faust's suicide attempt is linked with a reference to Christ and Beckett's own birth. Beckett later alluded to what he called his old chestnut, "Birth was the death of him" (*CDW* 425), meaning both that his birth coincided with the death of Christ and that birth is the beginning of a process of dying, which is called "life." But the reference to Faust also suggests that the old chestnut works the other way as well: "Death was the birth of him." And that is where the homunculus comes in.

When the Unnamable, in his turn, relates that he has wasted his time "behind my mannikins" (1955–58: 306), he is referring to what in the French version is called "homuncules" (Beckett 1953b: 32).[9]

Oh Mon Cul: Another Figure of Script

In the first part of the trilogy, Moran has to find Molloy. Before he starts his quest, he has a row with his son, who wants to bring along his favorite stamps: Moran "spare[s his] son a grave temptation," as he calls it, "that of putting in his pocket his most cherished stamps, in order to gloat on them, during our journey" (1955–58: 110). He then refers—in German—to a passage from the second scene in the study in *Faust I*, which Beckett excerpted: "*Sollst entbehren*, that was the lesson I desired to impress upon him, while he was still young and tender" (110). Then he recapitulates what he knows about Molloy—first about the person (Beckett 1955–58: 111-15), then about the place Molloy comes from (133–34): Ballyba, its geography and agriculture. In the published text, this is only a two-page passage. It ends as follows: "What then was the source of Ballyba's prosperity? I'll tell you. *No, I'll tell you nothing. Nothing*" (134; emphasis added). But as Magessa O'Reilly has shown,[10] the tension between "I'll tell you" and "No, I'll tell you nothing" reflects the omission of a long passage on excrements. In the manuscript, "I'll tell you" was followed by the straightforward answer that Ballyba derived its riches "from its citizens' stools" (*HRHRC*, notebook III, p. 134). Magessa O'Reilly summarizes how, in this long omitted passage, Moran discusses "the luxurious vegetable production that is achieved thanks to the shit of Ballyba's citizens":

> Producing shit is, in fact, a civic duty. Each citizen has a quota of shit to produce, as determined by a committee. (. . .) At the end of every year, totals are calculated and diplomas are awarded to those whose contribution exceeded their quota. (O'Reilly 2006)

Finally, Moran recalls the case of a scientist named Kottman who suggested shit baths to alleviate certain nervous disorders. According to a detailed plan he submitted to the appropriate committee, none of the shit would be lost to fertilization as it would all be recycled. His plan was turned down, however, for fear the bathers would pollute the shit. (O'Reilly 2006)

This last aspect of Ballyba society suggests a link with psychology, but also with literary production. Beckett's Psychology notes, taken from Ernest Jones (*TCD* MS 10971/8/1), mention the act of "writing up diary" as one of the large number of acts that are considered to be "symbols for defaecation" (10971/8/18); another comparison is made with the "inability over a long period to write a letter & then producing an epistle" (10971/8/19) and with the "Infantile cloacal theory of birth," that is, the idea that "babies [are] made of faeces (cp. flowers from dung)." In the section on Freud's *Treatment of Neurosis*, the note "Les constipés se promènent" is followed by the explanation of the "Aim of psychoanalysis" as "to release pent-up energy & make it available for normal sublimation" (10971/8/23).

But the idea of submerging patients in shit baths, attributed to the fictitious "balnéo-thérapeute" Kottmann—obviously alluding to the German word for shit, "Kot"—may refer more specifically to Otto Rank and his book on *The Trauma of Birth*, in which he describes the situation of being in the mother's womb as *"inter faeces et urinas"* (*TCD* MS 10971/8/34), which Beckett jotted down in his notes. Further on in Otto Rank's book (1924: 162), on a page Beckett has read and taken excerpts from, there is a footnote referring to the psychoanalyst Herbert Silberer, who is also mentioned elsewhere in Beckett's psychology notes (*TCD* MS 10971/8/14ff.).[11] The footnote more specifically refers to an article by Silberer entitled "Der Homunculus." This article, published in 1914 in the journal *Imago*,[12] takes the creation of the homunculus in Goethe's *Faust* as a starting point, with the motto: "WAGNER: Es wird ein Mensch gemacht." Silberer draws attention to the homunculus as a motif that links alchemy to fertility myths and to excrements, according to the following reasoning: the primary aim of alchemy is not the creation of a homunculus, but the production of gold, and many alchemists believed that the ingredients employed to produce gold had to fully decompose first in order to become fertile, so that the fertilization or insemination could take place and the gold could start growing:

> Da ist vor allem der Gedanke an die spermatische Kraft des Kotes. (. . .) Was in der Alchemie bereitet werden soll, ist zunächst nicht der Humunculus, sondern das Gold, und die bemerkenswerte Verknüpfung von Gold und Dreck wird dem mythologisch und psychoanalytisch geschulten Leser nicht entgehen. Die Angabe, dass die erste Materie zu dem alchemistischen Werk ein verachtetes Ding oder Mist sei, findet sich in der Literatur sehr häufig. (39)

So, decomposition or putrefaction was a crucial phase in the creation of gold. Silberer refers to several legends (53) in which the origins of man are situated in mud or dung, in other words: shit as the prima materia (39). When he has brought alchemy down to earth in this way, Silberer makes a connection between the homunculus and the underground human form of the roots of the mandrake, which in its turn has often been attributed aphrodisiac qualities. According to Silberer, mandrake has sometimes been called "Homunculus" because of its roots having the shape of a human body. Silberer tells the legend of the mandrake, which according to popular belief, grows under the gallows: whenever a young thief is hanged, has an erection, and ejaculates, a mandrake grows where his sperm falls. This is the legend Didi refers to in *Waiting for Godot*: When Gogo suggests: "What about hanging ourselves?" Didi replies: "Hmm. It'd give us an erection." Estragon—according to the stage directions—gets "*highly excited*," exclaiming: "An erection!" To which Didi replies: "With all that follows. Where it falls mandrakes grow. That's why they shriek when you pull them up. Did you not know that?" (*CDW* 18). In the French version, this passage reads: "Là où ça tombe il pousse des mandragores." Here, the link between life and death is even more direct because of the homophony between where it falls ("ça tombe") and the grave ("sa tombe"). To Gogo, this new knowledge is all the more reason to commit suicide: his spontaneous reaction is: "Let's hang ourselves immediately!" (*CDW* 18).

For an author who is so focused on de-creation or the prevention of human procreation, Beckett shows a remarkable interest in the creation of homunculi, be it in the guise of the human-shaped root of the mandrake, or in the form of another "mannikin." *En attendant Godot* was written between *Malone meurt* and *L'innommable*, in both of which Beckett made his characters refer to their respective homuncules (cf. supra). Just before Malone mentions his "little creature," a direct link is made between the Rankian return to the womb[13] and the idea of the homunculus:

> Yes, an old foetus, that's what I am now, hoar and impotent, mother is done for, I've rotted her. (. . .) All the stories I've told myself, clinging to the *putrid mucus*, and swelling, swelling, saying, Got it at last, my legend. But why this sudden heat, has anything happened, anything changed? No, the answer is no, I shall never get born and therefore never get dead, and a good job too. (. . .) But what matter whether I was born or not, have lived or not, am dead or merely dying. (1955–58: 225; emphasis added)

In the midst of this "putrid mucus," Malone has the feeling he has "never been born entirely" (as Jung said) or "never been properly born"; or, in Rankian terms, the feeling he is part of the womb *inter faeces et urinas*.

Beckett carefully maintained his distance from all these psychological theories, and remained as skeptical as he was of Goethe's "onwardness." This is already clear from the distorted name of Ernest "Erogenous" Jones in his Psychology notes, or the distorted sentence "Die Merde hat mich wieder." This is not merely a pun à la *Finnegans Wake*. It also indicates the way Beckett, in his ironical treatment of these source materials, uses them accordingly. His writing method fully exploits the alchemists' notion of putrefaction. He did not use Joyce's method of decomposition followed by recombination, decomposing source texts in order to recombine the fragments. Decomposition is an analytical activity, which Joyce used solely in function of his synthetic enterprise of putting "Allspace in a Nothall." Instead, Beckett amassed a huge amount of notes and kept decomposing them in an analytical way, allowing them to putrefy. He applied, in a more radical way than Joyce, what is described in the passage on Shem the Penman: "(crap in his hand)" and "(says he was dejected)" (*FW* 185). Death and putrefaction are a necessary stage in order to find a form that accommodates the mess. Beckett was highly skeptical of all the things he read during the 1930s, and he seems to have found his own writing method by parodying the alchemists' method: he collected and recollected his ingredients—a huge mass of notes—not in order to compose a work in progress, the way Joyce recombined his notes, but rather in order to decompose a work in regress.

MEDIUM: Holes

Beckett's own coinage "work in regress" is certainly adequate, but it needs to be nuanced, for it may imply a teleological process that would exclude digressions and elaborations. If the "progress" in Joyce's *Work in Progress* suggests too much onwardness (*Vorwärtsstreben*), the *Rückwärtsstreben*, or regress, is no less Faustian. Faust's reward at the end of Goethe's *Faust II*— "Wer immer strebend sich bemüht, / Den können wir erlösen"—does not even specify whether this striving should be forward or backward in order to be redeemed. Perhaps the final words "Nohow on" in *Worstward Ho* may also be read as a recognition that the striving toward lessness or nothingness is an equally autokinetic, Faustian mechanism, marked by the persistent and untranslatable word "on." It is also a form of not giving in to the death wish. Shortly after Faust's suicide attempt, Mephistopheles urges Faust to put on his coat to go out into the world, "Damit du, losgebunden, frei, / Erfahrest, was das Leben sei" (lines 1542–43). But Faust replies that whatever he wears, he will continue feeling "die Pein / Des engen Erdelebens" (lines 1544–45). Faust is too old to fool around and too young to "be without wishes":

> Ich bin zu alt, um nur zu spielen,
> Zu jung, um ohne Wunsch zu sein.
> Was kann die Welt mir wohl gewähren?
> Entbehren sollst du! sollst entbehren! (1546–49)

When Moran tries to impress the lesson "*Sollst entbehren*" upon his son (1955–58: 110), he adds: "And should this undertaking make me odious in his eyes and not only me, but the very idea of fatherhood, I would pursue it *none the less*" (110; emphasis added). The "*nihilo minus*" characterizing this pursuit, also marks the writing process of Beckett's works. It is not so much a pursuit "of," or a movement "toward." The emphasis in Beckett's works on the "way"—as Friedhelm Rathjen pointed out[14]—is also applicable to his ateleological writing process, characterized by a continuous initiating. This movement is a crucial element in the dynamics of Beckett's writing, no matter how often a form of stasis is being suggested. In this respect, his work is just as "purgatorial" as Joyce's, according to his own description in "Dante. . .Bruno.Vico..Joyce."[15]

This dynamics has a consequence for the published version of the text, as S. E. Gontarski points out: "The abstracted, the undone final version is dialectically dependent on the work's realistic, psychological origins, the nothingness on the being, the absence on the presence, on what is excised" (1985: 17). This dialectical interdependence may imply that the writing process is an integral part of the oeuvre. Against this background, it is interesting to note that Adorno's comments on *L'innommable* describe Beckett's work by means of a verb:

> Absolutes Wegwerfen, weil Hoffnung nur dort ist wo nichts zurückbehalten wird. Die Fülle des Nichts. Dies die Erklärung des Beharrens auf dem Nullpunkt. [Adorno 1994: 73]

> (Absolute throwing away, because hope is only where nothing is retained. The fullness of nothingness. This the explanation for insistence on the zero point.)

This reflection is followed by the final note:

> Nicht Abstraktion sondern Subtraktion" (73)

> (Not abstraction but subtraction)

Adorno's nuanced distinction is applicable to Beckett's writing process. Usually, concrete realistic details are gradually deleted as the writing proceeds. For instance, the "nightlight" in the early sketches of *Stirrings Still* became a more abstract light in the later versions of the first paragraph (see chapter 8). But sometimes the concrete objects remain, whereas more abstract elements gradually disappear. A good example is the first sentence of the fourth paragraph of *Stirrings Still*, which was originally longer: "To his ears too throughout this afterlife a clock afar striking the hours and half hours" (*RUL* MS 2935/1/4). Beckett deleted "this afterlife" until the sentence ended up as a perfectly "realistic" description: "A clock afar struck the hours and half-hours."

Adorno's subtle distinction between abstraction and subtraction reinforces the nominalist premise that only individual things are real. Abstraction potentially implies the creation of universals, which is different from Beckett's writing procedure toward less "-ness." It is easy to create a concept like "Nothingness," which is merely a word, a "motion of the air produced by the tongue," as Boethius defined it (Windelband 1958: 1: 296). As a *flatus vocis*, "Nothingness" does not solve the key question formulated by Adorno with reference to *L'innommable*: "Ist das Nichts gleich nichts?" (73).

The "nominalist irony" Beckett regarded as a necessary stage toward his "sehr wünschenswerten Literatur des Unworts" (in his July 1937 letter to Axel Kaun; Beckett 1984: 54) was characterized as a "Wörterstürmerei" (an assault against words) (53). Beckett insisted that this "Programm" had nothing to do with Joyce's last work—"Es sei denn, Himmelfahrt und Höllensturz sind eins und dasselbe" (Unless perhaps ascension to Heaven and descent to Hell are somehow one and the same) (53). Against this background, the confrontation between Faust and Mephistopheles in Goethe's *Faust* is elucidating. When Faust asks Mephistopheles, "Wie nennst du dich?" (what is your name?), the latter replies that his question is rather trifling for someone who has such contempt for the word and is only interested in penetrating the depth of beings, not deluded by outward appearances (lines 1327–30). Mephistopheles himself proves to be a master of linguistic cynicism:

Mit Worten lässt sich trefflich streiten,
Mit Worten ein System bereiten,
An Worte lässt sich trefflich glauben,
Von einem Wort lässt sich kein Jota rauben. (1997–2000)

And yet, that was precisely the task Beckett set himself in the German letter to Axel Kaun, one year after he read Goethe's *Faust*: to bereave Joyce's "whole" of a single Jota and create a hole in the "Sprachgewebe" (the tissue of language). The persistent image of the veil, which he knew through Schopenhauer, was revived during his reading of *Faust*, notably the "Monolog vom farbigen Abglanz" at the beginning of *Faust II*, from which Beckett excerpted the long "Schleier" passage (*RUL* MS 5005, f. 4r). Beckett compared his "hole"-program to Beethoven's Seventh Symphony and its "sound surface" torn by large black pauses (1984: 53). He had already formulated this strategy in *Dream of Fair to Middling Women*, when Belacqua announces his intention of writing a book, focusing on "the silence, communicated by the intervals, not the terms, of the statement" (138), which he compares to Beethofen's [*sic*] "compositions eaten away with terrible silences" (139).

Holes were the key to Beckett's poetics in the 1930s, as these early statements indicate. The question is whether they also apply to his later compositions. The image of the veil suggests that the writing process inevitably involves creating some kind of verbal tissue first, without which there would be nothing to bore holes into. Beckett's program surpassed the level of the metaphor, but his description to Kaun accounts for only the first of at least two different approaches.

1. Perforative Decomposition

The first modus operandi fully exploits the Beethovian pauses. In a text like *Not I*, the ellipses represent the visible holes in the *Wortfläche* of the published text:

. . . .out. . .into this world. . .this world. . .tiny little thing. . .before its time. . . (*CDW* 376)

The ellipses were part of the text from the very first version onwards, but their length changed during the writing process. After four versions with three-dot ellipses (and an initial four-dot ellipsis), Beckett tried out a few versions with only two dots:

. . birth . . into this world..this world . . tiny little thing..before its time . . in a godfor - . . what? . . ~~little~~ girl? . . yes . . tiny little girl . . into this . . before her time . . godforsaken hole . . (*RUL* MS 1227/7/12/5)

But after three versions (*RUL* MS 1227/7/12/6; 7; 8) and one translation (*RUL* MS 1396/4/26) with two dots, Beckett decided to switch over to three dots again. Here, the text with its godforsaken holes takes the shape of what Beckett had called "compositions where into the body of the musical statement he [Beethoven] incorporates a punctuation of dehiscence" (1992a: 139).

A striking example of the "compositions eaten away with silences" (139) or pauses is *Happy Days*. In *Krapp's Last Tape*, the number of pauses is perhaps less spectacular, but it is interesting to reconstruct the gradual way in which they were carefully introduced in the typescripts:[16]

Ts1	43 pauses
Ts2	59 pauses
Ts3	77 pauses
Ts4	80 pauses
Ts5	80 pauses

Ts6	81 pauses
Ts7	81 pauses
TsLDB	84 pauses

At first sight, this survey may give the impression that Beckett was doing much the same thing as Joyce: "always adding to it" (Knowlson 1996: 352)—albeit *ex negativo*, always adding more holes, pauses and moments of "hesitation." In a different way, Joyce also kept adding moments of "hesitency" [*sic*] to his *Work in Progress* as one of the book's major leitmotifs. In 1889, the *London Times* published a letter that was allegedly written by the leader of the Irish Parliamentary Party, Charles Stuart Parnell, who almost managed to achieve Home Rule for the Irish. He eventually did not succeed because of circumstances that damaged his political career, one of them being this letter in the *London Times*. According to this document, Parnell condoned the so-called Phoenix Park murders of 1882, when two men were mistakenly assassinated instead of the viceroy. The letter turned out to be a forgery, and in February 1889 the journalist Richard Piggott was unmasked as the forger of the letter thanks to a misspelling of the word "hesitancy" as "hesitency." This word recurs in numerous disguises throughout *Finnegans Wake*. For instance: "hasitancy" (*FW* 16.30); "Hesitency" (*FW* 35.20); "hisshistenency" (*FW* 146.34). As a leitmotiv, the textual "hesitensies" (*FW* 187.30) constantly remind the readers of the possibility of forgery. For instance, at a certain point the spelling of "HeCitEncy!" (*FW* 421.23) suggests that the forger may be the male protagonist, Humphrey Chimpden Earwicker, or HCE. The "hesitency" motif, marking the moment when Irish history might have taken a different course, also reflects a more general interest in roads not taken and the "hesitency" that characterizes the "history of the world," which Joyce said he was going to write after *Ulysses*.

This also applies to the composition history and the way it forges ahead. In Beckett's case, the moments when the writing process might have taken a different course are incorporated in his text. But this introduction of decomposition into his composition is not simply a matter of adding more holes, pauses or hesitations. In the first typescript, Krapp "(*hesitates*)" three times. The first time he hesitates before the word "myself." He is satisfied with the new light above his table and with the darkness that surrounds him:

> I like to get up and move about in it, then back here to. . .(*hesitates*)
> . . .myself. (Ts1, f. 1r)

After the addition of one extra hesitation in the second typescript, the number increases quite spectacularly in the third:

Ts1: "(*hesitates*)" 3 times
Ts2: "(*hesitates*)" 4 times
Ts3: "(*hesitates*)" 11 times

But then the number decreases again:

Ts4: "(*hesitates*)" 10 times
Ts5: "(*hesitates*)" 10 times
Ts6: "(*hesitates*)" 8 times
Ts7: "(*hesitates*)" 8 times

An example of the systematic way in which Beckett inserts these moments of hesitation in the third typescript is the word "viduity." In the first typescript, Krapp's recollection of his dying mother reads:

> there is of course the house on the canal where mother lay dying, in the early autumn, after her long widowhood

In the second typescript, Beckett changes "widowhood" into "viduity" and exploits this moment dramatically by expanding it into a short scene:

> there is of course the house on the canal where mother lay a-dying, in the early autumn, after her long viduity (A gives a start), and the - (A switches off machine, gets up, goes backstage into darkness and comes same way with a dictionary (*A givesa[sic] start*), and the - (*A switches off machine*, wind backs[sic] tape a little *winds back tape a little, bends his ear closer to machine*) - a-dying, after her long viduity, and the -
>
> *A switches off machine, turns face front. Puzzled.*
>
> ^A. -^ Viduity? (*Pause. He gets up, goes backstage into darkness, comes back with a* large dictionary *volume of the Concise Oxford* ^*or Johnson's dictionary and quotes example*^, *lays it on the table, sits down, looks up viduity, reads, nods, closes dictionary, switches on machine, resumes his pose.*) (Ts2, f. 3r)

The introduction of "viduity" creates a completely different kind of hole by means of a lexical loss: *A* (as Krapp was initially named in this second version, later changed into "Crapp" with a capital *C*) must have known the word "viduity" as a younger man, but now he has completely forgotten its meaning. This lost word is no longer part of his vocabulary. To stress the lexical loss, Beckett added two hesitations in the next version of this scene:

> there is of course the house on the canal where mother lay a-dying, in the early autumn, after her long ~~viduity~~ ^ . . . (*hesitates*) . . . viduity^ (*Krapp gives a start*), and the - (*Krapp switches off machine, winds back tape a little, bends his ear closer to machine*) - a-dying, in the early autumn, after her long ~~viduity~~ ^ . . . (*hesitates*) . . . viduity^, and the - (*Krapp switches off machine, raises his head, stares blankly before him. His lips move in the syllables of "viduity." No sound. He gets up, goes backstage into darkness, comes back with an enormous dictionary, lays it on table, looks up the word, reads, (quotes definition if possible), nods, closes dictionary, switches on machine, resumes his posture.*) (Ts3, f. 3r)

The word "viduity" is twice replaced by " . . . (*hesitates*) . . . viduity"; but in the next version the hesitation is omitted again: "there is of course the house on the canal where mother lay a-dying, in the early autumn, after her long viduity (*Krapp gives a start*), and the—" (Ts4, f. 3r-4r), which is repeated when Krapp winds back the tape. As if to compensate for the twice-omitted hesitation, Beckett adds a passage that was drafted on the back of the last page of this typescript and added to page 4r:

> Krapp (*reading from dictionary*). State of being - or remaining - a widow - or widower. (*Looks up. Puzzled.*) Being - or ~~remain?...~~ remaining? . . . ~~(Peers (Returns to~~ Peers again at dictionary. Reading.) "Deep weeds of viduity . . ." Also of an [~~an~~] animal, especially a bird . . .the vidua or weaver-bird. . . . black plumage of males. (*looks up. With relish.*) The vidua-bird! (Ts4, f. 4r)

No extra hesitation is added, but Krapp relishes in a word that has the same stem as the verb "viduare," to empty.

Other holes through which the text was emptied were interjections such as ". . . er . . .": "before embarking on a new . . . er . . . review ^conspectus^" (Ts1, f. 1r). Or simply an ellipsis, which sometimes gradually enlarged into an explicit hesitation:

> Eyes like . . . moonstones (Ts1, f. 2r)
> Eyes like . . . moonstones. (Ts2, f. 3r)
> Eyes like - moonstone! (*Pause.*) (Ts3, f. 4r)
> eyes! Like . . . (*hesitates*) . . . ~~moonstone~~ ^chrysolite! (*Pause.*)
>   (Ts4, f. 4r)

Even after the composition process, this kind of incorporation of a "punctuation of dehiscence" continued. In the case of *Not I*, for instance, Beckett's notes for the Anthony Page production on 16 January 1973 are far less elaborate than the theatrical notebooks he kept during the productions of other plays. But the notes for *Not I* are nonetheless remarkable. They are contained on a single sheet of paper and only indicate the precise insertion of 26 pauses and 6 hesitations (*RUL* MS 1227/7/12/11). According to John Fletcher, Beckett compared the pauses in *Waiting for Godot* to the holes, through which silence could enter, "pouring into this play like water into a sinking ship."[17] The metaphor is different, but it suggests yet another form of decomposition.

2. Centrifugal/Centripetal Decomposition

Still, this insertion of pauses and other holes into the text during the composition and postcomposition process is only one method of admitting the chaos and accommodating decomposition. It is the textual equivalent of Watt's "intent of undoing" as a method to find Knott, translated by Chris Ackerley as follows: "To find him, I abandoned all; to learn him, I forgot all; to have him, I rejected all; to love him, I reviled all. To him I brought this homeless body, this unknowing mind, these emptied hands, this emptied heart. To the temple, to the teacher, to the source—of nought" (2005: 155).

But this is a translation. Watt formulates his method by means of an inversion "of the sentences in the period," starting from nought:

> *Of nought. To the source. To the teacher. To the temple. To him I brought. This emptied heart. These emptied hands. This mind ignoring. This body homeless. To love him my little reviled. My little rejected to have him. My little to learn him forgot. Abandoned my little to find him.* (1981 [1953]: 164)

According to Augustinian principles, "the only way one can speak of nothing is to speak of it as though it were something" (Beckett 1981 [1953]: 74). In Watt's case, this comes down to speaking of nothing by means of what it is Knott. A similar approach applies to Beckett's writing.

The second method of accommodating decomposition consists of starting from a hole and weaving the text around it. Beckett's most famous play is built around the absence of Godot. Whether or not Godot exists remains a mystery, and even if he does, his existence is "obscene"—offstage. This kind of absence creates a central emptiness, which Beckett also employed in other plays, such as *Not I*.

The first draft of *Not I* did not yet start with the stage directions regarding the lighting of the mouth (which goes back to the "Kilcool" fragments preserved in Trinity College Dublin). The first unit of text, starting with the word "birth," initially focuses on the place of birth, which is referred to as a "hole":

> birth into ~~the~~ ^this^ world . . . this world . . . of a ~~small~~ ^tiny^ baby ~~boy or girl~~ ^in a small^ . . . what? . . . girl? . . . [~~in xx xx~~] . . . birth then into this . . . ^vast^ place of ^a tiny^ ~~a small~~ baby girl in a small ~~place~~ ^hole^ ~~in the lowlands~~ ^on the coast^ ~~by the name of named~~ in the [~~downs~~] ^bog^ named . . . what?.. ~~the [xx xx]downs?~~ no . . . no! . . . the [~~downs~~] ^bog!^ . . . small hole in the downs ^bog^ named . . . named . . . no matter . . . (*RUL* MS 1227/7/12–1, f. 1r)

From the nameless hole the text moves on to the first concrete image, which Beckett called a "life scene." In the beginning, this scene mentioned a grandchild:

> coming up to 65 walking in a field with ~~her~~ ^my^ youngest grandchild ~~looking~~ ^searching^ for cowslips to make a ball . . . when suddenly all went out . . . all that ^early^ april morning light . . . and ~~she~~ ^I^ found ~~her~~^my^self in the dark . . . (RUL MS 1227/7/12/1, f. 1r)

Apart from the grandchild, the age (65, which later became 70), and the change of "her" to "my" (which was already undone again in the second draft), this opening scene remained largely intact in all the later versions, as Beckett's own synopsis shows:

> NOT I—synopsis
> 1. Premature birth
>   Parents unknown
>   No love at any time
>   At age of 70 in a field picking cowslips suddenly finds herself in the dark (. . .) (*RUL* MS 1227/7/12/10)

This kind of synthetic exercise is rather rare in Beckett's manuscripts. As Beckett explained to Martin Esslin, *Joyce* was the "synthesiser"; when he described himself as an "analyser," he added: "I try to take as much of the detail away as possible."[18]

The manuscripts, however, nuance this statement. As pointed out in chapter 7, our view of Beckett's writing method is to a large extent influenced by the author's own efforts to contrast his method with Joyce's. In general, it is of course undeniable that Joyce's tendency to amplify is thoroughly different from Beckett's approach, but here and there the manuscripts suggest that the dichotomy is perhaps not that black and white. Against the background of Beckett's statement about the synthesizer and the analyzer, it is interesting to note that apart from the "Synopsis" of *Not I*, Beckett also made an "Analysis." In this analysis, he dissolves the text into fourteen segments: *Birth; Field; insentience; So far; buzzing; brain; memories; speculations; walking; punishment/suffering; interruptions; [beam]; speechless; voice* (RUL MS 1227/7/12/1, f. 6r).

Rosemary Pountney refers to a few passages in this analysis. Her selection corroborates the thesis of increasing ambiguity: "The notes most revealing of technique in Beckett's analysis show him intentionally working towards ambiguity in the text" (1988: 100). Pountney refers to the phrase "tho not explicitly stated" and the two parentheses "(*not made clear*)": "Two other notes, both underlined in red, state '*not made clear*,' meaning, presumably, intentionally ambiguous rather than requiring clarification" (100). Apart from these three instances, however, there are eight parentheses and notes, also marked in red, which indicate amplification or further illustration, such as "*amplify*" (four times) or "*add to*" or "*another ex.*" In response to these notes, Beckett wrote eight passages which he explicitly called "addenda" (*RUL* MS 1227/7/12/1, f. 5v and 4v).

For instance, under the penultimate heading *speechless* in the Analysis, after the example of the "supermart," Beckett indicated in red ink: "*another ex.*" Among the addenda (*RUL* MS 1227-7-12-1, f. 5v), he subsequently wrote not just one but two examples of speechlessness:

> practically speechless ... all her days ... not quite ... [even] to herself ... never out loud to herself ... but not quite ... not quite speechless ... sometimes sudden urge ... once or twice a year ... ^always^ winter for some reason ... the long [evenings] evenings ... sudden urge to ... tell ... then rush out & stop the first person she saw ... [man or woman or child] nearest lavatory ... start pouring it out ... steady stream ... wild stuff ... half the vowels wrong ... pine for pain ... that kind ... no one could follow ... till she saw the look she was getting ... then die of shame ... once or twice a year ... always winter for some reason ... now this ...
>
> *Ex. 2 of speechlessness*
>
> practically speechless ... how she survived ... that time in court ... guilty or not guilty what what had she to say for herself ... guilty or not

guilty... speak up woman... stood there... staring at nothing... waiting to be led away... glad of the hand on her arm...

The phrase "that time in court" introduces a new "life scene" and implicitly already contains the key to Beckett's next play, *That Time*. The words "that time" announce the more or less sudden recollection of a past life scene. In the example of the courtroom, the whole scene is almost complete from the first jotting onwards, but it is followed by a refining process. For instance, Beckett briefly considered replacing "that time in court" by "that time in the dock" (*RUL* MS 1227-7-12-6, f. 5r). In the subsequent typescript, he replaced it by "court" again.

As Philip Laubach-Kiani points out, the writing process of some of the images in Beckett's works are characterized by descriptive elaboration. Thus, for instance, the scene in the supermarket (to illustrate "how she survived") does not contain many details when it occurs for the first time in the drafts:

> ... how she survived ... even shopping ... ^busy shopping center^ ... just handed in the list... with the shopping bag... then stood there waiting... any length of time... motionless... staring ~~at nothing~~ ^into space^ ... till it was back in her hand... the bag... then paid & went... not as much as goodbye... how she survived... (*RUL* MS 1227/7/12/1, f. 3r)

Initially, the scene could have taken place anywhere; the specifics about the "busy shopping center" were added at a later stage in the left margin. The "shopping bag" became an "old black shopping back" in the fourth typescript (*RUL* MS 1227/7/12/5, f. 3r).

There are, of course, numerous other instances where Beckett cuts all the specifics, but this undoing is not always systematic. When Beckett carefully adds a few particulars, it is often in the description of recollections. Especially in these cases, the genesis of the text can be regarded as a reconstruction of the process of reminiscence (see chapter 8).

In terms of both micro- and macrogenetics, the genesis of *Not I* shows that Beckett's writing method is not only marked by undoing or "boring holes"—to use his own metaphor—but also by the second method, characterized by centrifugal and centripetal tendencies "autour du pot," that is, around the hole from which "she" is expelled ("out ... into this world") the way her words are expelled from her mouth.

The "Usual Vanishing Point"

Another example is the short piece *Come and Go/Va-et-vient*. In the published text, three women are sitting next to each other. When the first woman exits, the two others start talking about her, the one whispering to the other, who is surprised and exclaims a sentence like "God grant not" or "God forbid" or "Please God not" (*CDW* 354–55; Beckett 1999a: 207–9). When the third woman returns, they sit together until another one disappears in the "ob-scene." The same scenario is repeated three times. The central absence—the whispered words the audience cannot hear—can only be filled with speculations based on the three surprised reactions.

The idea of writing around an absence of information was the starting point. In the manuscript entitled "GOOD HEAVENS" (marked by Beckett: "Before / Come & Go"), Beckett simply indicates that the first scene is a conversation between *A*, *B*, and *C*, after which *C* exits: "1 Conversation ABC Exit C" (*RUL* MS 1227/7/16/4). This scene will later be elaborated as textual material surrounding the central hole. Instead of weaving this "textus" first, Beckett immediately draws a pagewide dividing line and jumps to the next scene, starting from the central absence in a conversation between *A* and *B* (without *C*): "*A whispers in B's ear.*" The original exclamation in response to the whispering ("You don't tell me!") is replaced by "Good heavens!" The same substitution in blue felt-tip pen is applied to all the subsequent whispering scenes; and with the same blue felt-tip Beckett added the title "GOOD HEAVENS" in the top margin of the manuscript's first page.

One of the reasons for consulting the manuscripts may be an elementary curiosity and the hope of finding a simple answer to the question: what are they whispering? The *avant-texte* gives a few clues. After the whispering and the initial reaction, woman *B* says: "I did not know he had been discharged" (*RUL* MS 1227/7/16/4). But from this piece of information one can only conclude that, at the moment when Beckett was typing this second version, he considered the possibility of making the content of the whispering somewhat more explicit. The decision to omit this explicitness again in the next versions is evidently just as, if not more, important in order to reconstruct the dynamics of the writing process.

To embed the whispered scenes in a textual surrounding, Beckett worked out a deliberately shallow first scene ("slipshod writing"; *RUL* MS 1227/7/16/5) in the next version (the first typescript), featuring three women, one of whom reads a passage from a dime novel to the others:

Curtain up. Poppy with closed book on ~~kbees~~ *knees. Pause.*
Viola   How mild it is for August.
Pause.
Rose   Read, Poppy.
       Poppy opens book at place marked.
Poppy Chapter seven. "Her my own rose at last—"
Rose   (*wearily*). Hermione.[19]
Poppy "Hermione[20] rose at last from the steaming sweet-smelling foam and stood all pink and dripping before the great cheval-glass, inspecting her luscious forms. Caressingly she passed her hands—"

Here, the reading is interrupted because of a missing piece of information. As Philip Laubach-Kiani points out (2003: 268), even this scene is marked by a lack of information—this time in the narrative of the dime novel: "Viola: Where is Aubrey at this point?" Poppy turns back a page and reads: "Aubrey stretched out to the flames his long hairy legs, took a sipo of his brandy ^Sandeman^, relit his cigar and resumed alone the collection of obscene postcards." This "collection" is immediately followed by a "recollection." When Viola asks "Are his trousers off then?" Rose replies: "Not in my recollection." Between the collection and recollection it is again Viola who effectuates a decomposition of the (ob)scene. Rose prompts Poppy to resume her reading where she left off:

Rose   "Caressingly she passed her hands . . ."
Poppy "Over her sple^n^did bosom glowing from the bath, her belly and quivering flanks, then falling to her knees plunged them between her thighs in an extasy of anticipation."
Viola This is careless ^slipshod^ writing.
Rose   You mean one cannot plunge one's knees between one's ~~thing~~^gh^s?
Poppy Come come, it is clear from the context what is meant.
Rose   You are right, Poppy. Purism can go too far. ~~Please~~ ^Pray^ proceed. (*RUL* MS 1227/7/16/5, f. 1r-2r)

Again, Poppy reads a few sentences, until she excuses herself and exits. The idea of the exit is the core of the piece. Beckett's schematic structure of the whole play looks as follows:

I	V.R.P.
II	V.R.
III	V.R.P.
IV	P.R.
V	V.R.P.
VI	V.P.
VII	V.R.P.

Scenes 2, 4, and 6 contain the crucial absences, but the whispering is only applied to tell the terrible news about the respective terminal illnesses. These are each time preceded by another whispering with a positive confidence, giving evidence of the whisperer's thriving will to live. In scene 6, for instance, Vi (who has just been informed in scene 2 that Poppy has only three more months to live "at the outside") tells Poppy how young she is looking and asks her if she has been using any special makeup.

> Vi   (. . .) Have you been using something on your skin? (*Poppy moves into Rose's seat and whispers in Vi's ear.*) Heavens! The croquet champion!
> Poppy He no longer holds the title. He makes me so happy.

The mention of cosmetics is interesting with regard to Beckett's concern about finding a form (cosmos) to admit the chaos and accommodate the mess. In spite of everything, the will to live is emphasized, even if it is only for three more months. Instead of using the whispering for both the happy and the sad secrets, Beckett decided to smooth down the emotional highs and use the whispering only to perforate the plain of their habitual lives with three variations of what comes down to the same end. What (in the published version) seems to be a way of "boring holes" appears to be the result of a writing process that is marked by the second method, starting from a hole. From a genetic perspective, this hole is the vanishing point around which the entire composition takes shape, comparable to the hole in the canvas of Vermeer's painting *Lady Writing a Letter* (see chapter 2). The little hole in the lady's left eye is the material trace of Vermeer's method to determine the vanishing point. Similarly, in the genesis of *Come and Go* and *Not I*, the centripetal tendency of the writing process toward the "ineffable departure" becomes visual. This second writing method, which does not differ that much from Joyce's "rumors"-around-the-"woid" technique in *Finnegans Wake*, is summarized by Beckett in a letter to Jocelyn Herbert.[21] In this document, written on 16 June—Bloomsday—1966, Beckett refers to his writing as a "work in regress with usual vanishing point in view." As in Vermeer's painting, the material traces of this vanishing point indicate how the whole relates to the hole.

SMALL: "Blanks for When Words Gone"

The idea of starting from the missing words and writing around this lacuna was a method Beckett often applied. The short text *Ceiling* starts from the whiteness of the ceiling, which is transposed to the blankness of the page: "~~On coming to himself his first sight was of white~~" (*HRHRC* Lake 17.1, f. 1r). In the case of *Stirrings Still*, one of the paralipomena in the *avant-texte* mentions: "Each tale of his end takes off with good prospects." But this line is immediately followed by the remark: "No words for his end" (*RUL* MS 2935/1/1, f. 1r). And yet the next lines read:

Some of the attempts to tell his end.

Hereunder / Hereinunder / Hereinbelow scenes ^snippets^ from his close.
Here ends snippet one.

With or without change ^of voice^ after the hiatus.

Around the same time Beckett wrote a few French jottings in his "Super conquérant" notebook (*RUL* MS 2934), starting from the notion of "lacunae":

lacunes
embellissements
amour propre
impossible passage du dit à l'écrit (RUL MS 2934, f. 2v)

On the facing recto, Beckett nonetheless tried to formulate the impossible transition from the spoken to the written word.[22] The lacuna eventually became the core of the third section of *Stirrings Still*. The lack of knowledge about what happens "where never till then" creates a lacuna, comparable to what *terra incognita* must have been to the early cartographers. No matter how much they would have liked to draw precise contours of coastlines, mountains, and names of cities, they could only fill in the blanks with the line: "Hic sunt leones" (Here are lions). Confronted with the ultimate existential margin, Beckett refused to just draw some vague contours; he honestly admitted that "what has so happily been called the unutterable or ineffable" could only be hinted at by means of words or, to quote Geert

Lernout's pun, "Here are lines." One of these lines is "oh how *and here a word he could not catch* it were to end where never till then" (*CSP* 264; emphasis added). Beckett thus drew the contours of what we do *not* know, fully aware that "any attempt to utter or eff it is doomed to fail, doomed, doomed to fail" (Beckett 1981 [1953]: 61)—and yet persisting.

The crucial "and yet" touches the core of manuscript genetics with reference to Beckett's writings, for the manuscripts are the laboratory where Beckett keeps seeking the right words in spite of the futility of the attempt. In this sense, Adorno is probably right in arguing against the notion of the absurd: "Gegen den Terminus 'absurd.' Er setzt als Normales ein Sinnvolles voraus. Aber eben dies ist die Illusion[,] das Absurde ist das Normale." [1994: 69] (Against the term "absurd." It presupposes something meaningful as normal. But that is precisely the illusion, the absurd is the normal.) In the manuscripts, Beckett keeps looking for the right words to utter the ineffable departure, even though the attempt is doomed to fail:

> And yet it is useless not to seek, not to want, for when you cease to seek you start to find, and when you cease to want, then life begins to ram her fish and chips down your gullet until you puke, and then the puke down your gullet until you puke the puke, and then the puked puke until you begin to like it. (1981 [1953]: 43)

In *Proust*, Beckett had defined habit as "the ballast that chains the dog to its vomit" (1999a [1931]: 19), echoing Proverbs 26:11: "As a dog returneth to his vomit, so a fool returneth to his folly." Fully aware of the futility of the attempt, Beckett deliberately started his last work with the word "folie"/"folly."

The starting point of *Comment dire* is a lacuna in the *avant-texte* of the previous work *Stirrings Still*. The first line of the first version temporarily ended in an impasse: "Tout ~~tout le temps~~ ^toujours^ à la même distance comme c'est *comment dire*? (. . .)" (*RUL* MS 2933/1, f. 1r; emphasis added). This blank spot is the point of departure in Beckett's "next next to nothing," *Comment dire*, which can be read as a failed attempt to write one sentence. In its most complete version, the sentence reads: "folie vu tout ce ceci-ci que de vouloir croire entrevoir loin là là-bas à peine"—in Beckett's own translation: "folly seeing all this this here for to need to seem to glimpse afaint afar away over there"—and then the attempt at finishing the sentence is aborted. The text ends with the words "comment dire," or "what is the word." These words recur seven times throughout the poem, not counting the title and the final repetition of the penultimate "what is the word."

If each moment when the phrase "comment dire" recurs can be regarded as a temporary deadlock, the text (whose genesis is its subject) can be divided into seven sections—seven failed attempts.

1. In the first section, the author is certain of only one word, "folie," but he does not find the right word to express what it is that he designates as a "folly": "folly - / folly for to - / for to - / what is the word - " (Beckett 2002: 113).

2. In the second section, the words "for to" are successively replaced by a few alternative variants: "folly from all this - "; "folly given all this - "; "folly seeing all this - "

3. The next problem is how to describe what is "given": "this this - / this this here - / all this this here - "

4. The attention is subsequently focused again on *what it is* that the author denotes as a folly:

see -
glimpse -
seem to glimpse -
need to seem to glimpse -
folly for to need to seem to glimpse -
what -
what is the word -

5. Because the "need to seem to glimpse" is transitive, the text is in need of a direct object. Since this object does not present itself—at least not directly—the attention temporarily shifts from "what" to the possibly easier question "where" (113).

6. The first word that comes to mind is "there": "there - / over there - / away over there - / (...) / afar away over there - " (115).

7. In the last section, the other vague description ("seeing all this this here") is reintroduced, further postponing the formulation of the direct object. This last section is a sort of recapitulation of the writing process so far, the result of which—in its longest version—is this unfinished sentence: "folly for to need to seem to glimpse afaint afar away over there what - / what - / what is the word - // what is the word" (115). Whereas the penultimate line "what is the word -" still has the potential meaning of "so far so good," the final repetition of the phrase (the only line in the poem that is not followed by a hyphen) only seems to express the more desperate meaning "so far and not further."

As a reenactment of a literary genesis, this text may be misleading for it is not a representation of this work's actual genesis. One could try to apply the above division into seven subsections to the typescripts and fair copies, but the danger of imposing such a teleological grid onto the genesis is that it distorts the actual writing process of *Comment dire*, which, for example, did not start with "folie" but with the word "mal." The "comment dire" motif was already present in the first draft, but its different expression ("quel est le mot") was less idiomatic:

> mal de ce -
> depuis -
> mal depuis ~~ce~~ ce -
> ~~[que]~~ ce -
> quel est le mot -
> le mot pour ce -
> ce ceci -
> ^ce ceci-ci^
> il n'y a pas ~~de mot~~ -
> ~~mal donc depuis ce ceci voir~~ -
> pas de mot pour ce ceci-[ce]ci
>
> (*RUL* MS 3316, f. 2r; emphasis added)

Even though there seems to be no word for "this this here," the search goes on. After another nine lines, the attempt is aborted. In the next version, the words "quel est le mot" are replaced by the phrase "comment dire -" (*RUL* MS 3316/1, f. 2r):

> ~~quel est le mot~~ ^comment dire -^
> ~~le mot pour ce~~ -
> ce ceci -
> ce ceci-ci -

Here, Beckett arrives at a deadlock again: "il n'y a pas de mot - / pas de mot pour ce ceci-ci"; but he deletes the obstacle and begins "from nought anew":

> ~~il n'y pas de mot~~ -
> ~~pas de mot pour ce ceci-ci~~
> mal donc de ce -
> (...)

The unknown element is called "ce ceci-ci sans nom," but as this is a form of naming in itself, the lines are crossed out and replaced by "ceci-ci -" (*RUL MS* 3316, f. 2r). The hyphen, which in *Not I* separated the words "- monde . . .mis au monde" from what preceded this birth (RUL MS 1396/4/27, f. 2r), now separated Beckett's last words from the "ineffable departure." On the next verso page, Beckett briefly considered omitting the hyphens ("sans traits?"), but instead of employing the standard expression "traits d'union," he referred to them as "traits de disunion" (*RUL MS* 3316, f. 2v).

After two more versions starting with the word "mal" (f. 3r), Beckett decided to replace it by "folie" (f. 2v). The need to see ("vouloir voir") is diverted from the direct object to its place: "où ça / comment dire - / ^là^ / là-bas - / au-delà / {au} loin - / loin ^là^ là-bas / à peine" (*RUL MS* 3316, f. 2v). Twice the word "là" is added, and when Beckett arrives at the bottom of the page ("à peine"), he draws an arrow pointing to the left margin, where he writes: "loin là-bas à peine quoi -" (f. 2v). While the arrow points to the edge of the document to mark the place, Beckett simultaneously crosses out the "au delà" [beyond]. In the absence of a thinkable "au-delà," Beckett explores the edges and margins of existence, yet he refuses to attach a label to an unknowable "beyond." In their "terrible materiality" (Beckett 1984: 172), the words "loin là-bas" indicate the limits of the effable. And the "trait de disunion" in the margin of the physical document becomes what Adorno—in one of his notes on *L'innommable*—called the "Urbild einer materialistischen Metaphysik" (primal image of materialist metaphysics) (Adorno 1994: 69). Further one cannot.

Conclusion

The attempt to eff the ineffable departure turned it into an ever-shifting horizon "loin là là-bas," which became "afaint afar away" when Beckett translated *Comment dire* into English. With this subtle gesture, referring to the last line of James Joyce's *Finnegans Wake*, Beckett paid tribute to his mentor, from whom he learned the craft of writing and to whom his writing is paradoxically linked by means of a "trait de disunion": "A way a lone a last a loved a long the"—what is the word—

"riverrun" brings us to the genetic point that this word was not in the beginning. It only became the beginning of *Finnegans Wake* by gradual stages. Initially the first draft of the opening section started with the words "Howth Castle & Environs!" (*JJA* 44: 3; *BL* 47482a–83). Joyce subsequently added the words "brings us to"; in the second draft, the opening words became "brings us back to" (*JJA* 44: 45; *BL* 47471a–2); in the third draft, the "riverrun" first appeared as a "river" to which "run" was added subsequently.

While the first word only gradually appeared in the beginning, another one mysteriously disappeared from the end. In the fifth version (the third typescript) of the final section of *Finnegans Wake*, the last line read: "A way a lone *a lost* a last a loved a long the" (*BL* 47488–160; emphasis added). In the next typescript, the words "a lost" disappeared: "A way a lone a last a loved a long the" (*BL* 47488–178).

Although Paul Léon was Joyce's closest collaborator at this moment, it is hard to establish the typist's identity with absolute certainty. With reference to the 1984 revised edition of *Ulysses*, Beckett "blamed the mistakes on the printers more than on the typist" (Gussow 1996: 46). About his own cooperation with Joyce, Beckett told Mel Gussow that "Joyce dictated parts of *Finnegans Wake* to him" (46), and when Gussow asked him whether he edited or changed anything, Beckett answered "no"—"with a hint of a smile" (47). Whoever served as a typist during the last genetic phase of *Work in Progress*, he or she made a most remarkable pun in the paratext of book IV. In a typewritten message to the printer preceding an addition to the galleys of book IV, Joyce or one of his helpers typed: "as I had to add several corrections in hand I am sending you now *the fool text* typewritten as follows" (*JJA* 63: 334; *BL* 47488–226; emphasis added).

Fifty years later, Beckett opened his last text with the word "folie." Although he repeatedly stressed that his own "work in regress" differed from Joyce's approach, the latter's "Work in Progress" is far from a celebration of nineteenth-century onwardness. By constantly "writing its own wrunes" (*FW* 019.35–36), it "autokinatonetically" (*FW* 614.30) undermines the idea of progress for the sake of progress, characterizing the project of modernity. The awareness that this project has become autokinetic marks modernism as a crisis of modernity. Beckett radicalized this crisis of modernity by indicating (for instance in *Watt*, with its lacunae and addenda) that the published text is not quite a finished product. His self-translations were another way in which he decomposed his compositions. Both Joyce and Beckett thus turned their manuscripts into functional tools in their critique of modernity's *Vorwärtsstreben*. That is why not only Joyce is a paradigmatic author for manuscript genetics—as Daniel Ferrer argued[23]—but Beckett as well. As opposed to Edgar Allan Poe, who claimed that all works of art should begin at the end (Poe 1986: 487), Beckett was "untouched by the teleological hypothesis" (Beckett 1999a [1931]: 92). He started writing without necessarily knowing where his creation would end, which is part of the attempt to find a cosmos that can accommodate chaos. In that sense, Beckett's "work in regress" shares the "chaosmos" with Joyce's "work in progress," as well as a poetics of process.

Joyce's openness to the aleatory was the engine of a textual machinery that could not fail because everything could become part of it; Beckett was convinced that his writing could not *but* fail, and therefore resolved to fail better. Consequently, his writing also included failure, which in a paradoxical way turns it into an even more radical chaosmos.

Since writing processes are characterized by a dialectics of repetition and invention (Ferrer 2002: 48), there is another reason why Beckett is a paradigmatic author for manuscript genetics. According to Daniel Ferrer, textual criticism focuses on the repetition (marking the variants between versions as textual departures from the invariant repetition), whereas genetic criticism focuses on the invention. In Beckett's writing method, both aspects are so intertwined that the invention is dependent on the repetition. In the example of the note "per lungo silenzio fioco" in the manuscripts of *Stirrings Still*, the consideration of incorporating the explicit reference to Dante ("hoarse from long silence") in the draft was undone almost as soon as it was introduced. As a consequence, the original "faint" eventually remained unaltered. And yet there is a difference. Between "faint" and "faint" an intertextual recollection and its decomposition have left their mark.

In his attempts to take a distance from Joyce, Beckett described his approach as boring holes in the veil of language. But as the manuscript analyses indicate, he also applied another technique, which shows some resemblances with Joyce's idea of writing a book around a central absence. Around the lack of information about HCE's "crime" Joyce weaves a gigantic web of rumors based on a "woid." The insistence on the absence of guilt only arouses suspicion, the way the word "Guiltless" initiated the most creative period in the genesis of *Finnegans Wake*. This mechanism characterizes many of Beckett's writings as well, up to and including his very last work.

In the copybook containing the drafts of *Comment dire*, Beckett has added a few words in the top margin of the first version (*RUL* MS 3316, f. 2r). Laura Cerrato deciphers them as "Weep ! for end" but they are written in a difficult handwriting toward the end of Beckett's life. Another plausible transcription is "Keep ! for end"[24]—which might be interpreted as a note by the author to himself, indicating that whatever he would write next, this text had to be kept for the end, to round off his oeuvre with an open ending. In that sense, this deliberately unfinished text was conceived as Beckett's literary testament, presenting the genesis of his works as an integral part of his writings. This view is reflected in the decision to preserve his manuscripts and to entrust them to university libraries such as Trinity College Dublin and the University of Reading, for the manuscripts both draw attention to, and are part of, the composition that accommodates decomposition.

In "Genesis: A Fallacy Revisited," W. K. Wimsatt described his enterprise as an attempt to "rescue poems from the morass of their origins," arguing: "If the art work has emerged at all from the artist's private world, it has emerged into some kind of universal world. The artist was not merely *trying* to do something worthy of notice in that world. He has done it" (1968: 194). The "morass of its origins" includes all the "discarded drafts and notes" (Pountney 1988: 101), the false starts, deletions, and tryouts that did not make it into the published text. In linguistic terms, these side paths are thus presented as a negligible past counterfactual hypothesis (irrealis). But it is precisely because, in the case of many authors, the notes and drafts are *not* entirely discarded (that is, not destroyed) that it becomes possible to study them from a chronological perspective and read the subjunctive of the *avant-texte* as a potential (conjunctivus potentialis).

To a certain extent, the drafts and notes allow us to reconstruct a process of writing, even though it "can only be approximately inferred from the existing documents" (Deppman, Ferrer, and Groden 2004: 11). The mere fact of their existence may appeal to our inquisitiveness. These documents deserve to be studied because they are "this this here," "ceci-ci" (*RUL* MS 3316, f. 2r), "ici bas" (*RUL* MS 1396/4/25), not somewhere "au delà." If, according to Monroe Beardsley, "the objective critic's first question" should be "What have we got here?" this also applies to manuscripts, that is, to the work of literature in all its variant forms. What we have got here are documents. The works by Joyce and Beckett continue to be in pro- and regress thanks to "the fool text" of the manuscripts. Whatever the tasks the author sets himself—to eff the ineffable departure or to put Allspace in a Notshall—the full text is a folly and therefore appropriately ends with a fool stop

Notes

Chapter 1. Genetics and Poetics

1. Published in 1831. The preface (of 1818, most probably written by Percy Shelley) states that it originated in "a playful desire of imitation." Mary and Percy Shelley, together with Byron and Polidori, had been reading ghost stories, and the underlying aesthetics of the novel was modeled after great examples with the intention to "innovate upon their combinations" (M. Shelley 1992: 11).

2. The first change (maker > creator) was made by Mary Shelley (MWS); the later revisions were suggested by Percy Shelley (PBS).

3. "Unlike perspective, the grid does not map the space of a room or a landscape or a group of figures onto the surface of a painting. Indeed, if it maps anything, it maps the surface of the painting itself. (. . .) Considered in this way, the bottom line of the grid is a naked and determined materialism" (Krauss 1985: 10).

4. This mathematical interest is reflected in his statement "about my *poetics*" in "A"-12, which he presents in mathematical terms: "An integral / Lower limit speech / Upper limit music" (Zukofsky 1993: 138). Regarding this upper limit, Bach's *Kunst der Fuge* served as a sort of poetical guideline: "From the spring of *Art of Fugue*: / The parts of a fugue should behave like reasonable men / in an orderly discussion" (Zukofsky 1993: 127). For a more detailed discussion, see Van Hulle 2006b.

5. For instance, in cahier 71, page 95v-96r: "Je crois que pour fondre avec plus d'unité, il faudrait mettre cela quand elle joue du pianola, ne faire en somme qu'une seule scène." See also page 93v.

6. 27 March 1903. Second document preserved under MS number 36,639 at the National Library of Ireland (page 24).

7. See Van Hulle 2004a: 38–39. The variations between the different versions of this quotation "perform" what the text is about and nicely illustrate the link between biogenetics and textual genetics: "~~Diversité~~ ^différentiation^ ~~Cette Cette variété~~ ^La variété^ que je ~~ne trouvais pas da dans la vie, dans~~ ^que j'avais^ cherchée en vain ~~dans la vie dans l'amour~~ ^dans la vie^, ~~que je n'av que~~ dans le voyage . . ." (cahier 73:16r)

8. "Au contraire la musique, elle, m'aidait à m'oublier et par là à descendre en moi-même, à y découvrir de nouveau la *vérité* que j'avais cherché en vain dans la vie, dans le voyage, (. . .)" (Proust 1987–89: 3: 1168, esquisse XVII).

9. "Das Anschwellen der Komposition beruht auf einem doppelten Vorgang, einem Bohrungsprozess und einem Ankristallisieren und Einbezogenwerden von aussen" (Mann 1994: 488–89).

10. The root/soil metaphor shows some resemblances to the metaphors Friedrich Schleiermacher employed to explain his view on hermeneutics: "Hence a work of art,

too, is really rooted in its own soil. It loses its meaning when it is wrenched from this environment" (Schleiermacher, quoted in Gadamer 1975: 148). Hans Georg Gadamer quotes this passage in *Wahrheit und Methode* (*Truth and Method*) to renounce traditional, Schleiermacherian hermeneutics: "The reconstruction of the conditions in which a work that has come down to us from the past fulfilled its original purpose is undoubtedly an important aid to its understanding. But it may be asked whether what is then obtained is really what we look for as the meaning of the work of art, and whether it is correct to see understanding as a second creation, the reproduction of the original production. Ultimately, this view of hermeneutics is as foolish as all restitution and restoration of past life. The reconstruction of the original circumstances, like all restoration, is a pointless undertaking in view of the historicity of our being" (1975: 148–49).

11. Richard Brown described a set of "Missing Typescripts," which were discovered in 1988 among the papers of Joyce's Maecenas Harriet Shaw Weaver. One of these documents is a typescript of the section with the "Roll on" quotation. This typescript contains revisions that never made it into *Finnegans Wake*. They were made in an early stage of the composition process. More than fifteen years later (in August 1938), when Joyce gave the section its final destination, he most probably forgot he ever made these early revisions in the "missing typescript."

12. Beckett first wrote "Mr Knott" and only subsequently replaced "Knott" by "Hackett"; he did not replace it in the next lines; this transcription does replace respectively "Mr K" and "Mr Knott" by "Mr [Hackett]" in these lines too, on the assumption that this was implied by the substitution in the first line.

13. The rest of the exclamation reads: "How variously ^With what choice of emotions sensations^ the corner turned! The seat seen! The suspense charged between the 2 operations!" (*RUL* MS 2935/1/1).

Chapter 2. Methodology

1. In this moment of iconicity, McEwan charges Robbie's preparation with a sense of expectation similar to the tuning of an orchestra before a concert performance, after numerous rehearsals: "Methodically, and with pleasure in his own efficiency, as though preparing for some hazardous journey or military exploit, he accomplished the familiar little chores—located his keys, found a ten-shilling note inside his wallet, brushed his teeth, smelled his breath against a cupped hand, from the desk snatched up his letter and folded it into an envelope, loaded his cigarette case and checked his lighter" (2001a: 89–90).

2. "A savage and thoughtless curiosity prompted her to rip the letter from its envelope (...) and though the shock of the message vindicated her completely, this did not prevent her from feeling guilty. It was wrong to open people's letters, but it was right, it was essential, for her to know everything" (113).

3. "The scene by the fountain, its air of ugly threat, and at the end, when both had gone their separate ways, the luminous absence shimmering above the wetness on the gravel—all this would have to be reconsidered" (113).

4. "Naturally, she had never heard the word spoken, or seen it in print, or come across it in asterisks. No one in her presence had ever referred to the word's existence, and what

was more, no one, not even her mother, had ever referred to the existence of that part of her to which—Briony was certain—the word referred. She had no doubt that that was what it was" (114).

5. Interview by M. Zeeman (Dutch television), on the occasion of the Dutch translation of *Enduring Love*.

6. The attempt to put oneself in the position of an author accords with Hirsch's point of view as explained in *Validity in Interpretation*: "The interpreter's primary task is to reproduce in himself the author's 'logic,' his attitudes, his cultural givens, in short, his world" (1971: 242). In a footnote, Hirsch explicitly adds: "Here I purposefully display my sympathies with Dilthey's concepts, *Sichhineinfühlen* and *Verstehen*" (242), two German notions that serve as an adequate description of Leopold Bloom's empathetic attempt to understand the cat in chapter 4 of *Ulysses*: "They call them stupid. They understand what we say better than we understand them. (. . .) Wonder what I look like to her. Height of a tower? No, she can jump me" (*U* 4:26–29).

7. For a more specific application of Popper's work to Beckett studies, see Feldman 2006b.

8. Another example is Raymonde Debray Genette's refutation of some (over)interpretations of Flaubert's *Madame Bovary* by showing that they were based on a copying mistake, notably the word "silencieusement" (silently). Many interpreters have commented upon this adverb, which after a more careful analysis of the manuscript appears to be "délicieusement." What happened to this delicious word is a clear case of "hermeneutic overburdening" (1994: 82).

9. "Quand je lis le berger de *l'Ensorcelée*, je vois un homme à la Mantegna, et de la couleur de la T . . . de Botticelli. Ce n'est peut-être pas du tout ce qu'a vu Barbey. Mais il y a dans sa description un ensemble de rapports qui, étant donné le point de départ faux de mon contresens, lui donnent la même progression de beauté" (Proust 1995: 298).

10. A good example is the German collection of essays *Rückkehr des Autors*, edited by Fotis Jannidis et al.

11. For instance, in the case of the changing number of leaves on the tree in *Waiting for Godot* mentioned in Beckett's theatrical notebook. In the General Editor's Note, James Knowlson writes: "The texts are now as close as possible to how Beckett wanted them to be" (*TN* 1: v). And yet, even after the performances under his own direction, Beckett's intentions could still change (see chapter 7).

12. For a more detailed discussion of this manuscript and of the "fioco" motif, see chapter 8.

Chapter 3. Strategies and Typologies

1. Raymonde Debray-Genette, "Génétique et poétique: Le cas Flaubert," in *Essais de critique génétique*, 21–67 (Paris: Flammarion, 1979).

Chapter 4. Introduction: "Work in Progress"

1. An even shorter competitor is the "woid" ("In the buginning is the woid"; *FW* 378.29), as Sebastian Knowles argues in the closing paragraph of *The Dublin Helix*: "'Woid' lays claim to a middle ground between the word and the void, a linguistic land-

scape that is a fusion of fact and fancy, sense and nonsense, the Word of God and the chaos of the void" (2001: 127).

2. *Finnegans Wake* famously opens with the second half of the sentence that starts at the very end of the book. This formal reflection of a circular view on history was inspired by the Italian philosopher Giambattista Vico (1668-1744), as is suggested in the novel: "The Vico road goes round and round to meet where terms begin" (*FW* 452.21-22). Vico postulated a cycle of three ages (the mythic or theocratic era, the heroic or aristocratic era, and the human era), followed by a period of renewal, which he called *ricorso*. The overall structure of *Finnegans Wake* shows a similar pattern. The text is divided into four books. Book I has eight chapters; book II contains four chapters; so does book III; and book IV consists of only one chapter, a *ricorso* which "brings us back to Howth Castle and Environs" on the first page of the novel. When asked (by the Danish author Tom Kristensen) whether he really believed in Vico's *Scienza nuova*, Joyce replied: "I don't believe in any science, but my imagination grows when I read Vico as it doesn't when I read Freud or Jung" (Ellmann 1983: 693).

3. In the schematic surveys, the four books of *Finnegans Wake* are indicated with Roman numerals, followed by the chapter number and the number of the section, e.g. I.2, section 1 = book I, chapter 2, section 1.

4. For instance, Wim Van Mierlo has discovered that in June and July 1925, Joyce was working in two notebooks at the same time, notebooks VI.B.09 and VI.B.19. When he went to Normandy, he put VI.B.19 aside and started a new notebook, VI.B.08. After his holiday, he continued jotting down notes in the second part of VI.B.19 in September-November 1925 (1997).

5. Luca Crispi presented his findings at the "Genetic Joyce and Beckett Studies" conference at the University of Antwerp, 16-17 March 2006. See also Slote 2006.

6. After the publication of *Finnegans Wake*, the work thus remained "in progress" since the errata were first published separately (1945), then included as an appendix (1946-47), then gradually incorporated (1950; 1957; 1964) until they were fully integrated in the text in the 1975 Faber and Faber edition. I wish to thank Sam Slote for this information.

Chapter 5. Decomposition

1. About the recycling of Wyndham Lewis's early Joyce criticism and some of his notes in VI.B.20, see also Van Hulle 2004a: 96-102. In the meantime, with the help of Geert Van den Eijnden, I have been able to identify several other scattered jottings derived from *The Art of Being Ruled*.

2. After a brief interruption, Joyce continued jotting down notes based on his reading of Lewis on page 60 of his notebook. Again, he clearly focused on the examples Lewis quotes from other sources: "Here is a very vivid description of a 'transformed *shaman*' named Tilu'wgi: '(. . .) He was so "bashful," that whenever I asked a question of somewhat indiscreet character, you could see, *under* the layer of its *usual dirt*, a *blush* spread over his face (. . .)'" (263-64; VI.B.20:60).

3. Joyce continued to focus on the examples mentioned by Lewis, such as the American anthropologist James Alexander Teit's account of rituals among the North American

Lilloets: "Among the Lilloets, on the attainment of puberty (...) a boy would tie his hair in a knot behind his head. For the first four days he painted his face red, after that yellow. His neck, chest, arms, and legs he also painted yellow. Repairing to the mountains, he built himself a *sweat-house*, where he sweated, fasted, and prayed" (265; VI.B.20:60).

From the Finnish anthropologist Edvard Alexander Westermarck's *The Origin of Sexual Modesty*, Lewis quoted a passage on *congress in* the *wood*: "In various islands belonging to the Malay Archipelago sexual intercourse takes place in the forest, not in the house" (266; VI.B.20:60). And "in the district of Lair in *New Ireland*, men and women, boys and girls, sometimes commit suicide when an indecent word is shouted to them as an insult" (266; VI.B.20:60).

4. "Languid Lola's" was added (in the left margin) to the fourth proofs for *transition* 13, dated by the printer 5 June 1928 (*BL* 47483–213). Around the same time (spring 1928), Joyce may have used the same note to add the word "languidous" (*FW* 427.13) to the second proofs (missing) for *transition* 12 (the word is already inserted in the printed text of the third proofs, dated by the printer 2 March 1928) (*BL* 47483–109).

5. Joyce noted down "flunkey" (VI.B.20:69) and crossed it out when he used it, possibly in the fable of the Ondt and the Gracehoper, just before the Gracehoper's song: "Flunkey Footle furlonghed foul, writing off his phoney, but Conte Carme makes the melody that mints the money" (*FW* 418.02–04). "Flunkey Footle" is added to the marked pages of *Two Tales of Shem and Shaun* (1932; *BL* 47486b–310v). The time gap between the writing of the notes (1926) and their use in the drafts (after 1932) is rather large, but still smaller than in the case of the other "Flunkey" in *Finnegans Wake*, which is part of chapter I.3 (*FW* 71.32), and was added to the galley proofs (first set) of book I (dated by the printer 12 March 1937 and received by Harriet Shaw Weaver on 25 February 1938 (*BL* 47476a–44v).

6. Joyce excerpted a few words from the continuation of this passage: "Behind the word is the mind or reason, which is the metaphysical enemy. In the schools of American psychology, deriving from William James, you find this war of words, or against words, being waged more epically and with more concentration than elsewhere. In examining the *tester*, or behaviorist-tester, at work for a moment, we shall be transporting ourselves to the so-called 'laboratory' where the word is actually being annihilated, or where the 'mind,' the 'intellect,' is being drilled out of it. And Professor Watson is the greatest exponent of behaviorism, and the king of testers. (...) There are for Watson two main points of behaviour, and two only. And into these two physiologically controllable forms the whole of the human personality is contained. There is no metaphysical or non-metaphysical element of personality. These two forms of behaviour are the big and the little; or, as he puts it, those affecting the large musculature of the animal, and those affecting the small. The former, the big, he calls *explicit* behaviour. The lesser, the small, he calls *implicit* behaviour" (340; VI.B.20:72).

Chapter 6. Recombination: S, M, L

1. Joyce himself tried to explain his linguistic experiment by pointing out to Miss Weaver that a large part of human life is passed in a state that cannot be expressed in "wideawake language," but even though the *Wake* is a "nightbook" compared to *Ulysses*

(the book of one day), and even though book IV announces dawn, it would be a defusing reduction to regard this text as nothing but a dream. T. S. Eliot's description of the mythic method in *Ulysses* as a way of presenting "the immense panorama of futility and anarchy which is contemporary history" is perhaps even more applicable to *Finnegans Wake*.

2. Ingeborg Landuyt, "'Words in Distress': A Genetic Investigation into James Joyce's Early 'Work in Progress'" (Ph.D. diss., University of Antwerp, 1999).

3. For a thorough investigation of notebook VI.B.34, see Luca Crispi's "The Mechanics of Creativity: A Genetic Study of James Joyce's *Finnegans Wake*, II.2" (2001): 177ff.

4. "It is one of Joyce's techniques following the commonplace idea that dreams are distortions of everyday life. The notebook units represent such life. At first (during the early stages of composition) Joyce is content to rearrange them. Later he distorts them more and more, making them less easy to recognize. Finally he uses the accidental mistranscriptions" (MacArthur 1987: 76–77).

5. A quarter century after the groundbreaking work of the editors of the *James Joyce Archive*, these few suggestions for the fine-tuning of the chronological arrangement of Joyce's manuscripts could only have been possible by the stimulating exchange of ideas among genetic Joyceans. In particular, I wish to thank Mikio Fuse for the excellent cooperation in view of the reconstruction of the writing sequence in this particular phase of "Work in Progress."

6. Presented at the "Genetic Joyce and Beckett Studies" conference at the University of Antwerp, 16–17 March 2006.

7. In /\b, the last notesheet based on VI.B.34 notes is *BL* 47486a–26r (*JJA* 61: 144). The second half of that page is based on VI.B.20. Joyce apparently continued taking excerpts from VI.B.20 on the first quarter of *BL* 47486a–26v. The rest of that page is derived from VI.C.01. The same scenario is applicable with regard to /\c: here, the last notesheet based on VI.B.34 is *BL* 47486a–47 (*JJA* 61: 175). The last quarter of that page is based on notes from VI.B.20, continuing on the first half of *BL* 47486a–54. The second half of this page is based on VI.B.17 and VI.C.01, in that order. In /\d, *BL* 47486a–57 (based on VI.B.34 and VI.B.20) and *BL* 47486a–58 (based on VI.B.20) preceded MS 47486a–59 (based on VI.B.20, VI.B.17, and VI.C.01). By analogy, it seems safe to say that, in /\a, *BL* 47486a–03 (based on VI.B.34 and VI.B.20) preceded *BL* 47486a–06 (based on VI.B.17 and VI.C.01).

8. The recto and verso of notesheet *BL* 47486a–3 cannot have been part of two piles simultaneously, but since this is the first of the whole series, the division between recto (/\a) and verso (/\b) indicates the start of the four-stack distribution system.

9. "De même la loi juive défendait aux Hébreux la reproduction en bois ou en pierre d'objets réels d'objets réels, animaux ou fleurs" (Gallois 1894: 20).

10. "Pendant le moyen âge, la *cryptographie* a été surtout cultivée par les moines et les kabbalistes; mais, comme en ces temps d'ombrageuse ignorance il était parfois dangereux de correspondre dans un langage mystérieux ou indéchiffrable, on y a surtout appliqué la *sténographie, modus sine secreti suspicione scribendi*, comme disaient nos pères, c'est-à-dire l'art de donner le change sur le sens de communications transmises" (Gallois 1894: 23).

11. "Il devait y avoir dans chacune d'elles [écuries] un homme intelligent pour recevoir

les dépêches apportées par un courrier, les remettre à un autre courrier, prendre soin des hommes et des chevaux qui arrivaient fatigués, et subvenir aux frais" (Gallois 1894: 25).

12. "Suidas, lexicographe grec du v° siècle de notre ère, dit que les courriers parcouraient d'un trait quinze cents *stades* (mesure itinéraire de cent vingt-cinq pas)" (Gallois 1894: 26).

13. Another example of this kind of distortion is the entry "leave little bag of / gloom behind" (VI.B.11:133). Mme Raphael copied it inaccurately and changed it into a "little bag of doom"; Joyce selected it and transferred it to the B-pile of the notesheets as "leave little bag of [doubt] behind"--the handwriting is unclear; but in any case the word-unit eventually made it into FW as "and leave your little bag of doubts (...) behind you" (*FW* 458.19-20).

14. "Une petite fille de neuf à douze mois, citée par Preyer, imitait de la façon la plus comique ce qu'elle voyait faire par sa bonne; elle baignait sa poupée, la corrigeait, la berçait, l'embrassait" (Queyrat 1920: 83).

15. See chapter I.1: "'E tekne mimeitai ten phusin'--This phrase is falsely rendered as 'Art is an imitation of Nature.' Aristotle does not here define art: he says only 'Art imitates Nature' and means that the artistic process is like the natural process" (second document preserved under MS number 36,639 at the National Library of Ireland, page 24).

16. "So ist die Bewegung die Brücke zwischen Worten und Dingen; und wie im menschlichen Körper es einen Kreislauf des Blutes gibt, wie die äußersten und feinsten Verästelungen der Arterien in die feinsten Verästelungen der Venen übergehen und das Leben zwischen ihnen liegt, so berührt sich die Wirklichkeit und die Sprache in der unzugänglichen Erscheinung der Bewegung. Die Worte berühren die Dinge nie, aber sie umschweben sie" (Mauthner 1923: 3: 86). Joyce read this part of the *Beiträge zu einer Kritik der Sprache* and excerpted a phrase from Mauthner's considerations regarding "movement." The note "wo ist die Reise" (VI.B.46:55) is derived from volume 3, page 85, where Mauthner notes that "the effort on the part of contemporary natural sciences to reduce every observation to periodical movements eventually collides with the idea that all our knowledge is subjective, that our language is an airy net of abstractions. We laugh at the child to whom a journey was promised, and which, confronted with mountains and lakes and forests far away from home, naively asks: 'Yes, but where is the journey?' We are just as naive if we ask the physicist: 'Yes, but where is the wind?'" (Mauthner 1923: 3: 85).

17. Hans Walter Gabler, "Explorations in Spaces of Writing." (January 1998) http://fb14.uni-mainz.de/~enb/forfritz.htm.

18. The second draft reads: "I am perfectly proud of this great ~~man~~ ^civilian^, ~~Mr~~ H.C. Earwicker, ^long life to him,^ my once handsome husband ^to ~~bee~~ seen from my improved looks^ who is as gentle as a woman and ~~very~~ ^a greatly^ attractable when he always sits fornenst me^, poor ass,^ to make our ^polite^ conversations about ^lawful^ business & pleasure when he is after his 3rd or 4th mug ^of 4 ale & shag^ and he never chained me to a chair since this ^native^ island was born" (*BL* 47471b-40).

19. The same fusion metaphor recurs frequently in Joyce's letters; see, for example, *L I* 128 (20 July 1919); *L I* 204 (9 October 1923).

20. Most references to "Sam" are probably not allusions to Samuel Beckett. For in-

stance, "Sam knows miles bettern me how to work the miracle" is already part of the fair copy of chapter 1+2 of book III (*BL* 47483-157), date in the JJA "April 1926." Sam or Sammy recurs elsewhere, e.g. "skeezy Sammy" (*BL* 47483-127) was already part of the fair copy of the "Dave the Dancekerl" episode, i.e., most probably in April 1926, more than two years before Joyce first met Beckett. "Sammy, call on" (*FW* 222.36) could theoretically be a reference to Beckett (ca. 1930), but given the earlier Sammies (1926) it does not seem very likely that Joyce is explicitly referring to Beckett.

21. "Ich kann aber dem Reize nicht widerstehen, mit einigen Worten wenigstens anzudeuten, wie die Geschichte der Philosophie (. . .) sich als eine langsame Selbstzersetzung des Metaphorischen ausdeuten liesse. Freilich darf man da nur die Philosophien betrachten, die historisch aufeinander beruhen, und muss von dem Denkgeschäft der Inder absehen, welche bereits in alter Zeit das Wirklichkeitsbild als ein *Blendwerk der Maya* betrachteten, als eine angeborene Täuschung, hervorgerufen durch falsche Analogien, also doch wohl durch Metaphern" (Mauthner 1923: 2: 473; emphasis added).

22. Daniel Ferrer, "Joyce as Paradigmatic Author for Genetic Criticism." Paper presented at the "Genetic Joyce and Beckett Studies" conference, University of Antwerp, 16-17 March 2006.

Chapter 7. Introduction: "Work in Regress"

1. The subtitle of this chapter, "Work in Regress," is taken from a letter to Ruby Cohn (9 January 1972), preserved at the University of Reading; with many thanks to Mark Nixon.

2. "Eine Abkürzung der unendlich langen Sprachentwicklung findet statt, mehr nicht. Das Kind lernt sprechen, aber es lernt nicht die Sprache. Wenn man hier unter Sprache die Summe der menschlichen Erfahrungen verstehen will" (Mauthner 1923: 1: 73). Source discovered by Vincent Deane.

3. Israel Shenker, "A Portrait of Samuel Beckett, the Author of the Puzzling *Waiting for Godot*," *New York Times*, 6 May 1956.

4. "Beckett Symposium," *New Theatre Magazine* 11, no. 3(1973): 12; emphasis added.

5. Samuel Beckett quoted by Tom F. Driver, "Beckett by the Madeleine," *Columbia University Forum* 4, no. 3 (1961): 23.

6. In Beckett's *Texts for Nothing*, the narrator calls himself a scribe: "I'm the clerk, I'm the scribe, at the hearings of what cause I know not" (*CSP* 117).

7. Most of Beckett's Mauthner notes are derived from volume 2 of the *Beiträge*. Several researchers have investigated this interesting cluster of notes; see, for example, Ben-Zvi 1980; 1983; Feldman 2006a; Garforth 2005; Hulle 1999; Pilling 1992; 2005; and Skerl 1974.

8. The French text reads: «On dirait un saule.» Against the backdrop of Beckett's marginalia in his copy of *A la recherche du temps perdu*, it is interesting to note that one of the idiosyncratic pronunciations of the hotel manager in Balbec is "saule" instead of "sole."

9. For a detailed discussion of this text's structuring patterns, see also Pountney 1988, which includes a montage of the six thematic "families" in the appendix.

Chapter 8. Recollection

1. "C'est dans la tranquillité de la décomposition que je me rappelle cette longue émotion que fut ma vie. (. . .) Décomposer c'est vivre aussi, je le sais, je le sais, ne me fatiguez pas, mais on n'y est pas toujours tout entier. D'ailleurs de cette vie-là aussi j'aurai peut-être la bonté de vous entretenir un jour" (Beckett 1951a: 39); "It is in the tranquillity of decomposition that I remember the long confused emotion which was my life. (. . .) To decompose is to live too, I know, I know, don't torment me, but one sometimes forgets. And of that life too I shall tell you perhaps one day" (Beckett 1955–58: 25).

2. The translation was revised by Joyce and several friends, and eventually published under the title "Anna Lyvie Plurabelle" in *Nouvelle Revue Française* 19, no. 212 (1 May 1931); 633–46.

3. The passage between ^. . .^ is an addition in the margin.

4. Not to be confused with criticism, according to David Hayman (1995: 8); see also chapter 2.

5. See Knowlson 1996: 117; 727 n. 123: letter to MacGreevy in which Beckett mentions that he is "thinking of Keats and Giorg[i]one's two young men (. . .) for a discussion of Proust's floral obsessions." In another note, Knowlson mentions that "July" in the date "7 July 1930" "may be an error for August" (727 n. 121).

6. See Jacques Aubert's introduction to "Anna Lyvia Pluratself ": "Un envoi de Samuel Beckett à Philippe Soupault en date du 5 juillet 1930 signale qu'un premier fragment de deux grandes pages dactylographiées sans interligne était prêt à cette date. Ce texte atteignit le stade des épreuves en placards (c'est un jeu de celles-ci daté au tampon par l'imprimeur du 15 octobre 1930 que nous reproduisons) mais fut retiré *in extremis* par les auteurs" (Aubert in Joyce 1985: 417).

7. Paragraph 35 suggests that the hearer could "be named H. Aspirate. Haitch."

8. This coincidence of birth, suffering, and death is hinted at in the first line of *A Piece of Monologue*: "Birth was the death of him."

9. "I simply know next to nothing about my work in this way, as little as a plumber of the history of hydraulics. There is nothing/nobody with me when I'm writing, only the hellish job in hand. The "eye of the mind" in *Happy Days* does not *refer* to Yeats any more than the "revels" in *Endgame* [refer] to *The Tempest*. They are just bits of pipe I happen to have with me. I suppose all is reminiscence from womb to tomb. All I can say is I have scant information concerning mine—alas" (Beckett in a letter to James Knowlson, 11 April 1972, quoted in Knowlson, "Beckett's Bits of Pipe," *Samuel Beckett: Humanistic Perspectives*, ed. Morris Beja, S. E. Gontarski, and Pierre Astier [Ohio, 1982], 16).

10. I wish to thank Mark Nixon for his transcription of this correspondence between Beckett and Herbert preserved at RUL.

11. See Van Hulle 2004b.

12. In his notes on Goethe's *Faust*, for instance, Beckett noted down the line "Die Träne quillt, die Erde hat mich wieder" (*RUL* MS 5004: 59). In his *Whoroscope* notebook, he changed this line into "Die Merde hat mich wieder" before he incorporated it as one of the Addenda in *Watt* (Beckett 1981 [1953]: 251).

13. Cf. note 9 above; letter from Samuel Beckett to James Knowlson, 11 April 1972.

14. With an arrow linking Mercier's 9.50 arrival to Camier's.

15. He asks Mercier why he wants to know, and Mercier answers: "Ce sont des mots qui me bruissent dans la tête depuis hier, dit Mercier, et me brûlent les lèvres" (These words rustle in my head since yesterday and they're burning my lips) (Beckett 1974: 100).

16. Bruno Clément, paper presented at the "Beckett at 100" conference in Tallahassee, Florida, 9–11 February 2006.

17. John Pilling has traced this intertextual reference (Lat. "sola diaeta curari") to the *Tardes passiones* II.xii of Caelius Aurelianus, a physician who lived in the fifth century (Pilling 1996).

18. I wish to thank Mark Nixon for drawing my attention to this document *RUL* MS 2937/1–3.

Chapter 9. Decomposition: L, M, S

1. With many thanks to Mark Nixon.

2. For a thorough discussion of these notes, see Feldman 2006a. See also Frost and Maxwell 2006.

3. Cf. also the corresponding note derived from Windelband (1958: 50): "On the way downward fire passes over, by condensation, into water and earth; on the way upward earth and water, by rarefaction, pass over into fire; and these two ways are alike" (TCD MS 1967/25r).

4. See Ackerley 2005: 54.

5. "For Watt's concern, deep as it appeared, was not after all with what the figure was, in reality, but with what the figure appeared to be, in reality" (Beckett 1981 [1953]: 225–26).

6. "D.--What other plane can there be for the maker?
B.--Logically none. Yet I speak of an art turning from it in disgust, weary of its puny exploits, weary of pretending to be able, of being able, of doing a little better the same old thing, of going a little further along a dreary road.
D.--And preferring what?
B.--The expression that there is nothing to express, nothing with which to express, nothing from which to express, no power to express, no desire to express, together with the obligation to express" (Beckett 1984: 139).

7. *Goethes Faust*, ed. Robert Petsch (Leipzig: Bibliographisches Institut, n.d.).

8. "To decompose is to live too, I know, I know, don't torment me, but one sometimes forgets" (*Molloy*; Beckett 1955–58: 25).

9. "Sous les cieux, sur les routes, dans les villes, dans les bois, dans les chambers, dans les montagnes, dans les plaines, au bord des mers, sur les flots, derrière mes homuncules, je n'ai pas toujours été triste, j'ai perdu mon temps, renié mes droits, raté ma peine, oublié ma leçon" (Beckett 1953b: 32).

10. "Genetic Joyce and Beckett Studies" conference, 16–17 March 2006, University of Antwerp.

11. In this context, Molloy's theft of one of Lousse's silver objects may be a reference

to Silberer: "I had stolen from Lousse a little silver, oh nothing much, massive teaspoons for the most part, and other small objects whose utility I did not grasp but which seemed as if they might have some value" (Beckett 1955-58: 63).

12. Herbert Silberer, "Der Homunculus." *Imago* 3 (1914): 37-79.

13. Toward the end, Watt returns to the station and waits in the waiting room, which may be a reference to the womb (something Beckett underlined in his psychology notes on Ernest Jones: "Symbolisation is an unconscious process, the subject is unaware of the meaning of the symbol, even of the existence of symbol, which he accepts as the reality. (. . .) It is true that the symbol may be ambivalent (as *room* for *womb* or for *woman*)" (*TCD* MS 10971/8/11-12). On the same page of the Psychology notes, Beckett noted down the word "manikin" in the section about "True Symbolism": "Important characteristic is the hostility provoked by correct interpretation of symbol. E.g. Punchinello as phallic symbol, male organ, comic *manikin*" (*TCD* MS 10971/8/11; emphasis added).

14. Friedhelm Rathjen, "Neitherways: Long Ways in Beckett's Shorts." Paper presented at the "Beckett at Reading" conference, 30 March-2 April 2006, University of Reading.

15. "Hell is the static lifelessness of unrelieved viciousness. Paradise the static lifelessness of unrelieved immaculation. Purgatory a flood of movement and vitality released by the conjunction of these two elements" (Beckett 1929: 253).

16. Ts1: Corrected typescript, numbered I by Samuel Beckett (HRHRC Beckett folder 4.2); Lake 1984, nr. 226.

Ts2: Corrected typescript (HRHRC Beckett folder 4.2); Lake 1984, nr. 227.

Ts3: Corrected typescript (HRHRC Beckett folder 4.2); Lake 1984, nr. 228.

Ts4: Corrected typescript; (HRHRC Beckett folder 4.2); Lake 1984, nr. 229.

Ts5: Thermofax copy; Lake 1984, nr. 230.

Ts6: Corrected proofs for Faber and Faber; Lake 1984, nr. 232.

Ts7: Processed typescript (computer printout; mimeographed acting version) of *Krapp's Last Tape*; Lake 1984, nr. 372.

TsLDB: Carbon copy of typescript of French translation "La dernière bande," with a few corrections and additions in red and blue inks and in pencil; Lake 1984, nr. 234.

17. *Waiting for Godot*, an educational edition with afterword and notes by John Fletcher (London, Faber and Faber, 1971), 120; cf. Knowlson in Beckett 1994 (General Editor's Introduction): xiv.

18. "Beckett Symposium," *New Theatre Magazine* 9, no. 3 (1973): 12.

19. The beat and offbeat on the syllables "mi" and "ne" are marked in black ink by Beckett.

20. The beat and offbeat on the syllables "mi" and "ne" are marked in black ink by Beckett.

21. Preserved at the University of Reading; many thanks to Mark Nixon for sharing his transcription.

22. "Le tiers à qui avant de mourir il fit part de confia l'incident se dépêcha avant de mourir à son tour d'en faire part de le confier à son tour à son [deuxi] autre deuxième tiers qui lui à son tour avant de mourir à son tour se dépêche en l'absence de tout tiers à qui en faire part le confier à son tour de la consigner par écrit.

Inexact par rapport à la confidence reçue inexacte elle aussi par rapport à l'originale ce document est donc doublement suspect. En raison surtout de lacunes indûment comblées" (*RUL* MS 2934, f. 3r).

23. Daniel Ferrer, "Joyce as Paradigmatic Author for Genetic Criticism." Paper presented at the "Genetic Joyce and Beckett Studies" conference, University of Antwerp, 16–17 March 2006.

24. I wish to thank Mark Nixon and John Pilling for their help and advice regarding the transcription of Beckett's late manuscripts.

Works Cited

Abbott, H. Porter. 1996. *Beckett Writing Beckett: The Author in the Autograph.* Ithaca and London: Cornell University Press.
Ackerley, C. J. 2004. *Demented Particulars: The Annotated "Murphy."* Tallahassee, Fla.: Journal of Beckett Studies Books.
———. 2005. *Obscure Locks, Simple Keys: The Annotated "Watt."* Tallahassee: Journal of Beckett Studies Books.
Ackerley, C. J., and S. E. Gontarski. 2004. *The Grove Companion to Samuel Beckett.* New York: Grove Press.
Adorno, Theodor. 1994. "Skizze einer Interpretation des 'Namenlosen.'" In "'Gegen den Trug der Frage nach dem Sinn': Eine Dokumentation zu Adornos Beckett-Lektüre," edited by Rolf Tiedemann, 18–77. *Frankfurter Adorno Blätter* 3. Munich: edition text+kritik.
Atherton, James S. 1959. *The Books at the Wake: A Study of Literary Allusions in James Joyce's "Finnegans Wake."* London: Faber and Faber.
Attridge, Derek, and Daniel Ferrer. 1984. "Introduction: Highly Continental Evenements." In *Post-structuralist Joyce: Essays from the French,* 1–13. Cambridge: Cambridge University Press.
Aubert, Jacques. 1985. Introduction to "Anna Lyvia Pluratself." In *Cahiers de l'Herne: James Joyce,* 417–18. Paris: L'Herne.
Ballard, J. G. 2001. *The Atrocity Exhibition.* London: Flamingo/Harper Collins. (Orig. pub. 1969.)
Barthes, Roland. 1970. *S/Z.* Paris: Éditions du Seuil, 1970.
———. 1977. "The Death of the Author." In *Image—Music—Text,* translated by Stephen Heath, 142–48. Glasgow: Fontana.
Beach, Sylvia. 1959. *Shakespeare and Company.* Lincoln: University of Nebraska Press. (Orig. pub. 1956.)
Beckett, Samuel. 1929. "Dante . . . Bruno.Vico..Joyce." *transition* 16–17, 242–53.
———. 1951a. *Molloy.* Paris: Éditions de Minuit.
———. 1951b. *Malone meurt.* Paris: Éditions de Minuit.
———. 1953a. *Watt.* New York: Grove Press.
———. 1953b. *L'innommable.* Paris: Éditions de Minuit.
———. 1955–58. *Molloy, Malone Dies, The Unnamable.* New York: Grove.
———. 1957. *Murphy.* New York: Grove.
———. 1958. *Nouvelles et textes pour rien.* Paris: Éditions de Minuit.
———. 1970a. *Mercier et Camier.* Paris: Éditions de Minuit.
———. 1970b. *More Pricks Than Kicks.* London: Calder and Boyars. (Orig. pub. 1934.)
———. 1974. *Mercier and Camier.* New York: Grove Press.

———. 1981. *Watt*. London: Calder. (Orig. pub. 1953.)
———. 1984. *Disjecta*. Edited by Ruby Cohn. New York: Grove. (Orig. pub. 1937.)
———. 1990. *The Complete Dramatic Works*. London: Faber and Faber.
———. 1992a. *Nohow On*. London: Calder.
———. 1992b. *Endgame*. Edited by S. E. Gontarski. Vol. 2 of *The Theatrical Notebooks of Samuel Beckett*. London: Faber and Faber.
———. 1992c. *Krapp's Last Tape*. Edited by James Knowlson. Vol. 3 of *The Theatrical Notebooks of Samuel Beckett*.
———. 1993a. *Dream of Fair to Middling Women*. Edited by Eoin O'Brien and Edith Fournier. New York: Arcade.
———. 1993b. *Company/Compagnie and A Piece of Monologue/Solo: A Bilingual Variorum Edition*. Edited by Charles Krance. New York and London: Garland.
———. 1994. *Waiting for Godot*. Edited by Dougald McMillan and James Knowlson. Vol. 1 of *The Theatrical Notebooks of Samuel Beckett*. New York: Grove Press.
———. 1995. *The Complete Short Prose 1929–1989*. Edited by S. E. Gontarski. New York: Grove Press.
———. 1999a. *"Proust" and "Three Dialogues with Georges Duthuit."* London: Calder.
———. 1999b. *The Shorter Plays*. Edited by S. E. Gontarski. Vol. 4 of *The Theatrical Notebooks of Samuel Beckett*. London and New York: Faber and Faber, and Grove Press.
———. 2001. *Comment c'est/How It Is: A Critical Genetic Edition*. Edited by Magessa O'Reilly. London and New York: Routledge.
———. 2002. *Poems 1930–1989*. London: Calder.
Benjamin, Walter. 1996. "Die Aufgabe des Übersetzers." In *Walter Benjamin: Ein Lesebuch*, edited by M. Opitz, 45–57. Frankfurt am Main: Suhrkamp. (Orig. pub. 1923.)
Ben-Zvi, Linda. 1980. "Samuel Beckett, Fritz Mauthner, and the Limits of Language." *PMLA* 95, no. 2 (March): 183–200.
———. 1983. "Fritz Mauthner for Company." *Journal of Beckett Studies* 9: 65–88.
Berkeley, George. 1957. *A Treatise Concerning the Principles of Human Knowledge*. New York: Liberal Arts Press.
Bernstein, Michael André. 1994. *Foregone Conclusions: Against Apocalyptic History*. Berkeley and Los Angeles: University of California Press.
Bishop, Tom, and Raymond Federman, eds. 1997. *Samuel Beckett*. Cahier de l'Herne. Paris: Éditions de l'Herne.
Boldrini, Lucia. 2001. *Joyce, Dante, and the Poetics of Literary Relations: Language and Meaning in "Finnegans Wake."* Cambridge: Cambridge University Press.
Borges, Jorge Luis. 1970. "Kafka and His Precursors." Translated by James E. Irby. In *Labyrinths: Selected Stories and Other Writings*, edited by Donald A. Yates and James E. Irby, 234–36. Harmondsworth, UK: Penguin.
Boulter, Jonathan. 2001. *Interpreting Narrative in the Novels of Samuel Beckett*. Gainesville: University Press of Florida, 2001.
Bourdieu, Pierre. 1992. *Les règles de l'art: Genèse et structure du champ littéraire*. Paris: Seuil.
Brater, Enoch. 1989. *Why Beckett*. London: Thames and Hudson.

———. 1994. *The Drama in the Text: Beckett's Late Fiction*. New York and Oxford: Oxford University Press.
Bryden, Mary, Julian Garforth, and Peter Mills. 1998a. *Beckett at Reading: Catalogue of the Beckett Manuscript Collection at the University of Reading*. Reading, UK: Whiteknights Press and the Beckett International Foundation.
———. 1998b. "No Stars without Stripes: Beckett et Dante." Edited by Michèle Touret. In *Lectures de Beckett*, 163–82. Rennes: Presses Universitaires de Rennes.
Bulhof, Ilse. 1988. *Darwins "Origin of Species": Betovererende wetenschap*. Baarn, Netherlands: Ambo.
Burke, Edmund. 1998. *A Philosophical Enquiry into the Sublime and Beautiful, and Other Pre-Revolutionary Writings*. London: Penguin Classics.
Burrow, J. W. 1968. "Editor's Introduction." In *The Origin of Species*, by Charles Darwin, 11–48. London: Penguin Classics.
Califf, David J. 1995. "Clones and Mutations: A Genetic Look at 'Dave the Dancekerl.'" In *Probes: Genetic Studies in Joyce*, edited by David Hamen and Sam Slote, 123–47. European Joyce Studies 5. Amsterdam: Rodopi.
Camus, Albert. 1942. *Le mythe de Sisyphe*. Paris: Gallimard.
Carey, Phyllis. 1992. "Stephen Dedalus, Belacqua Shuah and Dant's Pietà." In *Joyce'n'Beckett*, edited by Carey and Ed Jewinski, 104–16. New York: Fordham University Press.
Carey, Phyllis, and Ed Jewinski, eds. 1992. *Joyce'n'Beckett*. New York: Fordham University Press.
Carroll, Lewis. 1988. *The Complete Works of Lewis Carroll*. London: Penguin.
Casanova, Pascale. 1997. *Beckett l'abstracteur*. Paris: Seuil.
Caselli, Daniela. 1997. "Looking It Up in My Big Dante: A Note on *Sedendo et Quiesc[i]endo*." *Journal of Beckett Studies* 6, no. 2: 85–94.
———. 1999. "Dante and Beckett: Authority Constructing Authority." Ph.D. diss., University of Reading.
———. 2005. *Beckett's Dantes: Intertextuality in the Fiction and Criticism*. Manchester and New York: Manchester University Press.
Cerrato, Laura. 1999. *Génesis de la poética de Samuel Beckett: Apuntes para una teoría de la despalabra*. Buenos Aires: Fondo de Cultura Económica.
Cohn, Ruby. 2001. *A Beckett Canon*. Ann Arbor: University of Michigan Press.
Compagnon, Antoine. 1992. "Ce qu'on ne peut plus dire de Proust." *Littérature* 88 (December): 54–61.
———. 1995. "Introduction." *Romanic Review* 83, no. 3: 394–99.
———. 1998. *Le démon de la théorie: Littérature et sens commun*. Paris: Seuil.
Connolly, Thomas E. 1961. *James Joyce's Scribbledehobble: The Ur-Workbook for "Finnegans Wake."* Evanston, Ill.: Northwestern University Press.
———. 1978. *The Personal Library of James Joyce*. Buffalo: Norwood Editions.
Connor, Steven. 1988. *Samuel Beckett: Repetition, Theory and Text*. Oxford: Blackwell.
———. 1992. "Authorship, Authority, and Self-Reference in Joyce and Beckett." In *Re: Joyce'n Beckett*, edited by Phyllis Carey and Ed Jewinski, 147–59. New York: Fordham University Press.

Contat, Michel, and Daniel Ferrer. 1998. Introduction to *Pourquoi la critique génétique?* edited by Michel Contat and Daniel Ferrer, 7–10. Paris: CNRS Éditions.

Crispi, Luca. 2001. "The Mechanics of Creativity: A Genetic Study of James Joyce's *Finnegans Wake*, II.2." Ph.D. diss., State University of New York at Buffalo.

Culler, Jonathan. 2002. *Structuralist Poetics*. London: Routledge. (Orig. pub. 1975.)

Dalton, Jack P. 1966. "Advertisement for the Restoration." In *Twelve and a Tilly: Essays on the Occasion of the 25th Anniversary of "Finnegans Wake,"* edited by Jack P. Dalton and Clive Hart, 119–37. London: Faber and Faber.

Danielewski, Mark Z. 2000. *House of Leaves*. 2nd ed. New York: Pantheon.

Dante Alighieri. 1995. *Inferno*. In *The Portable Dante*, edited and translated by Mark Musa. New York and London: Penguin.

———. 2002. *The Inferno*. Translated by Robert and Jean Hollander. New York: Anchor Books/Random House.

Darwin, Charles. 1959. *The Origin of Species: A Variorum Text*. Edited by Morse Peckham. Philadelphia: University of Pennsylvania Press.

———. 1987. *Charles Darwin's Notebooks 1836–1844*. Edited by Paul H. Barrett et al. Ithaca, N.Y.: Cornell University Press, 1987.

Darwin, Francis. 1995. *The Life of Charles Darwin*. London: Senate. (Orig. pub. 1902.)

Dawkins, Richard. 1976. *The Selfish Gene*. Oxford: Oxford University Press.

Deane, Vincent. 1994. "Bywaters and the Original Crime." In *"Teems of Times,"* edited by Andre Treip, 165–87. European Joyce Studies 4. Amsterdam: Rodopi.

———. 1998. Looking after the Sense. In *A Collideorscape of Joyce*, edited by R. Frehner and U. Zeller, 375–97. Dublin: Lilliput Press.

de Biasi, Pierre-Marc. 1985. "Paranoïa-genèse: Remarques sur l'identité des recherches en génétique textuelle." In *Leçons d'écriture: Ce que disent les manuscripts*, edited by A. Grésillon and M. Werner, 259–75. Paris: Minard.

———. 1993. "Vers une science de la littérature: L'analyse des manuscrits et la genèse de l'oeuvre." In *Symposium: Les enjeux (Encyclopaedia Universalis)*, 2: 924–37. Paris: Encyclopaedia Universalis.

———. 1996. "What Is a Literary Draft? Toward a Functional Typology of Genetic Documentation." In *Drafts*, edited by Michel Contat, Denis Hollier, and Jacques Neefs, *Yale French Studies* 89: 26–56.

———. 1997. "Les Désarrois de l'herméneute." *Le monde des livres*, February 14, 1997.

———. 2004. "Toward a Science of Literature: Manuscript Analysis and the Genesis of the Work." In *Genetic Criticism: Texts and Avant-textes*, edited by Jed Deppman, Daniel Ferrer, and Michael Groden, 36–68. Philadelphia: University of Pennsylvania Press.

Debray Genette, Raymonde. 1994. "Hapax et paradigmes." *Genesis* 6: 79–92.

De Graef, Ortwin. 2001. "Nothing out of Hermeneutics' Certain Course." *Image & Narrative* 3 (September). www.imageandnarrative.be/illustrations/ortwindegraef.htm.

Deleuze, Gilles. 1973. *Proust and Signs*. Translated by Richard Howard. London: Allen Lane/Penguin.

———. 1976. *Proust et les signes*. 4th ed. Paris: Presses Universitaires de France.

Deppman, Jed. 2007. "A Chapter in Composition: Chapter II.4." In *How Joyce Wrote*

'Finnegans Wake': A Chapter-by-Chapter Genetic Guide, edited by Luca Crispi and Sam Slote, 304–46. Madison: The University of Wisconsin Press.

Deppman, Jed, Daniel Ferrer, and Michael Groden, eds. Genetic Criticism: Texts and Avant-textes. Philadelphia: University of Pennsylvania Press.

Dettmar, Kevin J. H. 1999. "The Joyce the Beckett Built." In Beckett and Beyond, edited by Bruce Stewart, 78–92. Gerrards Cross, UK: Colin Smythe.

Eco, Umberto. 1979. The Role of the Reader: Explorations in the Semiotics of Texts. Bloomington and London: Indiana University Press.

———. 1990. The Limits of Interpretation. Bloomington: Indiana University Press.

———. 1992. Interpretation and Overinterpretation. Cambridge: Cambridge University Press.

Eeckhout, Bart. 1992. "'Amoroso ma non troppo': The Music of the 'Sirens' Chapter in Joyce's Ulysses." In BELL—Belgian Essays on Language and Literature, edited by Pierre Michel et al., 37–47. Liège: L³—Liège Language and Literature.

Eliot, T. S. 1969. "The Frontiers of Criticism." In On Poetry and Poets, by Eliot, 103–18. London: Faber and Faber. (Orig. pub. 1957.)

———. 1975. Selected Prose of T. S. Eliot. Edited by Frank Kermode. New York: Farrar, Straus and Giroux.

Ellmann, Richard. 1983. James Joyce. New and rev. ed. Oxford: Oxford University Press.

Elsschot, Willem. 2003. Kaas. Amsterdam: Querido.

Engelberts, Matthijs. 2001. Défis du récit scénique: Formes et enjeux du mode narratif dans le théâtre de Beckett et de Duras. Geneva: Droz.

Enzensberger, Hans Magnus. 1965. Gedichte: Die Entstehung eines Gedichts. Frankfurt am Main: Suhrkamp.

Falconer, Graham. 1988. "Où en sont les études génétiques littéraires?" Texte 8: 267–86.

———. 1993. "Genetic Criticism." Comparative Literature 45, no. 1: 1–21.

———. 1995. "La critique génétique: Un retour à l'histoire?" Romanic Review 86, no. 3 (May): 429–36.

Feldman, Matthew. 2005. "Beckett's Poss and the Dog's Dinner: An Empirical Survey of the 1930s 'Psychology' and 'Philosophy Notes.'" In Beckett the European, edited by Dirk Van Hulle, 69–94. Tallahassee: Journal of Beckett Studies Books.

———. 2006a. Beckett's Books: A Cultural History of the Interwar Notes. London: Continuum.

———. 2006b. "Beckett and Popper, or, 'What stink of artifice': Some Notes on Methodology, Falsifiability, and Criticism in Beckett Studies," edited by Matthijs Engelberts, Everett Frost, with Jane Maxwell. Samuel Beckett Today/Aujourd'hui 16: 373–91.

Ferrer, Daniel. 1985. "The Freudful Couchmare of /\d: Joyce's Notes on Freud and the Composition of Chapter XVI of Finnegans Wake." James Joyce Quarterly 22, no. 4 (1985): 367–82.

———. 1993. "Les carnets de Joyce: Avant-textes limites d'une œuvre limite." Genesis 3: 45–61.

———. 1996. "Clementis's Cap: Retroaction and Persistence in the Genetic Process." Yale French Studies 89: 223–36.

———. 1998. "The Open Space of the Draft Page: James Joyce and Modern Manuscripts."

In *The Iconic Page in Manuscripts, Print, and Digital Culture*, edited by George Bornstein and Theresa Tinkle, 249–67. Ann Arbor: University of Michigan Press.

———. 2001. "Les bibliothèques virtuelles de James Joyce et de Virginia Woolf." In *Bibliothèques d'écrivains*, edited by Paolo D'Iorio and Daniel Ferrer, 171–93. Paris: CNRS Éditions.

———. 2002. "Production, Invention, and Reproduction: Genetic vs. Textual Criticism." In *Reimagining Textuality: Textual Studies in the Late Age of Print*, edited by E. Bergmann Loizeaux and N. Fraistat, 48–59. Madison: University of Wisconsin Press.

———. 2004. "Towards a Marginalist Economy." In *Reading Notes (Variants 2/3)*, edited by Dirk Van Hulle and Wim Van Mierlo, 7–18. Amsterdam: Rodopi.

Ferrer, Daniel, and Jacques Aubert. 1998. Anna Livia's French Bifurcations. In *Transcultural Joyce*, edited by K. R. Lawrence, 179–86. Cambridge: Cambridge University Press, 1998.

Ferrer, Daniel, and Michael Groden. 1995. "Post-Genetic Joyce." *Romanic Review* 86, no. 3 (1995): 501–12.

Ferrini, Jean-Pierre. 2003. *Dante et Beckett*. Paris: Hermann.

Fischer-Seidel, Therese, and Marion Fries-Dieckmann. 2005. *Der unbekannte Beckett: Samuel Beckett und die deutsche Kultur*. Frankfurt am Main: Suhrkamp.

Fitch, Brian T. 1988. *Beckett and Babel: An Investigation into the Status of the Bilingual Work*. Toronto: University of Toronto Press.

Foer, Jonathan Safran. 2005. *Extremely Loud & Incredibly Close*. London: Hamish Hamilton/Penguin.

Foucault, Michel. 1979. "What Is an Author?" In *Textual Strategies: Perspectives in Poststructuralist Criticism*, edited by Josué V. Harari, 141–60. Ithaca, N.Y.: Cornell University Press.

Frost, Everett, and Jane Maxwell. 2006. "Catalogues of Beckett's Reading Notes and Other Manuscripts at Trinity College Dublin." *Samuel Beckett Today/Aujourd'hui* 16: 19–199.

Gabler, Hans Walter. 1998. "Explorations in Spaces of Writing." http://fb14.uni-mainz.de/~enb/forfritz.htm.

Gadamer, Hans-Georg. 1975. *Truth and Method*. New York: Continuum.

Gallois, Eugène. 1894. *La poste et les moyens de communication des peuples à travers les siècles*. Paris: Librairie J.-B. Baillière.

Gardner, Helen. 1978. *The Composition of "Four Quartets."* London and Boston: Faber and Faber, 1978.

Garforth, Julian. 2005. "Samuel Beckett, Fritz Mauthner, and the *Whoroscope* Notebook: Beckett's Beiträge zu einer Kritik der Sprache." In *Beckett the European*, edited by Dirk Van Hulle, 49–68. Tallahassee: Journal of Beckett Studies Books.

Genette, Gérard. 1982. *Palimpsestes: La littérature au second degré*. Paris: Éditions du Seuil.

Gillet, Louis. 1958. *Claybook for James Joyce*. London and New York: Abelard-Schuman. (Orig. pub. 1931.)

Goethe, Johann Wolfgang von. 1986. *Faust*. 2 vols. Stuttgart: Philipp Reclam.

Goethes Faust. N.d. Edited by Robert Petsch. Leipzig: Bibliographisches Institut.

Gontarski, S. E. 1977. "Crapp's First Tapes: Beckett's Manuscript Revisions of *Krapp's Last Tape*." *Journal of Modern Literature* 6, no. 1 (February): 61–68.

———. 1980. "The Making of *Krapp's Last Tape*." In *Samuel Beckett's "Krapp's Last Tape*," edited by James Knowlson, 14–23. London: Brutus Books.

———. 1985. *The Intent of Undoing in Samuel Beckett's Dramatic Texts*. Bloomington: Indiana University Press.

———. 1986. "Molloy and the Reiterated Novel." In *As No Other Dare Fail: For Samuel Beckett on His 80th Birthday by His Friends and Admirers*, 57–65. London: John Calder; New York: Riverrun Press.

———. 1995. "Introduction" and "Notes on the Texts." In *Samuel Beckett: The Complete Short Prose*, edited by S. E. Gontarski, xi–xxxii; 279–86. New York: Grove, 1995.

———. 2005. "Greying the Canon: Beckett in Performance." In *Beckett after Beckett*, edited by S. E. Gontarski and Anthony Uhlmann, 141–57. Gainesville: University Press of Florida.

Gontarski, S. E., ed. 1992. *The Theatrical Notebooks of Samuel Beckett: Endgame*. London: Faber and Faber.

Gontarski, S. E., and Anthony Uhlmann, eds. 2005. *Beckett after Beckett*. Gainesville: University Press of Florida.

Goodkin, Richard E. 1991. *Around Proust*. Princeton, N.J.: Princeton University Press.

Gothot-Mersch, Claudine. 1989. "L'édition génétique: Le domaine français." In *La Naissance du texte*, edited by Louis Hay, 63–76. Paris: José Corti.

———. 1994. "Les études de genèse en France de 1950 à 1960." *Genesis* 5: 175–87.

Greenaway, Kate. 1987. *Book of Games*. New York: St. Martin's Press. (Facsimile edition of the 1889 Routledge edition.)

Gregorio, Mario di, et al. 1990. *Charles Darwin's Marginalia*. 2 vols. New York: Garland.

Grésillon, Almuth. 1992. "Ralentir: travaux." *Genesis* 1: 9–31.

———. 1994a. *Eléments de critique génétique: Lire les manuscrits modernes*. Paris: Presses Universitaires de France.

———. 1994b. "La critique génétique française: Hasards et nécessités." In *Les sentiers de la creation*, edited by Maria Teresa Giaveri and Almuth Grésillon, 51–63. Reggio Emilia: Edizioni Diabasis.

———. 1995. "Critique génétique et 'textual criticism': Une rencontre." *Romanic Review* 86, no. 3 (May): 595–98.

Groden, Michael. 1977. *"Ulysses" in Progress*. Princeton, N.J.: Princeton University Press.

———. 1991. "Contemporary Textual and Literary Theory." In *Representing Modernist Texts: Editing as Interpretation*, edited by George Bornstein, 259–86. Ann Arbor: University of Michigan Press.

———. 1996. "Geneticated Joyce." *James Joyce Literary Supplement* 10, no. 1 (Spring 1996): 14–15.

———. 2004. "Genetic Joyce." In *James Joyce Studies*, edited by Jean-Michel Rabaté, 227–50. New York: Palgrave Macmillan.

Grossman, Evelyne. 1998. *L'esthétique de Beckett*. N.p.: Éditions SEDES.

Gruber, Howard E. 1974. *Darwin on Man: A Psychological Study of Scientific Creativity*. London: Wildwood House.
Gussow, Mel. 1996. *Conversations with (and about) Beckett*. London: Nick Hern Books.
Hart, Clive. 1960. "Notes on the Text of *Finnegans Wake*," *Journal of English and Germanic Philology* 59, no. 2 (April): 229–39.
———. 1962. *Structure and Motif in "Finnegans Wake."* London: Faber and Faber.
———. 1966. "The Hound and the Type-bed: Further Notes on the Text of *Finnegans Wake*." *A Wake Newslitter* 3, no. 4 (August): 77–84.
———. 1967. "His Good Smetterling of Entymology." *A Wake Newslitter* 4, no. 1 (February): 14–24.
Hatlen, Burton. 1997. "From Modernism to Postmodernism: Zukofsky's "A"-12." In *Upper Limit Music: The Writing of Louis Zukofsky*, edited by Mark Scroggins, 214–29. Tuscaloosa and London: University of Alabama Press.
Hay, Louis. 1979. "La critique génétique: Origines et perspectives." In *Essais de critique génétique*, edited by Louis Hay, 227–36. Paris: Flammarion.
———. 1984. "Die dritte Dimension der Literatur: Notizen zu einer 'critique génétique.'" *POETICA* 16, no. 3-4: 307–23.
———. 1985. "'Le texte n'existe pas': Réflexions sur la critique génétique." *Poétique* 62 (April): 147–58.
———. 1987. "Genetic Editing, Past and Future: A Few Reflections by a User." *TEXT* 3: 117–33.
———. 1988. "Passé et avenir de l'édition génétique." *Cahiers de textologie* 2: 5–25.
———. 1988. "Comment éditer une genèse?" In *Les édition critiques: Problèmes techniques et éditoriaux*, edited by Nina Catach, 166. Paris: CNRS-Les Belles Lettres.
———. 1993. "L'écriture vive." In *Les Manuscrits des écrivains*, edited by Anne Cadiot and Christel Haffner, 10–31. Paris: CNRS/Hachette.
———. 1995. "Critiques de la critique génétique." *Romanic Review* 86, no. 3 (May): 403–18.
———. 1996a. "Pour une sémiotique du mouvement." *Genesis* 10: 25–58.
———. 1996b. "History or Genesis?" *Yale French Studies* 89: 191–207.
———. 2002. *La littérature des écrivains: Questions de critique génétique*. Paris: José Corti.
Hay, Louis, and P. Nagy. 1982. *Avant-texte, texte, après-texte*. Paris: CNRS.
Hayman, David. 1963. *A First-Draft Version of "Finnegans Wake."* London: Faber and Faber.
———. 1964a. "Tristan and Isolde in *Finnegans Wake*: A Study of Sources and Evolution of a Theme." *Comparative Literature Studies* 1, no. 2: 93–112.
———. 1964b. "A List of Corrections for the Scribbledehobble." *James Joyce Quarterly* 1, no. 2 (Winter): 23–29.
———. 1966. "*Scribbledehobbles* and How They Grew: A Turning Point in the Development of a Chapter." In *Twelve and a Tilly*, edited by Jack P. Dalton and Clive Hart, 107–18. London: Faber and Faber.
———. 1990. *The "Wake" in Transit*. Ithaca and London: Cornell University Press.
———. 1992. "Nodality and the Infra-Structure of *Finnegans Wake*." In *Critical Essays on*

James Joyce's "Finnegans Wake," edited by Patrick A. McCarthy, 129–42. New York: G. K. Hall; Toronto: Maxwell Macmillan.

———. 1995. "Genetic Criticism and Joyce: An Introduction." In *Probes: Genetic Studies in Joyce*, edited by David Hayman and Sam Slote, 3–18. European Joyce Studies 5. Amsterdam: Rodopi.

———. 1998. "Enter Wyndham Lewis Leading Dancing Dave: New Light on a Key Relationship." *James Joyce Quarterly* 35, no. 4/36, no. 1 (Summer/Fall): 621–31.

———. 1999. "Epiphanoiding." In *Genitricksling Joyce*, edited by Sam Slote and Wim Van Mierlo, 27–41. Amsterdam: Rodopi.

Haynes, John, and James Knowlson. 2003. *Images of Beckett*. Cambridge: Cambridge University Press.

Hesla, David H. 1971. *The Shape of Chaos: An Interpretation of the Art of Samuel Beckett*. Minneapolis: University of Minnesota Press.

Higginson, Fred H. 1960. *Anna Livia Plurabelle: The Making of a Chapter*. Minneapolis: University of Minnesota Press.

Hirsch, E. D., Jr. 1971. *Validity in Interpretation*. New Haven: Yale University Press.

———. 1982. "The Politics of Theories of Interpretation." *Critical Inquiry* 9, no. 1: 235–47.

Hisgen, Ruud, and Adriaan van der Weel. 1998. *The Silencing of the Sphinx*. Leiden: private edition.

Homer. 1924. *Odyssée*. Translated by Victor Bérard. 3 vols. Paris: Belles Lettres.

———. 1991. *The Odyssey*. Translated by E. V. Rieu. London: Penguin Classics.

Hulle, Dirk Van. 1999. "Beckett—Mauthner—Zimmer—Joyce." *Joyce Studies Annual* 10: 143–83.

———, ed. 2002. *James Joyce: The Study of Languages*. Brussels: Peter Lang.

———. 2004a. *Textual Awareness: A Genetic Study of Late Manuscripts by Joyce, Proust, and Mann*. Ann Arbor: University of Michigan Press.

———. 2004b. *Joyce and Beckett Discovering Dante*. Dublin: National Library of Ireland (Joyce Studies).

———. 2004c. "Note on Next to Nothing." *Variants: The Journal of the Europeans Society for Textual Scholarship* 2/3 (2004): 327–33.

———. 2005. "Introduction: Genetic Beckett Studies." In *Journal of Beckett Studies*, 13: 2 (2005): 1–9.

———. 2006a. "Samuel Beckett's *Faust* Notes." *Samuel Beckett Today/Aujourd'hui* 16: 283–97.

———. 2006b. "Growth and the Grid: Organic vs Constructivist Conceptions of Poetry." *Neophilologus* 90, no. 1 (July): 491–507.

Hulle, Dirk Van, and Wim Van Mierlo, eds. 2004. *Reading Notes*. Amsterdam: Rodopi.

Jackson, H. J. 2001. *Marginalia: Readers Writing in Books*. New Haven and London: Yale University Press.

James, William. 2000. "The Stream of Consciousness" (from: *Psychology: Briefer Course*). In *Pragmatism and Other Writings*, by James, 171–90. London: Penguin Classics.

Jannidis, Fotis, et al., eds. 1999. *Rückkehr des Autors: Zur Erneuerung eines umstrittenen Begriffs*. Tübingen: Niemeyer.

Joyce, James. 1931. *Anna Livie Plurabelle*. Translated by James Joyce, Philippe Soupault, Paul Léon, Ivan Goll, Eugene Jolas, Adrienne Monnier, based on the translation by Samuel Beckett and Alfred Péron. *Nouvelle Revue Française* 19, no. 212 (1 May 1931): 633–46.

———. 1939. *Finnegans Wake*. New York: Viking Press.

———. 1951. *Exiles*. New York: Viking Press.

———. 1957. *Letters of James Joyce*. Edited by Stuart Gilbert. London: Faber and Faber.

———. 1965. *The Workshop of Daedalus: James Joyce and the Raw Materials for "A Portrait of the Artist as a Young Man."* Edited by Robert Scholes and Richard M. Kain. Evanston, Ill.: Northwestern University Press.

———. 1966. *Letters of James Joyce*. Vol. 3. Edited by Richard Ellmann. London: Faber and Faber.

———. 1969. *Dubliners*. New York: Viking Press.

———. 1975a. *Finnegans Wake*. London: Faber and Faber. (Orig. pub. 1939.)

———. 1975b. *Selected Letters of James Joyce*. Edited by Richard Ellmann. London: Faber and Faber.

———. 1977–79. *The James Joyce Archive*. Edited by Michael Groden, Hans Walter Gabler, David Hayman, A. Walton Litz, and Danis Rose. New York: Garland.

———. 1984. *Ulysses*. Critical and synoptic edition. Edited by Hans Walter Gabler. New York: Garland.

———. 1985. "Anna Lyvia Pluratself." Translated by Samuel Beckett and Alfred Péron. In *Cahiers de l'Herne: James Joyce*, 418–21. N.p.: L'Herne. (Orig. pub. 1930.)

———. 1986. *Ulysses*. Edited by Hans Walter Gabler, with Wolfhard Steppe and Claus Melchior. New York: Vintage Books (Random House).

———. 1990. *James Joyce's Letters to Sylvia Beach 1921–1940*. Edited by Melissa Banta and Oscar A. Silverman. Oxford and Saint-Cyprien: Plantin.

———. 1991. *Stephen Hero*. Edited by Theodore Spencer. Rev. ed. by John J. Slocum and Herbert Cahoon. London: Paladin. (Orig. pub. 1944.)

———. 2000. *A Portrait of the Artist as a Young Man*. London: Penguin Books.

———. 2001–. *The "Finnegans Wake" Notebooks at Buffalo*. Edited by Vincent Deane, Daniel Ferrer, and Geert Lernout. Turnhout: Brepols.

———. 2002. *Finnegans Wake*. Bilingual edition. Translated by Erik Bindervoet and Robbert-Jan Henkes. Amsterdam: Athenaeum-Polak and Van Gennep.

Juliet, Charles. 1995. *Conversations with Samuel Beckett and Bram van Velde*. Translated by Janey Tucker. Leiden: Academic Press Leiden.

———. 1999. *Rencontres avec Samuel Beckett*. Paris_: P.O.L.

Jung, Carl Gustav. 1966–79. *The Collected Works of Carl Gustav Jung*. 2nd. ed. Vol. 18, translated by R.F.C. Hull. London: Routledge and Kegan Paul.

Killingsworth, M. Jimmie. 1993. *The Growth of "Leaves of Grass": The Organic Tradition in Whitman Studies*. Columbia: Camden House.

Klein, Scott W. 1994. *The Fictions of James Joyce and Wyndham Lewis*. Cambridge: Cambridge University Press.

Knowles, Sebastian D. G. 2001. *The Dublin Helix: The Life of Language in Joyce's "Ulysses."* Gainesville: University Press of Florida.

Knowlson, James, ed. 1985. *Happy Days: The Production Notebook of Samuel Beckett*. New York: Grove Press.
———. 1996. *Damned to Fame: The Life of Samuel Beckett*. London: Bloomsbury.
Knowlson, James, and Elizabeth Knowlson. 2006. *Beckett Remembering, Remembering Beckett: A Centenary Celebration*. New York: Arcade.
Knowlson, James, and John Pilling. 1979. *Frescoes of the Skull: The Later Prose and Drama of Samuel Beckett*. London: John Calder.
Krauss, Rosalind E. 1985. "Grids." In *The Originality of the Avant-Garde and Other Modernist Myths*, 9–22. Cambridge and London: MIT Press.
Lake, Carlton. 1984. *No Symbols Where None Intended: A Catalogue of Books, Manuscripts, and Other Material Relating to Samuel Beckett in the Collections of the Humanities Research Center*. Austin: University of Texas.
Lakoff, George, and Mark Johnson. 1980. *Metaphors We Live By*. Chicago and London: University of Chicago Press.
Landow, George P. 1997. *Hypertext 2.0: The Convergence of Contemporary Critical Theory and Technology*. Baltimore/London: Johns Hopkins University Press.
Landuyt, Ingeborg. 1997. "Shaun and His Post: *La poste et les moyens de communication* in VI.B.16." *Papers on Joyce* 3: 21–48.
———. 1999. "'Words in Distress'": A Genetic Investigation into James Joyce's Early 'Work in Progress.'" Ph.D. diss., University of Antwerp.
Landuyt, Ingeborg, and Geert Lernout. 1995. "Joyce's Sources: *Les grands fleuves historiques*." In *Joyce Studies Annual*, edited by Thomas F. Staley, 99–138. Austin: University of Texas Press.
Laubach-Kiani, Philip. 2003. "'Let us not speak': Die Genese einer *Konversationstragödie* von Samuel Beckett vor dem Hintergrund seiner Joyce-Rezeption." In *Schrift—Text—Edition: Hans Walter Gabler zum 65. Geburtstag*, edited by Christiane Henkes, Walter Hettche, Gabriele Radecke, and Elke Senne, 265–72. Tübingen: Max Niemeyer Verlag.
———. 2005. "'I Close My Eyes and Try and Imagine Them': Romantic Discourse Formations in *Krapp's Last Tape*." In *Beckett the European*, edited by Dirk Van Hulle, 125–36. Tallhassee: Journal of Beckett Studies Books.
Lawley, Paul. 2007. "Failure and Tradition: Coleridge/Beckett." *Samuel Beckett Today/Aujourd'hui* 18.
Lebrave, Jean-Louis. 1983. "Lecture et analyse des brouillons." *Languages* 69 (March): 11–23.
———. 1987. "Rough Drafts: A Challenge to Uniformity in Editing." *TEXT* 3: 135–42.
———. 1992. "La critique génétique: Une discipline nouvelle ou un avatar moderne de la philologie?" *Genesis* 1: 33–72.
Lernout, Geert. 1990. *The French Joyce*. Ann Arbor: University of Michigan Press.
———. 1994. "James Joyce and Fritz Mauthner and Samuel Beckett." In *In Principle, Beckett Is Joyce*, edited by Friedhelm Rathjen, 21–27. Edinburgh: Split Pea Press.
———. 1995. "The *Finnegans Wake* Notebooks and Radical Philology." In *Probes: Genetic Studies in Joyce*, edited by David Hayman and Sam Slote, 19–48. European Joyce Studies 5. Amsterdam: Rodopi.

———. 1998. "And yes I said yes Fritz but." In *A Collideorscape of Joyce: Festschrift for Fritz Senn*, edited by Ruth Frehner and Ursula Zeller, 294–305. Dublin: Lilliput Press.

———. 2000. "'Critique génétique" und Philologie." In *Text und Edition: Positionen und Perspektiven*, edited by Rüdiger Nutt-Kofoth, Bodo Plachta, H.T.M. van Vliet, and Hermann Zwerschina, 121–42. Berlin: Erich Schmidt.

———. 2002. "Genetic Criticism and Philology." *TEXT: An Interdisciplinary Annual of Textual Studies* 14: 53–75. Ann Arbor: University of Michigan Press, 2002.

Levin, Harry. 1960. *James Joyce: A Critical Introduction*. London: Faber. (Orig. pub. 1941.)

Lewis, Wyndham. 1927a. "An Analysis of the Mind of James Joyce" (chapter 16 of "The Revolutionary Simpleton"). *Enemy* 1, no. 1 (January): 95–130.

———. 1927b. *Time and Western Man*. London: Chatto and Windus.

———. 1989. *The Art of Being Ruled*. Santa Rosa: Black Sparrow Press. (Orig. pub. 1926.)

Litz, A. Walton. 1964. *The Art of James Joyce: Method and Design in "Ulysses" and "Finnegans Wake."* Oxford: Oxford University Press.

———. 1966. "Uses of the *Finnegans Wake* Manuscripts." In *Twelve and a Tilly*, edited by Jack Dalton and Clive Hart, 99–106. London: Faber and Faber.

Lüscher-Morata, Diane. 2005. *La souffrance portée au langage dans la prose de Samuel Beckett*. Amsterdam and New York: Rodopi.

MacArthur, Ian. 1987. "Mutant Units in the C Notebooks." *A Finnegans Wake Circular* 2, no. 4 (1987): 76–77.

Maeterlinck, Maurice. N.d. *Théâtre*. Vol. 1, *La Princesse Madeleine; L'Intruse; Les Aveugles*. Paris: Bibliothèque Charpentier. Fasquelle éditeurs.

Man, Paul De. 1986. "Conclusions: Walter Benjamin's 'The Task of the Translator.'" In *The Resistance to Theory*, 73–105. Theory and History of Literature 33. Minneapolis: University of Minnesota Press.

Mann, Thomas. 1959. *The Transposed Heads*. Translated by H. T. Lowe-Porter. New York: Vintage Books/Random House, 1959.

———. 1960. *The Magic Mountain*. London: Penguin.

———. 1979–95. *Tagebücher*. Edited by Peter de Mendelssohn and Inge Jens. Frankfurt am Main: Fischer.

———. 1990. *Gesammelte Werke in dreizehn Bänden*. Frankfurt am Main: Fischer Taschenbuch.

———. 1991. *Notizbücher. Edition in zwei Bänden*. Edited by Hans Wysling and Yvonne Schmidlin. Frankfurt am Main: Fischer.

———. 1994. *Über mich selbst: Autobiographische Schriften*. Frankfurt am Main: Fischer Taschenbuch.

Mauthner, Fritz. 1923. *Beiträge zu einer Kritik der Sprache*. 3 vols. 3rd ed. Leipzig: Verlag Felix Meiner.

Mayr, Ernst. 1985. "Darwin's Five Theories of Evolution." In *The Darwinian Heritage*, edited by David Kohn, 755–72. Princeton, N.J.: Princeton University Press.

McCarthy, Patrick A. 1992. "The Last Epistle of *Finnegans Wake*." In *Critical Essays on*

James Joyce's *"Finnegans Wake,"* edited by McCarthy, 96–103. New York: G. K. Hall; Toronto: Maxwell Macmillan.
McEwan, Ian. 2001a. *Atonement*. London: Jonathan Cape.
———. 2001b. "Beyond Belief." *Guardian Unlimited*, 12 September. www.guardian.co.uk/wtccrash/story/0,1300,550412,00.html.
———. 2005. *Saturday*. London: Jonathan Cape.
McGann, Jerome. 1983. *The Romantic Ideology: A Critical Investigation*. Chicago: University of Chicago Press.
———. 1991. *The Textual Condition*. Princeton, N.J.: Princeton University Press.
———. 2001. *Radiant Textuality: Literary Studies after the World Wide Web*. New York: Palgrave/St. Martin's Press.
McHugh, Roland. 1968. "A Structural Theory of *Finnegans Wake*." *A Wake Newslitter* 5, no. 3: 83–78.
———. 1972a. "Chronology of the Buffalo Notebooks." *A Wake Newslitter* 9, no. 2: 19–31.
———. 1972b. "Chronology of the Buffalo Notebooks (Cont.)." *A Wake Newslitter* 9, no. 3: 36–38.
———. 1972c. "Chronology of the Buffalo Notebooks—Corrigenda." *A Wake Newslitter* 9, no. 5: 100.
———. 1976. *The Sigla of "Finnegans Wake."* London: Edward Arnold.
———. 1988. "Gibbon in VI.A." *A Finnegans Wake Circular* 3, no. 4 (Summer): 77–78.
———. 1991. *Annotations to "Finnegans Wake."* Rev. ed. Baltimore: Johns Hopkins University Press.
McLaverty, James. 1984. "The Concept of Authorial Intention in Textual Criticism." *Library*, 6th ser., vol. 6, no. 2 (June): 121–38.
Melnyk, Davyd. 2005. "Never Been Properly Jung." In *Historicising Beckett/Issues of Performance*, edited by Marius Buning, Matthijs Engelberts, Sjef Houppermans, Dirk Van Hulle, Danièle de Ruyter. *Samuel Beckett Today/Aujourd'hui* 15: 355–62. Amsterdam and New York: Rodopi.
Melville, Herman. 2003. "Bartleby, the Scrivener." In *The Norton Anthology of American Literature*, 6th ed., 1086–1111. New York and London: Norton.
Mierlo, Wim Van. 1997. "The Freudful Couchmare Revisited: Contextualizing Joyce and the New Psychology." *Joyce Studies Annual* 8: 115–53.
———. 1998. "Indexing the Buffalo Notebooks: Genetic Criticism and the Construction of Evidence." In *Writing Its Own Wrunes for Ever: Essais de génétique joycienne*, edited by Daniel Ferrer and Claude Jacquet, 169–90. Tusson: Du Lérot.
———. 1999. "*Finnegans Wake* and the Question of History!?" In *Genitricksling Joyce*, edited by Sam Slote and Wim Van Mierlo, 43–64. Amsterdam: Rodopi.
Milesi, Laurent. 1994. "Killing Lewis with Einstein: 'Secting Time' in *Finnegans Wake*." In *'Teems of Times,'* edited by Andrew Treip, 9–20. European Joyce Studies 4. Amsterdam: Rodopi.
Milly, Jean. 1985. *Proust dans le texte et l'avant-texte*. Paris: Flammarion, 1985.
Neefs, Jacques. 1988. "La Critique génétique: L'histoire d'une théorie." In *De la genèse*

du texte littéraire. Manuscrit, auteur, texte, critique, edited A. Grésillon, 11–22. Paris: Du Lérot.

———. 1995. "La critique génétique, entre histoire et esthétique." *Romanic Review* 86, no. 3 (May): 419–27.

Nietzsche, Friedrich. 1956. "Über Wahrheit und Lüge im aussermoralischen Sinn." In *Werke in drei Bänden*, edited by Karl Schlechta, 309–22. Munich: Carl Hanser. (Orig. pub. 1873).

Nixon, Mark. 2004. "'What a tourist I must have been': The German Diaries of Samuel Beckett." Ph.D. diss., University of Reading.

———. 2005. "Writing 'I': Samuel Beckett's German Diaries." In *Beckett the European*, edited by Dirk Van Hulle, 10–23. Tallhassee: Journal of Beckett Studies Books.

———. 2006a. "'Scraps of German': Samuel Beckett Reading German Literature," edited by Matthijs Engelberts, Everett Frost, with Jane Maxwell. *Samuel Beckett Today/Aujourd'hui* 16: 259–82.

———. 2006b. "'Writing': Die Bedeutung der Deutschlandreise für Becketts schriftstellerische Entwicklung." In *"Obergeschoss Still Closed": Samuel Beckett in Berlin 1936/37*, edited by Lutz Dittrich, Carola Veit, and Ernest Wichner. Texte aus dem Literaturhaus Berlin 16. Berlin: Matthes and Seitz.

Norburn, Roger. 2004. *A James Joyce Chronology*. Houndmills: Palgrave Macmillan.

Nordau, Max. 1993. *Degeneration*. Translated by George L. Mosse. Lincoln and London: University of Nebraska Press.

Nutt-Kofoth, Rüdiger. 2000. "Schreiben und Lesen: Für eine produktions- *und* rezeptionsorientierte Präsentation des Werktextes in der Edition." In *Text und Edition: Positionen und Perspektiven*, edited by Rüdiger Nutt-Kofoth et al., 165–202. Berlin: Erich Schmidt.

Ogden, C. K. 1931. *Debabelization, with a Survey of Contemporary Opinions on the Problem of a Universal Language*. London: Kegan Paul.

———. 1932. "James Joyce's Anna Livia Plurabelle." *transition* 21 (March): 259–62.

Ogden, C. K., and I. A. Richards. 1972. *The Meaning of Meaning: A Study of the Influence of Language upon Thought and of the Science of Symbolism*. London: Routledge and Kegan Paul. (Orig. pub. 1923.)

O'Hanlon, John. 1979. "In the Language of Flowers." *A Wake Newslitter* 16, no. 1 (February): 9–12.

Oppenheim, Lois, ed. 2004. *Palgrave Advances in Samuel Beckett Studies*. Basingstoke: Palgrave Macmillan.

Ortner, Hanspeter. 2000. *Schreiben und Denken*. Tübingen: Niemeyer.

Palmer, Alan. 2004. *Fictional Minds*. Lincoln and London: University of Nebraska Press.

Parker, Hershel. 1984. *Flawed Texts and Verbal Icons: Literary Authority in American Fiction*. Evanston: Northwestern University Press.

———. 1987. "'The Text Itself'—Whatever That Is." *TEXT* 3: 47–54.

Petsch, Robert, ed. N.d. "Einleitung des Herausgebers." *Goethes Faust*. Leipzig: Bibliographisches Institut.

Pettit, Alexander, ed. 2000. *Textual Studies and the Common Reader: Essays on Editing Novels and Novelists*. Athens and London: University of Georgia Press.

Pierssens, Michel. 1990. "French Genetic Studies at a Crossroads." *Poetics Today* 11, no. 3 (Fall): 617–25.

Piette, Adam. 1996. *Remembering and the Sound of Words: Mallarmé, Proust, Joyce, Beckett*. Oxford: Clarendon Press.

Pilling, John. 1976. "Beckett's Proust." *Journal of Beckett Studies* 1. http://english.fsu.edu/jobs/num01/Num1Pilling.htm.

———. 1992. "From a (W)horoscope to *Murphy*." In *The Ideal Core of the Onion: Reading Beckett Archives*, edited by John Pilling and Mary Bryden, 1–20. Bristol, UK: Beckett International Foundation.

———, ed. 1994. *The Cambridge Companion to Beckett*. Cambridge: Cambridge University Press.

———. 1996. "A Short Statement with Long Shadows: *Watt*'s Arsene and his Kind(s)." In *Beckett On and On . . .*, edited by Lois Oppenheim and Marius Buning, 61–68. London: Associated University Presses.

———. 1997. *Beckett before Godot*. Cambridge: Cambridge University Press.

———, ed. 1999. *Samuel Beckett's "Dream" Notebook*. Reading: Beckett International Foundation.

———. 2004. *A Companion to "Dream of Fair to Middling Women."* Tallhassee: Journal of Beckett Studies Books.

———. 2005. "Beckett and Mauthner Revisited." In *Beckett after Beckett*, edited by Anthony Uhlmann and S. E. Gontarski, 158–66. Gainesville: University Press of Florida.

———. 2006. *A Samuel Beckett Chronology*. Houndmills and New York: Palgrave Macmillan.

Poe, Edgar Allan. 1986. *The Fall of the House of Usher and Other Writings*. London: Penguin Classics.

Ponge, Francis. 1992. *L'opinion changée quant aux fleurs*. In *Nouveau Nouveau Recueil 1940–1975*, 2: 101–32. Paris: Gallimard.

———. 1999. *Œuvres Complètes*. Vol. 1. Edited by Bernard Beugnot. Paris: Gallimard (Pléiade).

Popper, Karl. 2002. *The Logic of Scientific Discovery*. London and New York: Routledge Classics.

Pountney, Rosemary. 1987. "The Structuring of Lessness." Special issue on Samuel Beckett, *Review of Contemporary Fiction* 7: 55–75.

———. 1988. *Theatre of Shadows: Samuel Beckett's Drama 1956–76*. Gerrards Cross/Totowa, N.J.: Colin Smythe/Barnes and Noble Books.

Power, Arthur. 1974. *Conversations with James Joyce*. Edited by Clive Hart. London: Millington.

Proust, Marcel. 1987–89. *A la recherche du temps perdu*. 4 vols. Paris: Gallimard Pléiade.

———. 1989. *Remembrance of Things Past*. Translated by C. K. Scott Moncrieff. Revised by Terence Kilmartin. London: Penguin.

———. 1995. *Contre Sainte-Beuve*. Edited by Bernard de Fallois. Paris: Gallimard Collection Folio Essais. (Orig. pub. 1954.)

———. 2002. *Carnets*. Edited by Florence Callu and Antoine Compagnon. Paris: Gallimard.

Queyrat, Frédéric. 1920. *Les jeux des enfants: Étude sur l'imagination créatrice chez l'enfant*. Paris: Librairie Félix Alcan.

Quinones, Ricardo J. 1985. *Mapping Literary Modernism: Time and Development*. Princeton, N.J.: Princeton University Press, 1985.

Rabaté, Jean-Michel. 1985. "Pour une cryptogénétique de l'idiolecte joycien." In *Genèse de Babel: Joyce et la Création*, edited by Claude Jacquet, 49–91. Paris: CNRS.

———. 1995. "Pound, Joyce and Eco: Modernism and the 'Ideal Genetic Reader.'" *Romanic Review* 86, no. 3 (May): 485–500.

———. 1999. "Beckett et la poésie de la zone: (Dante . . . Apollinaire.Céline..Lévi)." In *Poetry and Other Prose*, edited by Matthijs Engelberts, Marius Buning and Sjef Houppermans. *Samuel Beckett Today/Aujourd'hui* 8: 75–90. Amsterdam: Rodopi.

Raby, Peter. "The Making of *The Importance of Being Earnest*." *Times Literary Supplement* 4629 (December 1991): 13.

Rank, Otto. 1924. *Das Trauma der Geburt und seine Bedeutung für die Psychoanalyse*. Leipzig/Wien/Zürich: Internationaler Psychoanalytischer Verlag.

Reich Gluck, Barbara. 1979. *Beckett and Joyce: Friendship and Fiction*. Lewisburg: Bucknell University Press.

Reiman, Donald H. 1987. "Versioning: The Presentation of Multiple Texts." In *Romantic Texts and Contexts*, 167–80. Columbia: University of Missouri Press.

Reynolds, Mary T. 1981. *Joyce and Dante: The Shaping Imagination*. Princeton, N.J.: Princeton University Press.

Ridley, Matt. 2000. *Genome: The Autobiography of a Species in 23 Chapters*. New York: HarperCollins, 2000.

Rorty, Richard. 1992. "The Pragmatist's Progress." In *Interpretation and Overinterpretations*, edited by Ed. Stefan Collini, 89–108. Cambridge: Cambridge University Press.

Rose, Danis. 1978. *James Joyce's The Index Manuscript: "Finnegans Wake" Holograph Workbook VI.B.46*. Colchester: A Wake Newslitter Press.

———. 1982. *Understanding "Finnegans Wake": A Guide to the Narrative of James Joyce's Masterpiece*. New York and London: Garland.

———. 1995. *The Textual Diaries of James Joyce*. Dublin: Lilliput Press.

Sardin-Damestoy, Pascale. 2002. *Samuel Beckett auto-traducteur, ou l'art de l'«empêchement».* Arras: Artois Presses Université.

Scheibe, Siegfried. 1982. "Zum editorischen Problem des Textes." *Zeitschrift der deutschen Philologie*, Sonderheft 101: 12–29.

———. 1995. "On the Editorial Problem of the Text." In *Contemporary German Editorial Theory*, edited by Hans Walter Gabler, George Bornstein, and Gillian Borland Pierce, 193–208. Ann Arbor: Michigan University Press.

———. 1998. "Variantendarstllung in Abhängigkeit von der Arbeitsweise des Autors und von der Überlieferung seiner Werke." In *Textgenetische Edition*, edited by Hans Zeller and Gunter Martens, 168–76. Beihefte zu *editio*, vol. 10. Tübingen: Niemeyer.

Schopenhauer, Arthur. 1922. *Sämtliche Werke*. Vol. 6, *Parerga und Paralipomena, zweiter Band*. Leipzig: Brockhaus.

———. 1969. *The World as Will and Representation*. 2 vols. Translated by E.F.J. Payne. New York: Dover, 1969.

———. 1987. *Die Welt als Wille und Vorstellung*. 2 vols. Stuttgart: Reclam.

Schork, R. J. 1994. "By Jingo: Genetic Criticism of *Finnegans Wake*." *Joyce Studies Annual* 5: 104–27.

———. 1998. "Sheep, Bones, and Nettles: St. Kevin's Childhood Miracles." In *Writing Its Own Wrunes for Ever: Essais de génétique joycienne*, edited by Daniel Ferrer and Claude Jacquet, 151–62. Tusson: Du Lérot.

———. 2000. *Joyce and Hagiography: Saints Above!* Gainesville: University Press of Florida.

Senn, Fritz. 1995. *Inductive Scrutinies*. Edited by Christine O'Neill. Baltimore: Johns Hopkins University Press.

Shattuck, Roger. 1996. *Forbidden Knowledge: From Prometheus to Pornography*. San Diego: Harcourt Brace.

Shelley, Mary Wollstonecroft. 1992. *Frankenstein*. London: Penguin Classics.

———. 1996. *The "Frankenstein" Notebooks: A Facsimile Edition*. Edited by Charles E. Robinson. Part 1. New York and London: Garland.

Shelley, Percy Bysshe. 2002. "A Defence of Poetry." In *Shelley's Poetry and Prose*, 2nd ed., edited by Donald H. Reiman and Neil Fraistat, 509–35. New York and London: Norton.

Shillingsburg, Peter. 1996. *Scholarly Editing in the Computer Age: Theory and Practice*. 3rd ed. Athens: University of Georgia Press.

———. 1997. *Resisting Texts: Authority and Submission in Constructions of Meaning*. Ann Arbor: University of Michigan Press.

———. 2006. *From Gutenberg to Google: Electronic Representations of Literary Texts*. Cambridge: Cambridge University Press.

Shklovsky, Viktor. 1965. "Art as Technique." In *Russian Formalist Criticism: Four Essays*, edited by Lee T. Lemon and Marion J. Reis, 3–24. Lincoln: University of Nebraska Press.

Skerl, Jennie. 1974. "Fritz Mauthner's 'Critique of Language' in Samuel Beckett's *Watt*." *Contemporary Literature* 15, no. 4 (Autumn): 474–87.

Slote, Sam. 1995. "Wilde Thing: Concerning the Eccentricities of a Figure of Decadence in *Finnegans Wake*." In *Probes: Genetic Studies in Joyce*, edited by David Hayman and Sam Slote, 101–22. European Joyce Studies 5. Amsterdam and Atlanta: Rodopi.

———. 1996. "Pressing Genetic Inquiries into Joyce." Paper presented at the Eleventh James Joyce Symposium, Zurich, 1996. http://www.antwerpjamesjoycecenter.com.

———. 1997. "'Every Splurge on the Vellum': The Silence in Progress of Dante, Mallarmé, and Joyce." Ph.D. diss., University of Wisconsin.

———. 1998. "'Did god be come': The Definitive Exgenesis of HCE." In *Writing Its Own Wrunes For Ever*, edited by Daniel Ferrer and Claude Jacquet, 103–18. Tusson: Du Lérot.

———. 2005. "On *Worstward Ho*." In *Beckett the European*, edited by Dirk Van Hulle, 188–205. Tallhassee: Journal of Beckett Studies Books.

———. 2006. "Prolegomenon to the Development of Wakean Styles: New Acquisitions at the National Library of Ireland." *James Joyce Quarterly* 42/43, nrs. 1–4 (Fall 2004– Summer 2006): 21–30.

Slote, Sam, and Wim Van Mierlo. 1999. *Genitricksling Joyce*. Amsterdam: Rodopi.

Sloterdijk, Peter. 1989. *Eurotaoismus*. Frankfurt am Main: Suhrkamp.

Smith, Frederick N. 2002. *Beckett's Eighteenth Century*. Basingstoke and New York: Palgrave.

Soupault, Philippe. 1931. À propos de la traduction d'Anna Livia Plurabelle. *Nouvelle Revue Française* 19, no. 212 (1 May): 633–36.

Spielberg, Peter. 1962. *James Joyce's Manuscripts and Letters at the University of Buffalo* Buffalo, N.Y.: University of Buffalo.

Stewart, Bruce, ed. 1999. *Beckett and Beyond*. Gerrards Cross, Bucks.: Colin Smythe.

Swift, Jonathan. 1986. *A Tale of a Tub and Other Works*. Edited by Angus Ross and David Woolley. Oxford: Oxford University Press.

Tadié, Jean-Yves. 1987. *La critique littéraire au XXe siècle*. Paris: Belfond.

Tanselle, Thomas. 1995. "Critical Editions, Hypertexts, and Genetic Criticism." *Romanic Review* 86, no. 3 (May): 581–93.

Taylor, Juliette. 2005. "'Pidgin Bullskrit': The Performance of French in Beckett's Trilogy." In *Historicising Beckett/Issues of Performance*, edited by Marius Buning, Matthijs Engelberts, Sjef Houppermans, Dirk van Hulle, Danièle de Ruyter. *Samuel Beckett Today/Aujourd'hui* 15: 211–23. Amsterdam and New York: Rodopi.

Venuti, Lawrence. 1998. "Strategies of Translation." In *Routledge Encyclopedia of Translation Studies*, edited by M. Baker and K. Malmkjaer, 240–44. London and New York: Routledge.

Vogelweide, Walther von der. 1994. *Werke*. Vol. 1, *Spruchlyrik*. Stuttgart: Reclam.

Wellek, René, and Austin Warren. 1973. *Theory of Literature*. 1949. 3rd ed. Harmondsworth, UK: Penguin.

Weller, Shane. 2000. "The Word Folly: Samuel Beckett's 'comment dire' ('what is the word')." *Angelaki: Journal of the Theoretical Humanities* 5, no. 1 (April): 165–80.

Werner, Michael. 1987. "Edition und Kulturtradition in Frankreich." *Editio* 1: 139–44.

Wheelock, Arthur K., Jr., and Ben Broos. *Johannes Vermeer*. 1995. The Hague: Cabinet of Paintings Mauritshuis; Washington: National Gallery of Art; Zwolle: Waanders Publishers.

Wimsatt, W. K. 1968. "Genesis: A Fallacy Revisited." In *The Disciplines of Criticism*, edited by Peter Demetz et al., 193–225. New Haven: Yale University Press.

Wimsatt, W. K., and Monroe C. Beardsley. 1946. "The Intentional Fallacy." *Sewanee Review* 54 (1946): 468–88.

———. 1954. "The Intentional Fallacy." In *The Verbal Icon: Studies in the Meaning of Poetry*, 3–18. N.p.:University Press of Kentucky, 1954.

Windelband, Wilhelm. 1958. *A History of Philosophy*. 2 vols. Translated by James H. Tufts. New York: Harper and Row. (Orig. pub. 1901.)

Woolf, Virginia. 2001. "Modern Fiction." In *The Norton Anthology: English Literature; The Major Authors*, 7th ed., 2408–14. New York and London: Norton.

Wordsworth, William. "Preface." In *Lyrical Ballads*, electronic scholarly edition by Bruce Graver and Ron Tetreault, www.rc.umd.edu/editions/LB

Wysling, Hans. 1967a. "Zu Thomas Manns 'Maja'-Projekt." In *Quellenkritische Studien zum Werk Thomas Manns*, edited by Paul Scherrer and Hans Wysling, 23–47. Bern: Francke.

———. 1967b. "Thomas Manns Verhältnis zu den Quellen." In *Quellenkritische Studien zum Werk Thomas Manns*, edited by Paul Scherrer and Hans Wysling, 258–324. Bern: Francke.

Wysling, Hans, and Yvonne Schmidlin. 1994. *Thomas Mann: Ein Leben in Bildern*. Zürich: Artemis and Winkler.

Young, Edward. 1759. *Conjectures on Original Composition*. London: Millar and Dodsley. http://eir.library.utoronto.ca/rpo/display/displayprose.cfm?prosenum=16.

Zimmer, Heinrich. 1936. *Maya: Der Indische Mythos*. Berlin: Deutsche Verlagsanstalt.

Zimmerman, Nadya. "Musical Form as Narrator: The Fugue of the Sirens in James Joyce's *Ulysses*." *Journal of Modern Literature*, 26, no. 1 (Fall 2002): 108–18.

Zukofsky, Louis. 1993. "*A*." Baltimore and London: Johns Hopkins University Press, 1993. (Orig. pub. 1978).

Index

Abbott, H. Porter, 4, 137
Ackerley, Chris, 143, 165–66, 180, 204n4
Adorno, Theodor, 113, 174–75, 188, 191
Aesop, 67
All That Fall (Beckett), 142
Anaximander, 162
Aragon, Louis, 2
Aramis, 84–85
Arikha, Avigdor, 155
Aristotle, 16, 201n15
Atherton, James S., 111
Aubert, Jacques, 203n6
authorial intention, 36–40
avant-texte, 29–30, 50, 57–58, 144, 184

Bach, Johann Sebastian, 101, 195n4
Ballard, J. G., 148
Barthes, Roland, 30, 38, 43, 72
Beardsley, Monroe C., 36–37, 39, 194
Beckett, Samuel, 1–6, 21, 23, 27, 30, 35–36, 39–40, 43–45, 47, 51, 77, 90, 100, 111–14, 117–94, 196n12, 197n11, 201n20. See also individual works
Beethoven, Ludwig van, 175–76
Benda, Julien, 81
Benjamin, Walter, 1
Bennett, Arnold, 84, 86
Bergson, Henri, 81
Berkeley, George, 102, 125, 144
Bernstein, Michael André, 2
Bianchi, Enrico, 152
Boethius, 175
Bourdieu, Pierre, 41
Boyd, Ernest, 84, 86
Brown, Richard, 196n11
Budgen, Frank, 67
Burnet, John, 163
Butor, Michel, 2
Byron, George Gordon Lord, 19–20, 195n1

Le Calmant/The Calmative (Beckett), 152
Campbell, Joseph, 55

Camus, Albert, 146
Carroll, Lewis, 30, 67, 83, 101
Casagrande, Gino, 149
Casanova, Pascale, 123
Caselli, Daniella, 152, 154
Ceiling (Beckett), 157–58, 187
Cerrato, Laura, 193
Chaikin, Joseph, 160
Chaucer, Geoffrey, 18
Clément, Bruno, 148, 204n16
Cluchey, Rick, 162
Cohn, Ruby, 127, 159, 202n1
Colum, Mary M., 84
Colum, Padraic, 98
Come and Go/Va-et-vient (Beckett), 184–86
Comment c'est/How It Is (Beckett), 154
Comment dire/what is the word (Beckett), 6, 188–91, 193–94
Compagnon, Antoine, 30–31, 37, 41–42
Company/Compagnie (Beckett), 136–40
Connolly, Thomas E., 113
Connor, Steven, 35–36
Conrad, Joseph, 115
Crispi, Luca, 59, 198n5, 200n3
critique génétique. See genetic criticism
Culler, Jonathan, 43
Cunard, Nancy, 154
Czaplicka, Mary, 80

Danielewski, Mark Z., 1
Dante Alighieri, 45, 121, 131, 138, 141–42, 146, 149–53, 155, 161, 166–68, 193
"Dante and the Lobster" (Beckett), 136, 150
"Dante...Bruno.Vico..Joyce" (Beckett), 123, 128, 130
Darwin, Charles, 18, 99
Dawkins, Richard, 16–17
Deane, Vincent, 202n2
de Biasi, Pierre-Marc, 9, 29, 41, 49–52, 56, 72, 76, 93, 105
Debray-Genette, Raymonde, 50, 197n8
de Gourmont, Rémy, 88

De Graef, Ortwin, 34, 39, 43
Deleuze, Gilles, 16
Deppman, Jed, 2, 61, 194
Dettmar, Kevin J. H., 122
Dickens, Charles, 77
Dilthey, Wilhelm, 197n6
Disjecta (Beckett), 4
Donne, John, 36
Douglas, James, 84
Dream of Fair to Middling Women (Beckett), 43, 133, 141, 175
Driver, Tom, 120, 202n5
Dujardin, Eduard, 134
Duthuit, Georges, 166

Eco, Umberto, 30, 33–34, 37, 43
écriture à processus, 49
écriture à programme, 49
Eeckhout, Bart, 101
Eliot, T. S., 35–36, 200n1
Ellmann, Richard, 105–6, 134
Elsschot, Willem, 14
empiricism, 41–42
Eh Joe (Beckett), 163
En attendant Godot/Waiting for Godot (Beckett), 123–26, 171–72, 180, 197n11, 205n17
Encyclopaedia Britannica, 57, 76, 89
endogenetics, 50–51
Engelberts, Matthijs, 139
Enzensberger, Hans Magnus, 40, 119–20
Esposito, Bianca, 151
Esslin, Martin, 113, 119, 181
Euclid, 64
exogenetics, 50–51
L'Expulsé/The Expelled (Beckett), 143

Feldman, Matthew, 141, 143, 197n7, 204n2
Ferrer, Daniel, 2, 5, 9, 23, 32, 41, 88, 100, 104, 192–94, 202n22, 206n23
Fichte, Johann Gottlieb, 133–34
figure of script, 148, 155, 157, 160, 168–69
Film (Beckett), 144
Fin de partie/Endgame (Beckett), 39, 136, 138, 154, 203n9
Finnegans Wake (Joyce), 4–5, 15, 17–20, 26, 33, 37, 44, 48, 50–52, 55–114, 120–21, 130, 141, 147, 172–73, 191–93, 196n11, 198n2, 199n5
Fizzles (Beckett), 4
Fletcher, Beryl, 39

Fletcher, John, 39, 180, 205n17
Footfalls/Pas (Beckett), 142
Foucault, Michel, 42–44, 152
Fourier, François Marie Charles, 80
Freud, Sigmund, 32–33, 170, 198n2
Frost, Everett, 204n2
Fuse, Mikio, 93, 200n5

Gabler, Hans Walter, 103, 201n17
Gadamer, Hans Georg, 196n10
Gallois, Eugène, 95–98, 200nn9–10, 201nn11–12
genetic criticism, 1–2, 7–52, 111, 114
genetic dossier, 30, 39
Goethe, Johann Wolfgang von, 164–65, 167–70, 173, 175, 203n12, 204n7
Goll, Ivan, 130
Gontarski, S. E., 35–36, 45, 114, 118–20, 134–35, 143, 160, 167, 174
Goodkin, Richard, 127
Greenaway, Kate, 55
Grésillon, Almuth, 9, 29–30
grey canon, 35
Groden, Michael, 2, 33, 41, 194
Grossman, Evelyne, 162
Gussow, Mel, 192
Gwynn, Stephen, 84, 87

Haeckel, Ernst, 18
Happy Days/Oh les beaux jours (Beckett), 176, 203n9
Harris, Frank, 78
Hatlen, Burton, 14
Hay, Louis, 7, 9, 31, 49
Hayman, David, 18, 33–34, 55, 58, 78, 104, 108, 203n4
Heraclitus, 81, 163
Herbert, Jocelyn, 141
Hirsch, E. D., 31, 38, 197n6
Hobson, Harold, 120
Hollander, Jean, 149
Hollander, Robert, 149
Homer, 9, 141
homunculus, 167–68, 171, 205n12

L'Innommable/The Unnamable (Beckett), 113, 169, 172, 175
intentio auctoris, 30
intentio lectoris, 35
intentional fallacy, 36

intentio operis, 30
ITEM (Institut des Textes et Manuscrits Modernes), 9

James, William, 134-36, 199n6
Jannidis, Fotis, 38, 197n10
Jenny, Laurent, 41-42
Joeres, Charlotte, 142
Jolas, Eugene, 50, 130
Jones, Ernest, 170, 172, 205n13
Joyce, Giorgio, 112
Joyce, James, 1-6, 16-23, 24, 27, 32-33, 44, 48-52, 53-114, 117-22, 130-32, 134, 141, 147, 166, 172-73, 175, 177, 181-82, 191-94, 196n11, 198n3, 199n5. *See also individual works*
Juliet, Charles, 119, 123
Jung, Carl Gustav, 142, 168, 198n2
Jünger, Ernst, 2

Kafka, Franz, 48
Kaun, Axel, 77, 113, 118, 175
Keats, John, 11, 203n5
Killingsworth, M. Jimmie, 10, 23
Knowles, Sebastian, 16, 197n1
Knowlson, James, 112, 118, 122, 135, 142, 145, 151, 154-55, 168, 197n11, 203n5, 203n9
Krance, Charles, 138
Krapp's Last Tape/La dernière bande (Beckett), 127-28, 132, 176-79, 205n16
Krauss, Rosalind, 13, 15, 195n3
Kristensen, Tom, 198n2

Landow, George, 72
Landuyt, Ingeborg, 83, 200n2
"Last Soliloquy" (Beckett), 160, 164
Laubach-Kiani, Philip, 128, 183, 185
Lebrave, Jean-Louis, 9
Lennon, John, 1
Léon, Paul, 69, 130, 192
Lernout, Geert, 18, 32-34, 37, 40-41
Lewis, Wyndham, 64, 66, 77-81, 105, 107, 163, 198n1, 199n3
Litz, A. Walton, 19, 72, 101
Lloyd, Horatio, 78

MacArthur, Ian, 92, 200n4
MacGreevy, Thomas, 112, 203n5
Malone meurt/Malone Dies (Beckett), 136, 169, 172

Mal vu mal dit/Ill Seen Ill Said (Beckett), 147
Mann, Thomas, 14, 22, 119, 195n9
Maitland, Margaret, 84, 87
Manning, Mary, 112
Mauthner, Fritz, 33, 51, 58-59, 100, 112-13, 117, 148, 201n16, 202n21
Maxwell, Jane, 204n2
McCarthy, Patrick, 110
McEwan, Ian, 24-28, 30, 196n1
McGann, Jerome, 11
McHugh, Roland, 89
Melnyk, Davyd, 142, 168
Mercier et Camier/Mercier and Camier (Beckett), 44-45, 129, 142, 144-46, 148, 153, 157, 204n14
Mierlo, Wim Van, 198n4
Milly, Jean, 15
Molloy (Beckett), 6, 113, 129, 137, 170, 173, 204n8
Mondrian, Piet, 13
Monnier, Adrienne, 130
Murry, John Middleton, 84-86

Nixon, Mark, 202n1, 203n10, 204n1, 204n18, 205n21, 206n24
Norburn, Roger, 112
Nordau, Max, 133
Not I/Pas moi (Beckett), 40, 132-35, 137, 142, 176, 180-83, 186

O'Reilly, Magessa, 170
Ortner, Hanspeter, 48-49

Palmer, Alan, 39
Parnell, Charles Stuart, 177
Péguy, Charles, 81
Petsch, Robert, 167, 204n7
A Piece of Monologue/Solo (Beckett), 138, 140, 203n8
Pilling, John, 112, 133, 141-42, 204n17, 206n24
Piggott, Richard, 177
Poe, Edgar Allan, 13, 89, 161, 192
Ponge, Francis, 3, 22
Pope, Alexander, 9
Popper, Karl, 16, 31-32, 40, 197n7
positivism, 41-42
Pound, Ezra, 106
Pountney, Rosemary, 39, 114, 119-20, 127, 182, 194, 202n9
Power, Arthur, 131-32
Proudhon, Pierre, 80

230 / Index

Proust, Marcel, 14–16, 31–32, 37, 49, 72, 81, 119, 122–23, 127, 129–32, 137, 163, 195n8, 197n9, 203n5
Proust (Beckett), 3, 129–32, 188

Queyrat, Frédéric, 98, 201n14
Quinet, Edgar, 67, 69

radical philology, 18, 32
Rank, Otto, 143, 163–64, 171–72
Raphael, France, 57, 91–92, 95–99, 201n13
Rathjen, Friedhelm, 174, 205n14
Richardson, Dorothy, 88
Ridley, Matt, 17
Robinson, Henry Morton, 55
Robinson, Peter, 18
Roger, Alain, 31–32
Rorty, Richard, 30
Rose, Danis, 57–58, 92, 96
Rousseau, Jean-Jacques, 80, 87

Sans/Lessness (Beckett), 120, 127
Sartre, Jean-Paul, 31, 148
Schädlich, Hans Joachim, 2
Schleiermacher, Friedrich, 195n10
Scheibe, Siegfried, 47, 49, 83
scholarly editing, 42
Schopenhauer, Arthur, 47, 49, 113, 126, 132, 146–47, 154, 175
Schork, R. J., 33
script acts, 37, 51
"Sedendo et Quiescendo" (Beckett), 166
Shakespeare, William, 141, 158–59, 203n9
Shelley, Mary, 11–12, 17, 195n1
Shelley, Percy Bysshe, 11–12, 17, 131, 195n1
Shenker, Israel, 118–19, 202n3
Shillingsburg, Peter, 29–30, 37–38, 40, 125
Silberer, Herbert, 171, 205n11, 205n12
Sinclair, May, 88
Slote, Sam, 17, 44, 78, 120–21, 198n5, 198n6
Sloterdijk, Peter, 147
Socrates, 164
Sorel, Georges, 81
Soupault, Philippe, 130, 203n6
Spielberg, Peter, 57
Stein, Gertrude, 77, 81
Stephen Hero (Joyce), 53
Stirrings Still/Soubresauts (Beckett), 21, 40, 44–45, 122, 137, 141, 144, 147, 154–57, 159, 166, 174, 187–88, 193

structuralism, 43
Sullivan, Edward, 62
Swedenborg, Emanuel, 67
Swift, Jonathan, 9, 89–90

Tadié, Jean-Yves, 41–42
Teit, James Alexander, 198n3
Textes pour rien/Texts for Nothing (Beckett), 125, 160
textual criticism, 42
Thales, 164
That Time/Cette fois (Beckett), 183

Ulysses (Joyce), 16, 27–28, 59, 83, 85–88, 90–91, 100–101, 145–46, 177, 197n6, 199n1, 200n1

Vaerting, Mathias, 78
Vaerting, Mathilde, 78
Vermeer, Johannes, 28, 45, 186
Vico, Giambattista, 51, 198n2
Virgil, 45, 146, 149–52, 155, 168

Wagenbach, Klaus, 48
Warren, Austin, 34
Warrilow, David, 138
Watt (Beckett), 21, 143, 148–49, 151, 154, 164–65
Weaver, Harriet Shaw, 15, 55, 60–63, 67, 72, 76, 77–78, 100, 102, 111, 196n11, 199n5
Wellek, René, 34
Werner, Michael, 41
Westermarck, Edvard Alexander, 199n3
Whitman, Walt, 10
Wilde, Oscar, 78
Wilson, Edmund, 84, 86
Wimsatt, W. K., 36–37, 39, 194
Windelband, Wilhelm, 162, 175, 204n3
Wittgenstein, Ludwig, 49
Woolf, Virginia, 84–85, 87–89, 100
Wordsworth, William, 6, 128–29
"Work in Progress" (Joyce), 5, 23, 50–51, 55–76, 83, 91, 114, 120, 130, 173, 177, 193
Worstward Ho (Beckett), 6, 144, 147, 173

Yeats, W. B., 203n9
Young, Edward, 10–11

Zeno of Elea, 110
Zimmer, Heinrich, 112–13
Zukofsky, Louis, 14, 195n4

Dirk Van Hulle, associate professor of English at the University of Antwerp, is the author of *Textual Awareness: A Genetic Study of Late Manuscripts by Joyce, Proust, and Mann*. He edits the online journal *Genetic Joyce Studies* and is co-director of the Beckett Digital Manuscript Project.

The Florida James Joyce Series
Edited by Sebastian D. G. Knowles
Zack Bowen, Editor Emeritus

The Autobiographical Novel of Co-Consciousness: Goncharov, Woolf, and Joyce, by Galya Diment (1994)
Bloom's Old Sweet Song: Essays on Joyce and Music, by Zack Bowen (1995)
Joyce's Iritis and the Irritated Text: The Dis-lexic Ulysses, by Roy Gottfried (1995)
Joyce, Milton, and the Theory of Influence, by Patrick Colm Hogan (1995)
Reauthorizing Joyce, by Vicki Mahaffey (paperback edition, 1995)
Shaw and Joyce: "The Last Word in Stolentelling," by Martha Fodaski Black (1995)
Bely, Joyce, Döblin: Peripatetics in the City Novel, by Peter I. Barta (1996)
Jocoserious Joyce: The Fate of Folly in Ulysses, by Robert H. Bell (paperback edition, 1996)
Joyce and Popular Culture, edited by R. B. Kershner (1996)
Joyce and the Jews: Culture and Texts, by Ira B. Nadel (paperback edition, 1996)
Narrative Design in Finnegans Wake: *The Wake Lock Picked*, by Harry Burrell (1996)
Gender in Joyce, edited by Jolanta W. Wawrzycka and Marlena G. Corcoran (1997)
Latin and Roman Culture in Joyce, by R. J. Schork (1997)
Reading Joyce Politically, by Trevor L. Williams (1997)
Advertising and Commodity Culture in Joyce, by Garry Leonard (1998)
Greek and Hellenic Culture in Joyce, by R. J. Schork (1998)
Joyce, Joyceans, and the Rhetoric of Citation, by Eloise Knowlton (1998)
Joyce's Music and Noise: Theme and Variation in His Writings, by Jack W. Weaver (1998)
Reading Derrida Reading Joyce, by Alan Roughley (1999)
Joyce through the Ages: A Nonlinear View, edited by Michael Patrick Gillespie (1999)
Chaos Theory and James Joyce's Everyman, by Peter Francis Mackey (1999)
Joyce's Comic Portrait, by Roy Gottfried (2000)
Joyce and Hagiography: Saints Above! by R. J. Schork (2000)
Voices and Values in Joyce's Ulysses, by Weldon Thornton (2000)
The Dublin Helix: The Life of Language in Joyce's Ulysses, by Sebastian D. G. Knowles (2001)
Joyce Beyond Marx: History and Desire in Ulysses *and* Finnegans Wake, by Patrick McGee (2001)
Joyce's Metamorphosis, by Stanley Sultan (2001)
Joycean Temporalities: Debts, Promises, and Countersignatures, by Tony Thwaites (2001)
Joyce and the Victorians, by Tracey Teets Schwarze (2002)
Joyce's Ulysses *as National Epic: Epic Mimesis and the Political History of the Nation State*, by Andras Ungar (2002)
James Joyce's "Fraudstuff," by Kimberly J. Devlin (2002)
Rite of Passage in the Narratives of Dante and Joyce, by Jennifer Margaret Fraser (2002)
Joyce and the Scene of Modernity, by David Spurr (2002)
Joyce and the Early Freudians: A Synchronic Dialogue of Texts, by Jean Kimball (2003)
Twenty-first Joyce, edited by Ellen Carol Jones and Morris Beja (2004)
Joyce on the Threshold, edited by Anne Fogarty and Timothy Martin (2005)
Wake Rites: The Ancient Irish Rituals of Finnegans Wake, by George Cinclair Gibson (2005)
Ulysses *in Critical Perspective*, edited by Michael Patrick Gillespie and A. Nicholas Fargnoli (2006)
Joyce and the Narrative Structure of Incest, by Jen Shelton (2006)
Joyce, Ireland, Britain, edited by Andrew Gibson and Len Platt (2006)

Joyce in Trieste: An Album of Risky Readings, edited by Sebastian D. G. Knowles, Geert Lernout, and John McCourt (2007)
Joyce's Rare View: The Nature of Things in Finnegans Wake, by Richard Beckman (2007)
Joyce's Misbelief, by Roy Gottfried (2007)
James Joyce's Painful Case: A Spoiled Priest, by Cóilín Owens (2008)
Manuscript Genetics, Joyce's Know-How, Beckett's Nohow, by Dirk Van Hulle (2008)

www.ingramcontent.com/pod-product-compliance
Lightning Source LLC
Chambersburg PA
CBHW020945230426
43666CB00005B/177